Discretion to Disobey

A Study of Lawful Departures from Legal Rules

Discretion to Disobey

A Study of Lawful Departures from Legal Rules

MORTIMER R. KADISH

AND

SANFORD H. KADISH

Stanford University Press, Stanford, California

1973

Stanford University Press
Stanford, California
© 1973 by the Board of Trustees of the
Leland Stanford Junior University
Printed in the United States of America
ISBN 0-8047-0832-0
LC 72-97201

To the memory of
Fanno and S.J.

Preface

To those of our generation who, like us, were deeply influenced by John Dewey and for whom the double threat of totalitarianism abroad and its McCarthyite approximation at home was a shaping experience, the absolute priority of democratic processes over any substantive advantages gained by deviating from them became a fundamental commitment. It was obvious that democratic processes might produce wrong decisions; but in the long run, we thought, those processes would prove justified more often than not. Dewey, and Pierce before Dewey, had found the justification of rationality in the long run. Like Dewey, if not like Pierce, we tended to identify democracy with rationality and placed our bets on the long run. The concept of process, in the sense of rational procedure, had become central in our address to social problems. We took to be the very strength of rational procedure that while it could eventuate in mistakes, it would come to recognize those mistakes for what they were and, in the long run, get things right or at least right enough.

Yet the long run has proven to be a very hard run indeed. We never expected that outcomes in the present—as much of the long run as people ever get to do much about—might seem serious enough to call for reevaluating the priorities of process and payoff for every social institution of any importance. Rightly or wrongly, we still see no alternative to process; and the attempt to cope with the tensions between process and payoff in a way that would remain as faithful as possible to the commitment to process is, broadly speaking, the problem that led to the writing of this book.

Historically the problem was inescapable. More and more, in the complex and turbulent conditions in which we live, incompatibilities between established processes and intended consequences, prescribed means and desired ends, justice and utility, spread and intensify. Forced upon us, they undermine a confidence perhaps once more general that a political or legal system, or any of the systems of rules defining the major practices of society, can be relied upon to meet often enough and quickly enough even the demands for which they were instituted. At the same time, only the hardiest skepticism could impeach the necessity for establishing procedures—for rules and abiding by the rules—in the central practices of contemporary society. We have been placed in a predicament. On the one hand, we are required to accept the results of such procedures even when we find them undesirable or mistaken, since that is what the acceptance of a procedure demands. On the other hand, the sense that we cannot accept whatever the mill grinds out—indeed, that sometimes, morally, we must not—becomes irresistible. Poised between procedure and payoff, we have fallen into a predicament of rules and are tempted to say of the social universe what John Donne said of the external one: " 'Tis all in pieces, all cohaerence gone; All just supply, and all Relation."

We have endeavored here to consider the predicament of rules in the domain of the law. For the most part people have faced that predicament by attempting to justify civil disobedience and revolution. It may be that the ultimate inadequacy of rules and legal systems imposes, when all the chips are down, a stance outside the legal system and a willingness to supersede established processes of law. But we suspect that this judgment may sometimes be premature, and that the issue depends at least partly on the nature of the system. In search, therefore, of some small measure of "just supply and . . . Relation," we have come to ask how even departures from the rules might under certain circumstances be incorporated into the legal order, and how the ability of the legal order to respond to social conflict and change might be increased beyond the conventional provisions for legal change. We freely admit that for those who regard the priority of process over payoff as absolute, no predicament exists; and we admit the same for those who simply reverse the priorities. For the rest of us who can find no comfort in absolute priorities, the predicament is acute. This book is an attempt to find a means of ameliorating that predicament through an examination of the possibilities of lawful departures from legal rules.

Of course, even to the extent that we may succeed, the most fundamental of questions will remain unsettled: what is to be done, here and now? But we cannot imagine that that question could ever be settled. In the hard business of resolving which shall yield, individual judgment or rule, there are only two things of which we are sure: nothing is simple; emphasis is everything. Even so, it cannot be said that the issue falls outside the province of good reasons. And it seems reasonable to hope that a general inquiry into rule departures and legal systems will leave us better equipped to deal with our predicament than before.

In writing this book we have incurred a number of debts that can be acknowledged even if they cannot be repaid. The early collaborative work began when both of us were on leave— Sanford H. Kadish, as a Fellow of the Center for the Study of the Behavioral Sciences in Stanford, California, and Mortimer R. Kadish, as a Fellow of the American Council of Learned Societies. The book was completed during leaves of absence from normal university duties made possible by a Ford Foundation project, Studies of Criminal Law and Social Policy, administered by the Earl Warren Legal Institute and the Center for the Study of Law and Society, Berkeley. We are grateful to these agencies for their generous investment of support and confidence.

We wish also to extend our warm thanks to Ellen Hershey, of the Stanford University Press, for her devoted and helpful editorial review of the manuscript, and to Joshua D. Kadish for his cheerful performance of the cheerless task of preparing the Index.

Professor Philip Selznick read a draft of the manuscript and gave us the benefit of his many critical insights. His generous colleagueship puts us especially in his debt.

An early version of Chapter Two first appeared as "On Justified Rule Departures," 59 *California Law Review* 905 (1971). A segment of that chapter was incorporated in "The Institutionalization of Conflict: Jury Acquittals," 27 *Journal of Social Issues* 199 (1971). In addition, early formulations of some of the material in the book were presented by Sanford H. Kadish in 1969 as the Addison Roach Lectures at the University of Indiana School of Law.

M.R.K.
S.H.K.

July 1973

Contents

Discretion to Disobey

CHAPTER ONE

Justification Before the Rules

How does a legal system affect a person's decisions? Through the practices it institutionalizes and enforces, plainly. Therefore one broad problem in the study of legal systems is the process of institutionalizing particular social and economic practices as part of the dynamics of social change. But we shall be concerned here with a narrower and more technical problem: in what ways, essential to the law, does the law institutionalize and enforce certain practices, whatever they may be?

Two ways have been distinguished: One is by establishing rules and procedures according to which a person may go about his business. If he is a private person, he sues, marries, makes contracts and wills, creates corporations and dissolves them. If he is an official, he performs various acts enabling private persons to sue, marry, and the like, and in general carries out the legislative, executive, administrative, and judicial functions of a public office. Failing to follow the established rules and procedures, the private person simply fails to secure their benefits, and the official fails to exercise his powers. So the first way legal systems affect a person's decisions is by creating channels through which his choices receive content and effect. The second way is through rules of law and commands of officials that exist to foreclose freedom of choice. The relationship of individuals to rules of this second kind—rules we shall refer to as mandatory rules—constitutes the subject matter of this book.

In our usage the statutes of the criminal law are mandatory

rules; so are the commands of policemen and the injunctions of courts, since they also legally foreclose choice. The court order to fulfill the terms of a contract is a mandatory rule, though the decision to make a contract is not mandatory. A court clerk may be required by a mandatory rule to marry all those who come before him who satisfy certain conditions; but if he fails to follow the proper procedure for marrying people, he may not be disobeying a mandatory rule but simply failing to perform a marriage. Likewise, the rules that define the procedure for enacting legislation are not mandatory rules; if they are not heeded, the legislature simply fails to enact a law. By contrast, constitutional prohibitions are mandatory rules, since officials are not free to ignore them even if no punishment is prescribed for doing so.

It seems natural, therefore, for people to regard mandatory rules as affecting their decisions by imposing, whatever the final meaning of the term, obligations. Such rules tell us what we have to do, not what we may do, nor what the law will help us do, nor what we shall be taxed for doing. Will it not seem, therefore, to receivers of the law that the law seeks to affect their decisions by imposing what they ordinarily think of as obligations? Adopting their point of view, mandatory rules may be defined as rules that lay upon us not merely potential liabilities but duties that, so far as the legal system is concerned, it is our obligation to perform—that is to say, legal obligations.* And they may be so defined quite apart from any particular jurisprudential theory of the origin, warrant, or legitimacy of the rules.

Some may say that the notion of an obligation has been taken too seriously. Mandatory rules do not affect conduct by imposing obligations, they would argue, but simply and directly by imposing sanctions on people who break them. According to this view people toss the seriousness of the sanctions and the probability of their incurring them into their decision mill

---

* Later we shall make the point that the obligations imposed by mandatory rules do not all equally constrain final actions. But this does not deny that all mandatory rules impose some obligations.

along with other possible consequences of prospective decisions. That is how the mandatory law affects their decisions, and that is all we ought to mean when we speak of how the law would have people consider what they are obliged to do. But though it would be a mistake to deny the importance of the prospect of sanctions (which, among other things, function to signal what is obligatory), it would also be a mistake to assume that the law affects people's decisions only by this means. This is so for several reasons.

First, the obligatory import of a mandatory rule may be produced by other means than the threat of sanctions, notably through the assumption of office by an official, as we shall later try to show.

Second, even if mandatory rules were invariably linked in a direct and immediate way with sanctions, it would not follow that they affected people's decisions only by the threat of sanctions. The strongest distinction exists between modes of social control that operate by the threat of sanctions and modes of social control that operate by virtue of their authority—and the name that has usually been given to that distinction is "law." If men can be persuaded to make their decisions in view of a mandatory rule they take to impose obligations on them, then conscience will have amplified the effect of threat. And conscience is always a more valuable mode of social control than fear—however useful fear may be—where government has no impenetrable shield to protect it from the governed and very modest resources at best to carry out its threats. Therefore it would be an odd kind of practical philosophy that concluded in the interests of keeping clear of illusions that for the receiver of the law nothing properly counts in the legal system except the threat of punishment.

Finally, and most important, the law as a system of threats simply does not constitute an adequate description of how the law traditionally has worked, or of how it works now, as it seeks to affect people's decisions. Not only does the mandatory law threaten violators with punishment, whether directly or indirectly, but it provides a schema of rights, privileges, liberties, obligations, and duties that serves as a guide to a person trying to determine what the law would have him do. As Prof. H. L. A. Hart observed:

It is sometimes urged . . . that by recasting the law in a form of a direction to apply sanctions, an advance in clarity is made, since this form makes plain all that the "bad man" wants to know about the law. This may be true but it seems an inadequate defense for the theory. Why should not law be equally if not more concerned with the "puzzled man" or "ignorant man" who is willing to do what is required, if only he can be told what it is?[1]

In short, legal systems provide frameworks for the evaluation of action, and there is a difference between the framework of obligations and that of sanctions. Different considerations are at work in each. Legal systems affect people's decisions not only by threatening violators with sanctions, but also by offering people a framework for justifying their actions. Hence the question arises of principal concern to this book—the justifying of one's actions before the rules of the law.

Now why, or whether, a person ought to seek to justify his actions before the law is a very different question from how he is to justify his actions before the law. The former question requires introducing considerations in some meaningful sense external to the system: a person's acceptance of the moral basis of the legal system; his view of himself as a citizen in a community; his more general moral scruples, such as the idea of fairness; or perhaps merely his sense of social utility. But our concern is the second question, not the first. To investigate how legal systems affect conduct through the provision of frameworks of obligations, it suffices that some sorts of moral or prudential considerations, of whatever strength, typically lead people to feel obligated to justify their actions before the law.

We shall use the term citizen to designate those who consider themselves constrained, to whatever extent, to determine their legal obligations in order to fix their conduct. Citizens apply the legal point of view to themselves. Similarly, an official in our usage is not merely a person who occupies a legal or political office, but one who seeks to reach his decisions according to the requirements of that office rather than according to his own convenience or interests. The fundamental questions of this book can now be stated: What limitations on actions of citizens and officials derive from the obligations imposed by the mandatory rules of a legal system? How do they know what decisions to make, given those rules, if they wish to act in a way that can be justified before the law?

The meaningfulness of these questions rests on the assumption that justifying departures from mandatory rules under the law is a genuine problem. We believe that legal systems may still fairly be called such even though they provide alternatives to unqualified obedience for citizens and officials confronted by mandatory rules. Moreover, we believe that our own legal system makes it possible on occasion for citizens and officials to justify legally their departures from the rules, even while acting as citizens and officials.

The jurisprudence of departures from rules, on which this book is an essay, considers those features of legal systems, whether or not they find direct and formal expression in the law, that a citizen or official may invoke in order to justify his departure from some mandatory rule. Our first step toward that jurisprudence will be to determine what kind of justification a citizen or official might properly offer for his actions and in what sense he might conceivably justify a departure from mandatory rules. If that analysis is correct, the jurisprudence of rule departures arises as no special consequence of the law or the nature of citizens and officials as such, but rather as the consequence of certain very general features of organized behavior of which legal systems avail themselves.

The Justification for Undertaking an Action

What kind of justification might a citizen or official properly offer for his actions if challenged to defend them? We shall follow the common view that in answering such a challenge he does not properly defend himself merely by showing that the action itself is desirable; at the same time he must also show that as a citizen or official he is entitled to perform that action. He misses the point offering merely the "justification of an action." He must offer the second, fuller response, which we call the "justification for (an agent's) undertaking an action." Legal systems seek to affect human conduct through the organization of contexts in virtue of which citizens and officials may argue to the justification of their undertaking an action. The distinction between the justification of an action and the justification for undertaking an action is essential to this analysis, and we must try to make it good.

Observe, first, that the distinction is rooted in ordinary experience. To justify fixing a leaky faucet oneself rather than hiring a plumber, it normally suffices to say that the faucet leaked, that plumbers are expensive, and that one has the time and can probably manage to do the job. The justification of the action is precisely the kind of justification required. To defend the dollar given to a panhandler, it is enough to say that the dollar can be spared and the fellow's story might have been true. In these cases it suffices to answer the challenge to one's actions on the merits, whether those merits be prudential or ethical.

A man asked by his wife, however, to explain his purchase of a hi-fi set cannot simply answer that the family needed one, that it seemed like a good buy, and that the money was in the bank, even if she agrees to all of these statements. He must also explain why he did not consult her first, in case she had some other use for the money. In other words, he must defend the appropriateness of his action as well as its merits. In some cases the challenge may extend to the concept of appropriateness itself. An employer might challenge his employee to explain his failure to promise the delivery of goods to a customer by a specific date, and the employee might respond that making such promises lay outside his competence. The employee has of course tried to justify his conduct by defending the appropriateness of his action. But the employer might not be satisfied. He could conceivably answer that the employee should have considered the merits of the case—the weight of advantage in making a sale and the attendant probability of exoneration, even reward—and ought therefore to have exceeded his competence.

Thus two component arguments are required to justify undertaking an action: an argument to the merits and an argument to appropriateness. The former supports the conclusion, a "proposition of merit," that the merits riding on an action outweigh the demerits (and suffices for the justification of an action). The latter supports the conclusion, a "proposition of appropriateness," that it is justifiable for the agent, given his position, to make a judgment and to act on it. Propositions of appropriateness characteristically appear in forms such as the following: "Actions of type A are (or are not) up to agent X"; "X has no choice but to do (or not do) A"; "X has (or does not have) freedom of action for A"; "X has the obligation to do (or not do) A"; "A is permissible (or not) for X"; "X has (or lacks) the privilege of doing A"; "A is (or is not) a legitimate action for X"; "X has (or does not have) the right to do A"; and so on. Propositions of merit, by contrast, appear in the use of predicates such as "desirable," "good," "best for all concerned," "advantageous," and the like. The two sorts of propositions are necessary and jointly sufficient to establish that an agent ought to undertake a given action.

Such, broadly speaking, is the justification for undertaking an action. In order for citizens and officials to justify undertaking their actions in the context of a system of laws, they must argue toward a proposition of merit establishing that the action to be undertaken is, in the context of a legal system, desirable or meritorious, and they must argue toward a proposition of appropriateness establishing that the contemplated action is indeed appropriate for a citizen or official to undertake. In studying the rule departures of citizens and officials, the complexity of the relationship between merit and appropriateness in general and in the legal system in particular will then be-

come a central issue, since it is almost always an appraisal of
the merits that induces people to depart from the rules. But two
questions must be answered before we can proceed. First, is the
distinction between propositions and arguments of merit, on the
one hand, and propositions and arguments of appropriateness,
on the other, a genuine distinction, or have we been taking ordinary ways of speaking too seriously? Second, even if the distinction is genuine, why must citizens and officials justify undertaking their actions rather than simply justify their actions?

Merit and Appropriateness

As a first step in making good the distinction between propositions of merit and propositions of appropriateness, it is important to see that the vocabularies of merit and appropriateness are used differently, even though they overlap. Consider,
for example, the following sketch of a justification for undertaking an action. The critical predicates, "right" and "wrong,"
occur in both propositions and in the conclusion:

Proposition of merit. The war in Vietnam is wrong and
should be ended.

Proposition of appropriateness. Whenever a war is wrong it
is right for a citizen to engage in any nonviolent action, legal
or not, that will in his judgment help end the war.

Conclusion justifying undertaking the action. Therefore, as
a citizen I am right to undertake any nonviolent action that
will in my judgment help end the war in Vietnam.

Plainly, "wrong" in "the war in Vietnam is wrong" and
"whenever a war is wrong" has a purely ethical or prudential
force. "Right" in the proposition of appropriateness ("it is
right for a citizen") is not used in exactly the opposite sense of
"wrong" in the proposition of merit, but is used in the sense of
granting the right to undertake an action. The idea would be
less ambiguously conveyed by some such language as "it is up to
me (or appropriate, permissible, legitimate)." "Right" in the
conclusion ("I am right to undertake") is used in yet another
sense, that of "fully justified."

If some agent X thinks that some action A ought to be undertaken, it cannot be the case, if the employment of vocabulary is as suggested, that X ought therefore to undertake A just as long as A lies within X's power. No doubt it is often true that if X thinks A is justified on the merits, he ought to undertake A if he can, but the conclusion does not follow from the premise. To reach the final conclusion of the previously given example, not only must the proposition of merit (that the war in Vietnam is ethically or prudentially wrong) be true, but the illustrating proposition of appropriateness must also be true; and the suppression of that proposition serves to hide what may often be the major point at issue.

The distinction between propositions of merit and propositions of appropriateness involves more than an elementary dialectical point, for propositions of appropriateness that justify undertaking an action determine the use made of propositions of merit. An agent may decide with a high degree of certainty that a particular act ought to be performed and that only he can perform that act, and yet he may also recognize the need to decide whether or not to proceed on that judgment. The risk of trying to justify the decision to undertake an action on purely moral grounds, even in cases of civil disobedience, follows: if one wants to consider a question of civil disobedience a moral question, one must be careful not to collapse the justification of the decision to undertake the act into the proposition of merit just because the proposition of merit is preeminently a moral proposition. One must not forget that a proposition of appropriateness is necessary to decide what to do about the proposition of merit.

Later we will consider just how propositions of appropriateness license or constrain action indicated by propositions of merit. But that they do so, that linguistic usage corresponds to the urgencies of experience when it discriminates between predicates as they function in propositions of merit and in propositions of appropriateness, is plain enough. To submerge one proposition into the other fails to confront precisely the nub of the problem involved in justifying the undertaking of an action: to resolve a tension between what an agent's judgment prompts him to do and what is or is not appropriate for an agent to do in a given context. To justify the undertaking of an action we must have considered the possibility that we might have to say, even if we did not want to, "I'd like to do such and such but I cannot, I am not free to," or "I wish I did not have to do this but I must," or whatever the locutions suitable in the circumstances. If under no circumstances could we imagine putting ourselves under such a tension in confronting the merits, there could never be a possibility of feeling that we had justified undertaking the action. So, in the example given, undertaking civil disobedience has been justified, however adequately or inadequately, just because a proposition of appropriateness prohibiting it might have been substituted for the highly permissive proposition of appropriateness that licensed it. If the proposition of appropriateness simply followed directly from the proposition of merit, and hence could not be discriminated from it, the civil disobedient's undertaking the action could never have been justified.

To be sure, it might be said that the tension between appropriateness and merit is itself a moral tension. Confronting that tension, according to this view, one simply includes any restriction imposed by propositions of appropriateness among the other advantages or disadvantages in terms of which one finally, by some sort of weighing process, reaches a conclusion. But the point is a purely dialectical one, for even in that weighing metaphor, which covers up the crucial problem of how precisely to weigh each element in the decision, propositions of appropriateness still function in a unique way.

It should also be seen that the argument to merit and the argument to appropriateness are not identical, just as the propositions they support are not. That the two arguments are in fact discriminated in practice as agents consider and reconsider undertaking an action is obvious in the example just given. The civil disobedient in that case distinguishes (or if he does not his

opponents will make him distinguish) his reasons for concluding that the war in Vietnam is unjust from his reasons for concluding that the individual citizen has the right to obstruct wars
he believes are unjust.

How could such a person support his proposition of appropriateness? To quiet doubts in his own mind or in the minds
of others he must do two things. First, he must explicate the
nature and extent of the commitment to which his proposition
of appropriateness leads, a matter separate from that of determining whether the war in Vietnam is justified morally, politically, or in any other sense. How wrong must a war be before
citizens are justified in undertaking acts of civil disobedience?
Does his proposition apply only to wars, or can it be extended
to other situations? Second, he must show why the commitment
to which his proposition leads is desirable. If, for example, his
view of appropriate action for citizens presupposes an anarchis-
tic conception of society, he must show why such a conception
should be accepted. Among the arguments supporting his proposition of appropriateness there must stand a more or less coherent political theory in virtue of which a certain class of actions becomes appropriate for citizens, a political philosophy
justifying that theory, and of course whatever arguments are
available in support of that theory and philosophy.

Let us put the matter generally, then, to apply to any domain
—political, legal, economic, familial, and so on—in which justification for undertaking an action is relevant: for any such
domain, the argument to appropriateness demands as a necessary condition an institutional program for the allocation of
authority to make decisions along with whatever arguments are
needed to sustain such an institutional program. The argument
to the merits, however, does not require an institutional program. To show that the war in Vietnam is wrong, it would suffice
to point up the attendant toll in life, physical destruction of the
country, disruption in the internal affairs of the United States,
and so on. There is no need to show the inconsistency of the
war in Vietnam with an institutional program, though the war's

disruptive consequences for a justifiable institutional program
would of course be part of the argument to the merits.

When Undertaking an Action Must Be Justified

As matters stand so far, anyone who wanted to consider decisions to abide by or depart from mandatory rules as, simply,
decisions to be made on the merits might easily concede that if
such decisions were justified as one justified undertaking an
action, then absorbing the proposition of appropriateness into
one of merit would be a mistake. But then he could simply deny
that departures from mandatory rules were of the kind that required justification for undertaking an action. What conditions
pertinent to the plight of citizens and officials call for that special kind of justification? Fortunately, political and moral philosophy have long since explored the circumstances under which
it is expected that people will not merely justify their action but
justify themselves before the rules.

People recognize that they must justify undertaking an action
when they see the action as affecting the interests and preferences of other persons, but not usually when they see it as affecting only themselves. Thus there was no need for Robinson
Crusoe to justify undertaking any action until his man Friday
appeared. Of course, Crusoe could have continued taking all
his actions on himself, merely expanding the range of those
actions to include Friday. But to have done so would have denied Friday's existence as a person. If Friday was to be his own
man, and not merely Crusoe's, Crusoe became obliged to justify
undertaking his actions, and hence to begin the search for propositions of appropriateness. So it is with citizens and officials.
To act in their roles preeminently entails affecting the interests
and preferences of other persons, since the rules of a legal system characteristically represent settled norms of conduct that
adjust the different interests and preferences of persons in the
legal community.

Of course, the principle that people must justify undertaking
an action when others are affected is based on a system of values,
and not on logical necessity. It flows from an underlying com-

mitment that other people are entitled to be treated as autonomous and free beings rather than as manipulable things—a commitment that has informed not only the Rechtsphilosophie of Kant and Hegel, but the entire Western liberal tradition.

Another consideration commonly advanced to induce people to relinquish their claims to act according to their perceptions of the merits of the case is that they might be mistaken even when they feel sure of their grounds. Therefore, the argument runs, a person must not presume to judge unless he has the right to risk being mistaken—and society allocates rights to risk mistakes in a certain domain partly according to an agent's competence in that domain. So it may be argued that a person's private life is his own business, not the government's, for who would know better where the shoe pinched and how to handle his private life? So also it has been argued that the government's power over the economic life of a society ought to be severely limited, since a government cannot adequately make judgments about the multifarious aspects of an economy.

There is much to this more or less classic argument, especially when the risk of being mistaken is seen to include both the probability of making a mistake and the seriousness of the mistake in question. In any domain, as the seriousness of the mistake risked in action increases, the acceptable probability of being mistaken decreases. Regardless of how the seriousness of a mistake is measured, then, the introduction and observance of propositions of appropriateness asserting that a given risk may be assumed by X but not by Y becomes an essential part of a society's structure. By establishing conditions under which an agent may act according to his own judgment and conditions under which he cannot, society minimizes the probability that we will afflict one another with our certitudes. In the domain governed by the law, the consequences of a possible mistake are always too serious to leave to chance, and it becomes the better policy for all members of the community to follow a general strategy for the assumption of risks.

One last set of considerations is essentially Hobbesian. When predictability and peace are considered desirable, rational

people are driven to demand a justification for undertaking
actions. And predictability and peace are prime ends of the law.

Why would a rational person prefer a society in which decisions are made within a system of licenses and constraints?
Why, in effect, would he opt for the social contract, the classic
way of insisting that a judgment of an action's merits alone is
insufficient as a justification for undertaking the action? Because, to make the predictability point first, if he knows that
there exist institutional limits on people's right to undertake
actions according to their judgment of the merits, then to that
degree he need not know the details of the circumstances surrounding other people's lives when he plans behavior depen-
dent on the behavior of others. If others fail him, he can make
a case showing why they ought not to fail him; and to the extent
that the institutional framework makes sanctions available,
whether the overt sanctions of the law or the covert ones of
guilt, he can hope for a measure of control. If another person
promises him something, he can exert a pressure to keep that
person to his promise even though circumstances arise that
make the promiser rue the promise. When a man signs a contract he can be reasonably sure that the other person will either
comply with the conditions of the contract or pay for the failure.
Business, in the broadest sense, becomes possible; the state of
nature has been overcome. And every rational person must desire that end as a condition for reaching his goals, regardless of
whether or not the particular arguments of appropriateness
generated by his society's institutions are justifiable.

The point about peace follows. In a society where decisions
were not made according to a system of rights and obligations
for undertaking action but according to what each thought
best at the moment, no one could anticipate what anyone else
would do next. Peaceable though he might otherwise be, each
person would therefore be compelled to wage the war of each
against all in order to protect his interests. To use a more modern phrase, he would be compelled by the logic of the preemptive strike; and as Hobbes in effect says, it is that logic, not

just a propensity to force or fraud, that precipitates the state of war.

Why, then, must decisions about compliance with mandatory rules be justified as one justifies undertaking an action? The reason is at least in part that legal systems serve in varying measure to protect persons and define the limits to their actions, to assign rights for the assumption of risks, and to increase predictability and secure peace.

Acting in Roles: Citizens and Officials

We now face the task of considering somewhat more closely just what goes into the justification for undertaking an action. Only then can we understand what is involved in attempting to justify a departure from a rule by a citizen or official.

The common concept of a social role offers a helpful basis for approaching the task, since it is precisely to the concept of their role that people turn when they want to understand what they can and cannot do. The union member, student, employer, father, physician, priest, citizen, or official—for citizens and officials are acting in roles, too—who asks himself whether an action is appropriate or not means to ask himself whether it is up to him in his role as union member, student, employer, father, physician, citizen, or official to undertake the action. Accordingly, given that nearly everyone has at one time or another tried to justify undertaking an action in a role, it should be possible to gain at least a rough idea of what constitutes the justification for undertaking an action by reconsidering what it means to act in a role.

From our point of view, which does not presume to take a position on sociological controversies concerning role theory, the notion of a role is pertinent because it refers to what one ordinarily has in mind when one speaks of acting in a certain capacity, or of being constrained by one's position, or of standing in a certain relationship to someone. Following common parlance, then, and abstracting from it only enough to suit our own purposes, we shall understand roles as established and continuing parts in a social enterprise or institution. As such, they serve an accepted social purpose, which is why one can refer to them to justify one's actions. They are "parts" because the life of the social institution or enterprise depends upon their performance. They are "established" first in the sense that, while their agents may sometimes alter them, those agents typically encounter the rules and purposes of the role substantially given; and second in the sense that agents can refer to their role to establish their authority to deal with others. Being perceived by those who enact them and by those who receive those enactments as framed for the occupancy of others who will, or may, come later, roles are conceived as intrinsically "continuing." Agents come and go—the role remains.

In such an intuitive sense of role, being a citizen or official would be to act in a role. Being a thief, on the other hand, would not be to act in a role in the community at large, though within the Mafia or the society of the *Threepenny Opera*, thieving would be doing an approved job of work and hence constitute a social role. Being a chess player also would not be to act in a role, since however socialized and regularized chess playing may be, chess players do not perform any social function—though as game players they might in an appropriate society, such as Hermann Hesse's Castalia.

To act in a role, then, suggests that at least the following considerations have a bearing on the justification of one's action. First, anyone who acts in a role engages in a certain more or less distinctive activity that constitutes his "participation in an interactive process,"* and that participation defines precisely

---

* "The role is that organized sector of an actor's orientation which constitutes and defines his participation in an interactive process. It involves a set of complementary expectations concerning his own actions and those of others with whom he interacts. Both the actor and those with whom he interacts possess these expectations. Roles are institutionalized when they are fully congruous with the prevailing culture patterns of value-orientation shared by the members of the collectivity in which the role functions." T. Parsons and E. A. Shils, eds., *Toward a General Theory of Action* (New York, 1962), p. 23.

what his role is. Second, for the sake of that participation he reaches judgments on how to act in a special context of evaluation that provides him with standards for supporting propositions of appropriateness and so determines how he is to manage his role.

In the remainder of this section we shall attempt to indicate how people acting in roles (with special emphasis on citizens and officials) engage in more or less distinctive activities and reach judgments in a special context of evaluation. We shall also reach the more general question of how people may determine the nature of the role they occupy.

The Role Activity

That one who acts in a role (or a "role agent," as we shall sometimes call him) must engage in a certain kind of purposeful activity follows from what is normally meant by a role. The parent who does not care for his or her children, and in a certain sort of way, fails to act as a parent. The officer who does not command fails to act as an officer. The congressman who takes advantage of his prerogatives but refuses to participate in the legislative process is no congressman. To act in a role is, plainly, to do certain sorts of socially useful things in a certain sort of way.

Since a person's role activity must have a social function, it must ultimately be sustained by the role activity of others. The parent who cares for his children does not do so as a parent, but merely as a matter of fact, on his own as it were, unless his activity is in some way recognized and sustained by society. The officer cannot act as an officer unless there are other people who in their roles will accept his commands. The congressman cannot function in his role without the acceptance of the entire legal system by the other members of society; and merely to influence legislation, to whatever degree, does not make one a congressman. Therefore it is a fundamental consideration guiding role conduct that others in their roles sustain one's role activity. If they do not, the activity ceases to be such activity. And others "sustain" role activity in the sense that a person acting in a role must depend on the cooperation of others acting in their roles to achieve the ends prescribed by his, and also in the sense that those others, seeing him as a participant with them in some social enterprise, impute a kind of legitimacy to his behavior, a legitimacy often expressed by the locution that it is proper for him to be doing what he is doing.

It is clear enough that an official performs various distinctive and socially sustained activities of the sort that characterize roles. But what are the activities that characterize the role of the citizen? Essentially they are the reciprocal of the official's activities. If officials are to perform their functions, others must consent to conduct their affairs in accordance with those official activities—and they must choose to do so, they must accept their role as citizens, if the legal system is to be a system that rules at least partly through the obligations it imposes rather than through brute force. Thus the citizen's activity consists of co-operating with the political-legal system by accepting the restrictions it imposes on his conduct as well as its positive obligations, even though the citizen need not necessarily heed every authoritative voice addressing him, as we will show later. The point is really a very old one. The citizen as citizen holds no office except insofar as the law may require, as it does in the case of jury members in our system; and he participates in the process of government only in the way the legal system provides for, as by exercising his right to vote. He respects the authority the legal system has allocated to make the political and legal order viable, and in acceding to the law he both sustains and is sustained by the activities of officials.

Judging in a Context of Evaluation

To act in a role does not merely mean to engage in a distinctive activity that is sustained by persons acting in other roles. It also means to make choices in a context of evaluation proper to a role. A context of evaluation determines not only whether a role agent's actions will be regarded as proper by others but how he himself will weigh his options in a given situation. What does a context of evaluation consist of? Given our concern with how a person might justify undertaking an action, the question is a critical one. Since by our definition roles must have social functions, we shall proceed by analyzing the elements of contexts of evaluation under the general categories of prescribed means and prescribed ends. Not every context of evaluation includes all the elements we shall mention, but some of them must be present to set standards for the propositions of appropriateness a person acting in a role must offer to justify undertaking an action.

Prescribed Means. One element of a context of evaluation, and hence one kind of standard for propositions of appropriateness, consists of what we shall call constraints on reasons — more or less explicit limitations on what reasons will be considered acceptable for undertaking actions in a particular role. Specifying acceptable reasons serves essentially as a means by which roles may be structured to achieve their ends. Thus a person acting in a role knows that certain considerations must not be taken into account; that other considerations may or may not be taken into account at his own discretion; and that still other considerations must always be taken into account. In the more complex roles the constraints on reasons include weights and priorities assigned to various aspects of the role's ends. Thus the appropriateness of a role agent's action depends in part on whether the action is in accord with that particular role's priorities. A person who gives great weight to that which is minimal or little to that which is overriding does not judge as a person in that role.

Only rarely are constraints on reasons adequately developed for all the occasions when a person acting in a role must make a decision. Nevertheless, if a role is to be differentiated from other roles, some set of constraints on reasons must be distinguishable. There is a special way of rebuking anyone who strays from such constraints, even with the best of intentions and the best of reasons, except that those reasons are not reasons of the role: "Remember," such a person is enjoined, "you are a soldier, not a social worker; a priest, not a judge; a parent, not a stranger." Similarly, officials of the legal and political systems may be told: "Remember, you are a judge, not a legislator; a prosecutor, not a defense attorney." The same holds for citizens: "Remember, you are a private citizen, not a judge. Perhaps you would have decided the case differently. That's not a relevant reason for refusing to comply." Such statements say in effect that reasons acceptable in one role are precluded in another.

Constraints on actions, rather than on reasons for actions, are another element in a context of evaluation. Whatever the constraints on reasons in a particular context of evaluation may be, there are times when no reason suffices to justify a role agent's undertaking or not undertaking a certain action. Constraints on action extend to the outcomes of any reasoning within a context of evaluation, rather than to the reasoning itself.

Constraints on actions are part of any role's context of evaluation in virtue of the distinctive and socially sustained activity that characterizes the role. Through those constraints the structure of a role seeks to guarantee that at least the essential ends of the role will be achieved, and that the achievement of other ends, perhaps those of other roles, will not be blocked. That a soldier may not leave the battlefield without the permission of his commander is a constraint on his action; his deferring to that rule, even in the face of death, is one of the things that makes him a soldier. Similarly, constraints on the actions of officials follow from the nature of their office, and are essential to achieving the ends for which the office was created. And the actions of citizens are of course constrained by the legal system.

A related kind of constraint on actions consists of specifications of actions that will count as actions in the role, rather than of actions that may not or must be taken. This element appears in the context of evaluation of roles that entail the exercise of delegated powers, such as the role of an official. An official must exercise his powers by certain procedures and within certain limits if his actions are to have any effect. For example, a judge who acts in excess of his jurisdiction has in effect taken no action at all: his action counts for nothing legally. Such constraints do not apply to the citizen, however, whose role need not entail any delegated powers. To say that a citizen has not acted as a citizen means only that he has not acted properly in his role. His actions count as actions nonetheless. One might say that a citizen who refuses to pay his taxes has failed to carry out his obligations as a citizen. His refusal still stands as an action, however, and one for which he may be held accountable.

Needless to say, there is always the possibility of serious disagreement over which actions constitute role actions and over proper procedure for exercising delegated powers in a role. Difficulties of this sort are commonly encountered in all but the simplest roles, and especially among bureaucrats jockeying for position. Still, contexts of evaluation provide a basis for settling such quarrels and appraising the actions of those acting in roles.

It must be emphasized that contexts of evaluation do not eliminate the possibility of acting at one's own discretion. To the contrary, discretion is intelligible only in terms of a context of evaluation, for a role agent acting at his own discretion must have a way of judging what considerations are relevant and what actions are proper within his role. Thus a trial judge is often required to act at his own discretion in sentencing a criminal, but he must set the sentence within certain prescribed limits on the basis of facts the law deems appropriate for him to consider. In general, then, constraints on reasons and on actions within a role often allow some discretion to persons acting in the role. And sometimes role constraints may specifically demand the exercise of discretion.

Prescribed Ends. All roles exist to achieve some end or ends, as we have seen. And the prescribed means just discussed are those constraints on role-agent conduct that have been fashioned to serve those ends. But sometimes a role's context of evaluation will extend to the ends of the role as well, so that the role agent may (or must) consider the mesh between the prescribed means and the role's ends in judging the appropriateness of undertaking some action. The familiar case in which the end of a role becomes part of its context of evaluation, though by no means the only one, as will be subsequently shown, ocurs when a role agent is required or permitted to act at his own discretion to achieve the end of his role. It is instructive to consider now the various types of ends that sometimes enter a role's context of evaluation.

The most immediate and least abstract type of end to which a role agent may have recourse in determining appropriate action is the specific task his role is designed to accomplish. For example, the mailman's role could conceivably authorize him to choose his delivery route, to decide his hours of delivery, to give preference to pieces of mail that deserved priority, and the like, so long as he acted in accordance with the end of delivering the mail. Normally, of course, the mailman's role does not allow recourse to ends, even the end of delivering the mail. But it could be structured so that the mailman would determine his actions in accordance with his conception of his task. The same could be said, in fact, for any official role—that action will be appropriate to the degree it is in the interest of accomplishing the task and inappropriate to the degree to which it is not.

Another type of end that may become part of a context of evaluation is a role's function within a larger institution, which may itself be embedded in an entire network of institutions. To the extent that a role is so structured, judging the appropriateness of undertaking action extends to the evaluation of the role's task in the light of the larger institutional ends that the task ends are designed to serve. When this happens both the role's prescribed means and its task ends become subject to modification and interpretation by the role agent as conflicts appear. The institutional organization of society then itself becomes a factor in making judgments in a role. Obviously officials and political leaders, at least those at high levels of government, must constantly reassess the relationship of their role activity to the larger institutional framework within which their roles function. But citizens also have institutional ends they may properly take into account in certain situations. Broadly speaking, those ends are part of the general end of ensuring that the society's system of rules and competences functions successfully. Contributing to that general end will then become a relevant consideration in differentiating appropriate from inappropriate action.

The third type of end that may become part of a context of evaluation derives from commitments to norms that transcend any institutionalized role. There can be no a priori objection to incorporating in the contexts of evaluation of at least some roles, including some of those in the legal and political systems, what we shall call "background ends." Whereas task ends and institutional ends may be invoked to justify actions that serve more or less established task requirements and institutions, background ends enable an individual role agent to conceive of what is proper in his role in a more liberal or open way— or, it must be conceded, in a narrower and more wrongheaded way—and so to alter the institutional pattern in which he finds himself. He may thus invoke ends that are recognized by his society but only incompletely realized by its structure, or even ends his society has completely ignored. He may even look further afield and invoke ends that perhaps no system of roles has ever achieved or could be expected to achieve in full measure: ends such as a finer justice, kindliness, respect for other people, or human creativity. In sum, background ends may serve as a basis for criticizing and humanizing institutional ends. Later we shall argue that background ends do in fact function in the structure of some legally defined roles as points of resistance against the prescribed means for achieving role ends.

Such, roughly, are the elements that may appear in the context of evaluation proper to a role: constraints on reasons for undertaking actions; constraints on actions themselves, and on what will count as role actions; and a variety of different types of role ends of increasing generality that a person may properly take into account under certain circumstances. Our case for the justifiability of departures from mandatory rules by citizens and officials will ultimately depend on the appeal to ends.

Knowing the Role

In order for an agent to respond to a challenge to some action of his undertaken in his role, he must first determine the nature of his role. Does the role's context of evaluation grant the role agent recourse to certain ends in justifying his actions? What tasks does it require him to perform? Such questions are not always easily answered. To determine the characteristics of a role one could reasonably consult the people who act in the role and study their behavior, but one still would not necessarily know what their reports and one's own observations signified, particularly if the two sources differed. Simply describing role behavior does not necessarily uncover the essential characteristics of the role itself. To complicate matters further, all roles need not be determinate in every respect. Roles change; roles grow; roles divide and collapse. But difficult as the task may be, it cannot be escaped by one challenged to defend undertaking some action in his role. How then are roles known?

The Ecology of Roles. The repeated observation that social roles must sustain each other suggests one direction in which an answer may be found. In order to discover what behavior is appropriate in a role and how to interpret the justification offered by role agents for their actions, one considers not only what the role agent says and does but also how persons in complementary roles respond. When do they object, and in what way? Will they refuse to cooperate, or extend cooperation only partially or provisionally? What sanctions will they administer? A role is shaped substantially by the demands of the complementary roles surrounding it; hence we may determine some of the characteristics of a role by studying its function in a complex of interdependent roles, or what we shall call the "ecology of roles." We speak of an ecology precisely because changes in specific roles tend to follow changes anywhere in the institutional environment and may radiate consequences for roles apparently far removed. By studying the ecology of roles we can see the consequences for other roles if the role in question should have one characteristic rather than another. Since there are such consequences, that a role has a given characteristic need no longer be left to simple observation; it can be confirmed against the requirements of the roles that it sustains and the roles that sustain it.

The Historical Reference. People also know the characteristics of their role, the obligations and privileges for which it provides, through the role's origins and history. In effect, roles are known through an explanation of how they got to be that way, and that is especially true of the more complex legal and political roles. But to comprehend the full meaning of a role's history, one must also trace the history of the role's developing ecology. A role's past development cannot be understood without reference to its past ecology any more than a role's present nature can be understood without reference to its present ecology. Tracing that large history also gives sense to precedents. This is so because roles are historical entities, by and large. They are established for those who come in time to fill them; and those who come in time to fill them are expected to value the way they were filled in the past. In fact, historical analysis is one means by which people often reach agreement on propositions of appropriateness.

The Systematic Reference. We said that roles are historical entities "by and large" because plainly a constitution may be written or an enterprise begun that creates a role full-grown. Such a role has no precedents. To assess its characteristics one must first turn to the constitution, statute, or agreement that produced it. If that step fails to produce a definitive result, it seems natural, as the history of constitutional law illustrates, to refer to the ecology of roles in which the constituted role was intended to operate. Nevertheless, in the case of a deliberately contrived social role one must always appeal first to the systematic reference—to the act that created the role.

Normative Judgments. A final means of determining the nature of a role deserves particular attention. It is the appeal, in some phases of some arguments about roles, to judgments of what a role should be in order to establish propositions about what it is.

Sometimes, despite ecological considerations, precedents and systematic references, disagreement over the nature of a role persists. At that point the parties to the controversy may find themselves making implicit appeals to differing normative judgments, and then continuing the argument over the role's nature by disputing one another's judgments of what the role ought to be like. For example, they might argue about whether a prosecuting attorney's role requires him to prosecute all known and provable cases that violate some portion of the penal code. A decision on the nature of his role may then depend partly on the case that can be made for the social values of having him do so.

Within the limits of ecology, history, and system, then, roles can be said to have the properties that they ought to have. Sometimes, no doubt, the constraints on the role prior to the appeal to normative judgments are so strong and definite that the normative judgment carries no weight. But at other times, particularly when events make roles as traditionally construed inadequate, it is natural to seek the nature of the role in what would be better for the role, the institution it serves, or society at large.

Rule Departures in Roles

We must now develop further the premise on which this inquiry into justified rule departures hinges: that in some roles a departure from a mandatory rule can at times be justified in terms of a proposition of appropriateness that leaves it up to the role agent to make judgments on discrepancies between prescribed means and ends and on conflicts among ends. To develop that premise further we must now show how such roles function, how they differ from other roles, and how they originate in a society. Just as the previous section considered the roles of citizen and official primarily in terms of the general properties they share with other roles, now we shall consider the potentialities of roles for justified departures from rules in general, whether they be social or moral conventions, the orders of a superior in a private organization, or the mandatory rules of the law. So doing will exhibit rule departures in legal systems as exemplifications of the possibilities of social organization in general, and not as mere quirks of the law.

Individuals and Roles

As a first step in understanding the rationality of roles that permit rule departures, let us consider the relationship of individuals to their roles not as abstract role agents, but as real people who must convince themselves that they ought to undertake a specific action required by their role. In his role a person may be a doctor, a judge, a senator, a mail carrier, but he is also a person with his own aspirations and ethics. Thus not one but two sets of considerations, broadly speaking, guide his conduct. The first consists of what we call "role reasons"—reasons based on the constraints of his role tempered by whatever discretion recourse to role ends may afford him. The second consists of reasons that he may recognize as an individual but that in his role he cannot take into account, or what we call "excluded reasons." Frequently a person committed to a role finds himself in situations where the role reasons for undertaking an action and the excluded reasons conflict. In such a case he does not simply weigh the role reasons equally against the excluded reasons, and then act according to whichever set of reasons is greater. Instead he acknowledges his obligation to his role by imposing an extra burden, or surcharge,* so to speak, on the

---

* See W. D. Ross's *The Right and the Good* (Oxford, Eng., 1930), where the idea of surcharge is used in a critique of utilitarianism. Our borrowed usage of the term as part of an account of what it means to accept a role commitment is logically independent of arguments over utilitarianism or other ethical theories.

excluded reasons, so that they must have significantly greater weight than the role reasons, rather than merely greater weight, in order to sway him. This is a familiar way of dealing with one's role commitments. Nearly everyone has had the experience of acknowledging that he would take a certain course of action if only he were not in a certain position. Usually this means that though the acknowledged merits of the case carry, in one's objective judgment, in favor of the action required, they are insufficient to overcome the demands of one's role. Very rarely, perhaps, it may mean that the excluded reasons never could carry against the role reasons, no matter what their weight.

In effect, in dealing with obligations of role, the surcharge imposed on excluded reasons is either finite, as in the first case, or infinite, as in the second. Imposing a finite surcharge is the practical result of being a person who at once accepts his obligation to a role and continues to think of himself as an individual with other commitments as well; imposing an infinite surcharge is the practical result of being a person who puts his obligation to a role unqualifiedly first. It is difficult to see how an absolutely unqualified commitment to any role can be defended. But a qualified commitment to a role, based on a finite surcharge, might be defended by seeking agreement on the whole institutional program in which that role exists, along with the implications of role deviation of the given sort for a large variety of wider interests. So the student who interrupts a class defends himself by condemning the university's structure and involvement with the military-industrial complex. He counters the accusation that he has taken his role obligations as a student too lightly by urging the overwhelming value of an alternative institutional program. In sum, in defending his judgment of the appropriate surcharge against his action, he engages in social philosophy.

That, very roughly, is how people manage their role commitments, quite apart from all consideration of whether the role somehow permits rule departures. We can now turn to the questions of how rule departures in roles become possible and why a rational society might want to make them possible.

How Rule Departures in Roles Become Possible

Roles, including those of citizen and official, may be structured to take account of the fact that individuals acting in roles nevertheless place for the most part only a finite surcharge on excluded reasons before departing from some role requirement. That fact is taken into account for some roles by incorporating into their contexts of evaluation a principle for acting in the role that, in effect, guides the agent in applying and sometimes extending the context itself. Though such a role may still require a role agent to act in a certain way, it may also permit him to conclude that complying with the role's prescribed means would obstruct the role activity or defeat the role's task or institutional ends. Or it may permit him even to conclude that the required action would defeat certain background ends, which by their nature could never be clearly delineated in the role's context of evaluation. In effect, the role agent is permitted to incorporate into his decision what would ordinarily be excluded reasons, or to put the matter differently, to convert excluded reasons for an action into role reasons. He is at liberty to act on his own judgment in certain circumstances, and he can expect his decision to be supported by others in related roles. This is the finesse that introduces flexibility into role behavior and reduces the instances in which people simply step out of their roles in order to do what must be done.

There is nothing unfamiliar in the extension of a liberty to depart from the rules. It is simply not true that every conception of a soldier's role requires the soldier to obey his superior officer no matter what he may be commanded to do. The soldiers who obeyed Lieutenant Calley's command to fire on civilians might have been expected, as soldiers, to assume the risks of disobedience instead. Central to the physician's role is the requirement that he preserve the life of his patient, but he may, when the costs in pain are great enough, and long before meeting the problem of euthanasia, act to reduce pain in a way that in some measure increases the danger to his patient's life. Few would say in such circumstances that he had failed to act as a physician. In the earlier example of the employee who lost a sale because he refused to act outside his competence, the employer's response was not to commend his dutifulness but to reprimand him for failing to depart from the rules to further the institutional end of his role—to profit the employer's business. Our point is not merely that persons acting in roles sometimes depart from the rules, but that rule departures may on occasion be necessary if one is to be a good soldier, a good doctor, a good employee, and so on.

Two requirements must be met if such rule departures are to be justified. First, extra weight must be given to achieving the role's ends through its prescribed means, including any discretion that the role may provide for; by the same token, an extra burden must be imposed on any reasons there may be for departing from the role's requirements. In effect, the procedure used when conscientious individuals depart from roles that do not provide for justifiable rule departures must be incorporated as a feature of roles that do provide for justifiable departures.

The second requirement is that there be a constraint on the reasons for undertaking the action. A person's reason for departing from a role's prescribed means or for failing to achieve its prescribed end must meet some standard of relevance; otherwise the valuable distinction would be lost between the flexibility afforded by roles providing for justifiable rule departures and the exploitation and misuse of such roles. That standard of relevance is provided by the same set of ends normally taken to guide discretionary action within the role: the task ends, institutional ends, and background ends. Those ends establish the terms on which the role agent considering a departure from a rule, or what is a species of the same thing, an unauthorized extension of his discretion, may hope to reach agreement with those who depend on him and those on whom he depends in the ecology of roles. If he can show that he departed from a

rule in order to achieve such an end, he will have begun to make
a case. Clearly, as the range of ends a role agent may invoke
to justify departing from a rule widens (to institutional ends
or, at the extreme, to background ends), the possibility of
justifying rule departures in a role widens also. And the wider
the possibility for justifying rule departures, the greater the
opportunity for role agents both to exercise their intelligence
and to commit egregious and uncontrollable violations.

Rule departures in role are made possible, then, by incorporating into the role a liberty, often of a sort that the role
agent takes advantage of at his peril, to undertake actions outside the role's prescribed means to achieve the role's ends. The
actions are of a sort that were the liberty not granted, they
could not be justified by the role agent through any appeal to
his authorized discretion, leaving him in the position of one
who broke with his role. The discovery of such rule departures
is not new. "An important feature of a large proportion of
social roles," a group of sociologists has observed, "is that the
actions which make them are not minutely prescribed, and that
a certain range of variability is regarded as legitimate. Sanctions
are not invoked against deviance within certain limits."[2] Our
point is merely that the nature of rule departures in role has
not always been squarely faced. "Deviance," which, if it means
anything, means a departure from some rule or expectation,
has often been hidden under the more common notion of
indeterminacy, as though to deviate from a rule or requirement
were the same as to assume responsibility for acting in ways
"not minutely prescribed."

Rule departures in role may seem less anomalous, however,
if we can suggest at least in a general way why they occur and
what purpose they serve in a rational society.

Why Justified Rule Departures Occur

When a role achieves its prescribed ends through its prescribed means, we shall speak of the role as adequately developed, or simply as adequate. A role is inadequately developed or inadequate, we shall say, when two or more of its pre-

scribed means for achieving the same end are incompatible; or when its prescribed means in a given case fail to achieve the end sought; or when, the end being multiple, the achievement of one end inhibits the achievement of another. The adequacy of a role, therefore, refers not to the value people place on it or even to its effectiveness as such in the world, but to the adequacy of its context of evaluation, from which, finally, propositions of appropriateness stem. Moreover, since roles do not usually impose requirements that are inconsistent as such (although a role with logically inconsistent requirements would indeed be inadequate), roles are not adequate or inadequate in themselves but with respect to their occasions. It is circumstances that render roles inadequate.

Clearly, then, roles basic to a society cannot be invented that will be adequate for all conceivable occasions. Even roles that grant discretion may be strained, warped, and ultimately shattered by time and circumstances. Hence roles that admit departure from rules are to be expected in any society that manages to respond successfully to radical changes. When unforeseeable circumstances develop, new interests or claims emerge, and perceptions of the balance between competing values change, a natural strategy is to place the responsibility on the role agents themselves to modify their roles as necessary while avoiding gratuitous deviation from role demands.

From another point of view, the inadequacy of roles under the pressure of unforeseeable circumstances is the pivotal consideration in any argument to appropriateness seeking to justify a rule departure in role. "Look," one says, "I have no choice, if I am not to make a mess of things." The other parts of the argument include justifying the degree of surcharge placed on the excluded reasons in question and showing that the role ecology affords agents in the role a liberty to depart from the rule.

The purpose of permitting justifiable rule departures in role is now surely obvious: they offer, suitably hedged, fair gambles for answering social needs that might otherwise go unanswered, where those needs are measured by the ends for which the role was initially instituted. They offer the chance of avoiding the consequences of inadequacy. Thus the soldier commanded to fire at a designated target is obliged by his role to obey, since that is the way to defeat the enemy. But suppose he believes the troops are friendly and withholds fire. If he is wrong, he may be punished. But if he is right, must he necessarily still be punished? Might he not, on a perfectly rational construction of the military role, be applauded for initiative? Similarly, the sentencing judge, whose role obliges him to serve justice by applying the criminal statutes, finds himself mandated to impose a heavy, and as he has reason to believe, destructive sentence on a youth convicted on a marijuana charge. If he breaches the sentencing restraints imposed by law, should he necessarily be impeached or even criticized? In that breach might lie society's peace. In the facilitation, toleration, or flat prohibition of rule departures, the issue is social utility. It is by no means obvious that prohibition is always the best choice, or even the inevitable choice.

Thus far we have emphasized the positive aspects of rule departures in order to make sense of them as options in legal systems. But there are also major disutilities and risks in establishing roles allowing for rule departures, and these negative aspects often will overbalance the positive. Later in this book we shall address ourselves more directly to this problem.

Types of Roles

We shall now offer a summary view of different types of roles in an effort to show concretely that the notion of justified rule departures is not necessarily anomalous. To be sure, justifying in a role an action that contravenes a mandatory rule of the role seems highly illogical. But while justified rule departures are indeed anomalous for some roles, and with excellent reason, they are not so for others.

The notion of a justified departure in role by a clerk is indeed anomalous. A clerk's role denies him recourse to any of its ends to justify actions outside its prescribed routine. To determine the appropriateness of an action the clerk consults "the book"— a set of rules and procedures established to eliminate any need for him to consider independently what ought to be done. If a case cannot be decided in this manner he must refer it to a higher authority, using formalized procedures ("forms") for submitting questions and receiving answers. The clerk's context of evaluation consists simply of prescribed means. Deviation from those means is his cardinal sin.

The notion of a justifiable rule departure in role is out of place even for roles that, unlike the clerk's, make use of the agent's judgment to achieve role ends. Agents authorized to make decisions in the light of role ends face no problem of justifying rule departures, since the rule in effect obliges them to act on their own judgment. In sentencing within the statutory range of penalties, a judge is simply following the rule. Even when he is authorized to decide whether or not to apply certain rules (as some proponents of the realist school of jurisprudence regard a judge's authority with respect to precedents), no question of rule departures arises. For rules are then in no way mandatory but simply tools that he may use at will to achieve the ends of his role.

Similar conclusions follow even when there are no prescribed means at all to guide a role agent in achieving his role end. There, least of all, despite the absolute reliance on the agent's judgment, are departures from rules possible, for the agent is constrained by only one rule: "Accomplish your mission!" The only problem he faces is the technological one of finding a way to achieve the role end. Thus the only role requirement for the spy is to accomplish his mission, and for the philosopher-king, to succeed in governing. But for the complete freedom to do as they think best in accomplishing their ends, the spy and the philosopher-king must pay the price of absolute responsibility in the event of failure. They may not know failure. Their roles forbid it.

At this point it may seem that to talk about justified rule

departures must be to confuse departing from rules with some kind of discretionary action, a major component in the roles of officials and perhaps of citizens. But the ordinary typology of roles omits the possibility of what we shall call "recourse roles" — roles that enable their agents to take action in situations where the role's prescribed ends conflict with its prescribed means, including grants of discretion, broad or narrow. Recourse roles provide for such situations by establishing conditions under which agents may be justified in undertaking actions that depart from role requirements. In short, they extend a liberty in handling obligations.

The problem of conflicting obligations must be handled one way or another in any case. One way, of course, is to organize obligations so that they will not conflict; but as we have seen, this solution is not always feasible. Another is to convert obligations into instrumentalities and authorize the choice of whichever serves a specified purpose. But still another way parallels the process of moral decision, in which the decision among conflicting obligations is left to the agent as his responsibility. Whether any role indeed incorporates this last means of handling conflicting obligations must of course rest on an investigation of that role.

One might challenge the existence of recourse roles on the ground that if a role can be said to grant its agents liberty to depart from a mandatory rule, there is no departure at all. Rather the rule in fact accommodates the qualification exemplified by the agent's action. We shall deal more fully with this objection later. For now we may remark that it secures what force it has by blurring the distinction between the decision problem an agent faces and the total situation after the decision has been made. To say that the rule in question really permitted the departure in the first place is not the same as to say that after the process of decision is over a rule could be devised to allow for it.

This book attempts to show that the roles of citizens and officials may sometimes function as recourse roles by virtue of the way they are embedded in the legal system. If it is a mistake to perceive them as being without any limitations whatsoever, so it is often a mistake to perceive them as necessarily modeled on the role of the clerk. Citizens and officials may sometimes be justified in undertaking a departure from the mandatory rules of the legal system.

To be sure, we have so far given no evidence that official and citizen roles are sometimes organized this way. This is the task of the succeeding chapters. Chapter Two considers departures from the rules by officials of our legal system; Chapter Three considers departures from the rules by citizens; Chapter Four considers the possibilities of extending and contracting society's provision for citizens and officials to depart from the rules and the utilities of doing so; and Chapter Five considers the implications of the analysis for the theory of legal systems.

CHAPTER TWO

Justified Rule Departures
by Officials

IN CONSIDERING justified departures by officials from the mandatory rules of a system—rules or commands that aim to impose a legal obligation on those they address—it will be helpful to clarify the kinds of mandatory rules at issue. Two kinds of mandatory rules may be distinguished. The first is the kind that most naturally comes to mind: rules that require compliance with certain standards of behavior on pain of punishment. Rules of this type exhibit their mandatory character both in their form ("No one shall . . . ," "You shall not . . . ," "It is a crime to . . .") and in their explicit threat of punishment for noncompliance. We shall call them peremptory rules. Examples are the rules of criminal law, orders of courts, and the enforceable orders of administrative tribunals and individual officials, such as policemen. We put these aside for the next chapter.

The second kind of mandatory rule addresses itself to government officials as such and derives its mandatory import not necessarily from the threat of formal punishment, which may or may not exist, but from the inherently restricted role of those officials as recipients of a limited government authority that they undertake to exercise. We shall call such rules constraining rules of competence, in order to distinguish them from constitutive rules of competence, which are not mandatory but merely state what must be done to achieve a legal result. If an official does not follow a constitutive rule of competence, there is no question of his departing from a rule. No obligation has been denied; the official has simply failed to exercise his powers. If, for example, a court decides a case not within its jurisdiction, the decision may be deprived of legal force. As Prof. H. L. A. Hart has pointed out,

> The relationship between the conforming action and the rule [power-conferring rule, that is, in his terminology] is ill-conveyed by the words "obey" and "disobey," which are apposite in the case of the criminal law where the rules are analogous to orders.... Whereas rules like those of the criminal law impose duties, power-conferring rules are recipes for creating duties.[1]

Constraining rules of competence, by contrast, direct the official to undertake or not to undertake certain actions, and supply him with standards for making decisions in the course of exercising his official powers. To the extent the rules are constraining and not constitutive their disregard does not deprive his action of legal effect (though some rules, of course, may be both constraining and constitutive). Since our concern here is with constraining rather than constitutive rules of competence, we shall hereafter use the phrase "rules of competence" to refer to the former.

Some rules of competence, of course, are backed by criminal sanctions—rules against accepting bribes, for example. Their obligatory force is the same as the obligatory force criminal statutes have with regard to ordinary citizens; for this reason we defer their consideration to the next chapter. But other rules of competence are not accompanied by sanctions. Their obligatory force may derive from the peculiar relation of the official to his office; that is to say, they are role obligations the official incurs by venturing to act as an agent of government authority. For example, the jury has a duty to reach its verdict in accordance with the judge's instructions on the law; the administrative agency, to give controlling weight to one single factor or to disregard a certain factor entirely, or to consider some factor only in conjunction with other factors; the magistrate, to set bail on the basis of the need to ensure the defendant's presence at trial; the judge, to grant probation only in classes of cases defined by law; the court, to apply the law rather than follow its own inclinations.

But suppose the jury decides otherwise than in accordance with the judge's instructions. Suppose the administrative agency does not give proper weight to certain factors. Suppose the magistrate does not set bail solely on the basis of the need to ensure the defendant's presence at trial. Or suppose the judge, following his own inclinations, grants probation to an offender who is not legally entitled to receive it. Granting the mandatory character of the rules of competence involved, does the legal system necessarily condemn all such actions as illegitimate? In many, perhaps even most cases, no doubt it does. Yet we shall argue in this chapter that the American legal system does not always, or necessarily, do so and that its very organization may at various critical points furnish the justification for officials taking upon themselves actions that depart from some rule of competence.

Our use of the term departure merits a moment's comment. This chapter argues the thesis that an official, in virtue of the nature of his office and its place in the legal system, may sometimes be justified in taking upon himself the decision to depart from some rule of competence and hence from some incurred obligation. We use the neutral term departure that we used in the general discussion of the first chapter, rather than "breaking" or "violation," or the like, because "breaking" or "violation" implies flat-out that that has been done that ought not to have been done. The term departure, on the other hand, does not carry this implication, but leaves open the possibility that even though what was done is the sort of action that is not supposed to be done, still the undertaking of that action was justified.

As for the content of the term departure, we give it that variety of possible contents that will make it applicable to the different sorts of affairs we have found it convenient to include under the rubric, mandatory rule. The term is intended to encompass all cases in which some demand has been refused, whether in the sense of breaking or bending some rule, or of ignoring, disregarding, or failing to give adequate consideration to it. The different nuances of such expressions acknowledge that not all rules lie on the same logical level. There are prima facie significant differences between the rule of *stare decisis*, for example, and the instructions a judge may give to a jury on the law. The jury might be said to defy the judge's instructions and thereby to break the law, if following those instructions is required by a rule; but it is hard to see how a judge could break the rule of *stare decisis*, or even, in any clear way, defy it. Judges might ignore *stare decisis*, but the rule is too fluid to break and its authority too uncertain to defy. Some might prefer the term policy or principle for a rule of this order of generality and logical force. But, even so, if *stare decisis* or any other policy or principle is to have a determinate character and function in decision, it must be possible at some point to say that the official has in fact not met the obligation it imposes. And it is that fact, of failing to meet an obligation imposed by some authoritative demand, that gives force to a departure from a rule.

We turn now to the central issue. When and in what circumstances does our legal system provide grounds for concluding that an official is justified in undertaking to depart from a rule of competence? When and under what circumstances may he undertake such an act, not in the moral but in the legal context?

The Rule-of-Law Model and the Official's Role

The traditional understanding of the obligation of officials in our legal system with respect to rules of competence is epitomized in the concept of the rule of law. Over the years the phrase has acquired a variety of meanings associated with various attributes of the good legal order. It is sometimes used to embrace the rights of man in the large sense. It is also used to refer to procedural guarantees available to protect individuals against government action, such as those specified in the Bill of Rights. At other times it is used to refer to the substitution of legal procedures for force in resolving international disputes. For our purposes, however, its most relevant meaning is conveyed by the phrases "supremacy of law" and "a government of laws and not of men." So taken, the rule of law constitutes an ideal model of legal authority in which government by rules takes precedence over government by the will of those holding official power. Its roots go back to medieval times, when the theory prevailed that "law of some kind—the law either of God or man—rules the world."[2] It became entrenched in English constitutional law when the judges and Parliament invoked the supremacy of the law against the royal prerogative following the Stuart period.

As Dicey formulated the rule of law, it has two fundamental meanings. First, it means "the absolute supremacy or predominance of regular law as opposed to the influence of arbitrary power, and excludes the existence of arbitrariness, of prerogative, or even of wide discretionary authority on the part of government." Second, it means "the equal subjection of all classes to the ordinary law of the land administered by the ordinary law courts [and] excludes the idea of any exemption of officials or others from the duty of obedience to the law which governs other citizens or from the jurisdiction of the ordinary tribunals."[3] More recent formulations voice similar themes. According to Prof. F. Hayek, for example, the rule of law means that

government in all its actions is bound by rules fixed and announced beforehand—rules which make it possible to foresee with fair certainty how the authority will use its coercive powers in given circumstances. . . . Within the known rules of the game the individual is free to pursue his personal ends and desires, certain that the powers of government will not be used deliberately to frustrate his efforts.[4]

Essentially, then, the rule-of-law model requires those who exercise government authority to conform strictly to the rules. The expositors of the rules are the law courts, which perform their duties within the rigorous confines of common-law reasoning and principles. The legislature, and only the legislature, may alter those rules: in England, under the doctrine of parliamentary sovereignty, subject to no judicial review; in the United States, subject to written constitutional restraints interpreted by the courts. The process of determining the rights and liabilities of individuals under the rule of law excludes the official's personal judgment. As Léon Duguit observed, "No organ of the State may render an individual decision which would not conform to a general rule previously stated."[5] The person exercising government authority is obliged always to act in complete conformity with the rules. He is a wheel in the machine; he may never be its ghost.

This view of the legal official's role responds to considerations of fairness and protection against the abuse of power. By eliminating the effects of personal inclination in official decision making, it enhances equal treatment for all. And by requiring conformity with stated rules, it enables the governed to plan their conduct in accordance with predictable outcomes.

The rule-of-law model, therefore, protects in two ways against the official's injection of his personal will into the exercise of government power. First, it forbids any exercise of power that is not delegated by law and any action taken on the basis of considerations precluded by law. Second, it requires that the action authorized and the grounds for taking the action be sufficiently clear and complete to permit no major exercise of judgment by the official. Dicey spoke to the first principle when he observed that the rule of law "excludes the existence of arbitrariness, of prerogative." He explicitly embraced the second when he observed that the rule of law also excludes "wide discretionary authority on the part of the government."[6] By these two principles any discretionary judgment permitted to an official was rendered ipso facto a defect in the legal system. The first barred totally what we may term deviational discretion—the exercise of authority in ways or on the basis of considerations either unauthorized or prohibited by rules of competence. The second severely limited even legally delegated discretion. Thus, according to the rule-of-law model, the official's role could not be, in our term, a recourse role; and it could not even be a limited recourse role allowing the official to act at his own discretion in certain designated areas. The model's overall consequence was to lend support to a theory of legal reasoning in which the conclusions of that reasoning would follow inevitably, a theory that took its least sophisticated form in a "mechanical jurisprudence."

The sharp restriction of delegated discretion is today no longer regarded as one of the essential features of the rule-of-law model, at least not in anything like the sweeping sense Dicey had in mind. The expansion of the government's role to deal with problems of urbanization, industrialization, and technology in the public interest have made it inevitable that substantial discretionary authority be delegated to government officials. The courts continue to insist on a legislative statement of standards to control the exercise of discretion,[7] but in fact the standards held permissible—"public convenience and necessity," "unjust rates," "unfair methods of competition"[8]—are so broad that they scarcely function as realistic restraints. Prof. Kenneth C. Davis's view of discretion would generally find favor today:

No legal system in world history has been without discretionary power. None can be. Discretion is indispensable for individualized justice, for creative justice, for new programs in which no one yet knows how to formulate rules, and for old programs in which some aspects cannot be reduced to rules. Eliminating discretionary power would paralyze governmental processes and would stifle individualized justice. Those who would forbid governmental coercion except on the basis of rules previously announced seem to me to have misunderstood the elements of law and government.[9]

Therefore the contemporary problem is not the existence of discretionary government but how, again in Professor Davis's words, "to confine, to structure, and to check" its appropriate exercise.[10]

Despite the general acceptance of broad discretion by officials, what we have termed deviational discretion is characteristically seen as a usurpation of power incompatible with government by law. Why this is so seems obvious enough. Delegated discretion can be defended on grounds that some discretion is inescapable for a rational and just system of law and that a variety of constraints are available to foster the rational and principled exercise of discretionary authority. Deviational discretion is another matter. It entails not only an official's deciding the substantive issue without the guidance of legal rules, but also his disregarding the answer provided by law in favor of his own judgment on the merits. In sum, while delegated discretion hands the issue over to the official to decide, deviational discretion enables the official to take it on himself to determine whether to produce the decision the law provides or to fashion a different one.

Accordingly, deviational discretion must be distinguished from each of the three forms of discretion that Prof. Ronald Dworkin has enumerated, and about which the controversy over the judge's role has been waged. Deviational discretion is not discretion in its weakest sense, in which to do his role job according to its rules, an official must exercise judgment—though, of course, it entails the exercise of judgment. Neither is it discretion in the sense that no one will review the official's exercise of judgment—though normally when a deviational discretion exists no one will. Most important, it is not even discretion in the stronger sense in which "on some issue he [the official] is simply not bound by the standards set by the authority in question."[11] For in exercising deviational discretion the official *is* bound either to some specific rule or policy, or to functioning within a prescribed discretion. And he deviates from that to which he is bound.

In short, discretion is one thing; discretion to determine competence to exercise discretion is quite another. A community does not necessarily forfeit its claim to being governed by law when it grants officials authority to resolve certain substantive issues at their own discretion; but it seems that it does if it grants them freedom to redefine their authority and role to assume a competence denied by the rules. The obligation of officials to act in accordance with the rules is what it means to say that a system is governed by law, if one accepts the rule-of-law model; and this way of regarding the obligations of officials, and of citizens, too, for that matter, is formalized in the custom of referring to all departures from mandatory rules as violations.

The conventional rule-of-law model, then, provides no justification for officials to undertake to depart from the mandatory rules of competence the law prescribes. We want to argue, however, that the rule-of-law model is not necessarily the ideal model

for the functioning of legal systems; that it partially misde-
scribes the roles and obligations of officials in our legal system;
and that consequently it fails to define adequately what it means
to function as a legal system. While acknowledging that roles
structured according to the rule-of-law model do exist within
the American legal system, and indeed in many areas may even
be the prevailing roles, we shall argue in the following pages that
the American legal system also includes some official roles that
allow for deviational discretion—that is, for the exercise of an
official's judgment to depart from the explicit constraints on his
authority. Moreover, we shall argue that these familiar instances
of deviational discretion are not satisfactorily accounted for by
either the statement that when officials depart from rules they
lawlessly usurp legal authority or the statement that what officials do is the real law and what the laws says is not the law at
all. To support our case we will first examine the role of the
criminal jury in returning verdicts of acquittal and then attempt to use the jury discussion to develop some general conceptions concerning the nature of deviational discretion.

An Alternative Model: The Criminal Jury

The Development of Jury Power

At one time juries were held accountable for their mistakes
and misjudgments, and their verdicts were given effect only so
long as they were considered right. The earliest mode of control over jurors was the attaint, which allowed a party that had
lost a case to assemble a larger jury to find the facts anew; if the
larger jury found contrary to the first, it could attaint the members of the first, which meant loss of lands, fine, or imprisonment, and reverse their judgment. Though the attaint became
obsolete in the fifteenth century and in any event was apparently little used in criminal cases, another means to control jury
error took its place: the judges themselves assumed power to
punish jurors for delivering incorrect or corrupt verdicts.[12] Indeed, the practice was formalized by a statute in 1534 authorizing courts to punish jurors for delivering "any untrue verdict

against the King . . . contrary to good and pregnant evidence ministered to them."[13] But though the jury could be punished for an erroneous acquittal in criminal cases, the prisoner apparently could not, for new trials could not be ordered in criminal cases as they could in civil cases. At all events, the courts exercised their power to punish erring jurors from time to time[14] until 1670, when *Bushell's Case*[15] repudiated the practice and discharged the jurors who had acquitted William Penn of unlawful assembly.* The device of ordering a new trial was developed as a substitute means of controlling juries in civil cases. In criminal cases no comparable control evolved.

From the end of the seventeenth century to the present, therefore, the legal power of a jury in criminal cases has been substantial. They render a general verdict, which is to say they respond with a general finding of guilty or not guilty of the crime charged, both finding the facts and applying the law.† The varieties of special pleading developed in civil cases, by which questions of law were separated from questions of fact, were never extended to criminal proceedings. When criminal juries convict, a variety of checks and controls operate to ensure that they act in conformity with the law, including judicial power to set the verdict aside and grant a new trial. But when they acquit, there are no such controls. The acquittal is a *diktat*, a "sovereign power,"[16] for which stated reasons are neither expected nor permitted. The jurors may in no way be held to

---

* A plaque in the Old Bailey commemorates the incident in the following words: "Near this site William Penn and William Mead were tried in 1670 for preaching unlawful assembly in Gracechurch Street. This tablet commemorates the courage and endurance of the jury, Thomas Vere, Edward Bushell and ten others, who refused to give a verdict against them although they were locked up without food for two nights and were fined for their final verdict of not guilty. The case of these jurymen was reviewed on a writ of habeas corpus and Chief Justice Vaughan delivered the opinion of the court which established the right of juries to give their verdict according to their conviction." Scheflin, "Jury Nullification: The Right to Say No," 45 *So. Calif. L. Rev.* 168 (1972).

† Though the jury had the inherent authority to render a special verdict (finding the facts and permitting the judge to find the defendants guilty or not guilty depending on how he should find the law), this practice has fallen into disuse.

account for their verdict, or be made to explain it, or even be questioned about it. Their verdict is given conclusive legal effect, no matter how fully it may be proved contrary to law. Lord Devlin has summarized the situation aptly: "Whenever there is a trial by jury, the condemnation must be by a judgment which is both lawful and the judgment of the country. If his countrymen condemn a man and they exceed the law, he shall go free: if the law condemns him and nevertheless his countrymen acquit, he shall go free."[17]

What did this development mean for the legal authority of the criminal jury to acquit? What *is* the legal role of the jury with respect to the rules of the criminal law? From the end of the seventeenth century on, these questions underlay a classic debate in English and American law over whether the jury in criminal cases had the right to determine the law as well as the facts. The English debate revolved principally around an issue in seditious libel cases: should the jury be told that its sole task was to determine whether the accused was responsible for the publication, leaving the question whether the publication constituted criminal libel for the court to decide?[18]

Though technically the issue was the fairly modest one of whether the criminal jury had the same freedom in libel cases that it had in other criminal cases—i.e. the freedom to decide the whole question by a general verdict—the debates left little doubt that the substance of the controversy was whether a criminal jury could legitimately invoke its own conscience as a bar to conviction in all cases. Upon the enactment of Fox's Libel Act in 1792, the narrower issue was resolved in England: in seditious libel, as in all other criminal cases, "the jury . . . may give a general verdict of guilty or not guilty upon the whole matter put in issue"; it would not be required or directed to find guilt merely on proof of publication.[19] Whether this act was also designed to resolve the larger issue of the legitimacy of jury nullification has been argued both ways. At all events, subsequently in England the issue was never actively pressed, and the view came to prevail that the jury's duty is to apply the law given by the court, notwithstanding its power to do otherwise through a general verdict of not guilty.[20]

On this side of the ocean, however, the controversy continued vigorously. The seditious libel issue again provoked the debate. The New York trials of John Peter Zenger in 1735 and Harry Croswell in 1803, both for seditious libel, produced replays of the judicial debates in England.[21] But the enactment of laws modeled on Fox's Libel Act did not, as in England, put the issue to a practical rest. The larger controversy, carried on in the colonies in the eighteenth century and continued in state and federal courts on through the nineteenth, was whether the jury in criminal cases should explicitly be recognized as having the right to determine the issues of law as well as of fact, and often implicitly the right to reject the law when they found it unacceptable. The same issue appeared in a variety of guises. Did defense counsel have the right to argue issues of law to the jury in opposition to the view of the law expressed by the judge?[22] Was it proper to instruct the jury in a murder prosecution that they might return a verdict of guilty or not guilty of murder, but that they might not (because the judge found no evidence to justify it) return a verdict of manslaughter?[23] Was it proper to instruct the jury that they were duty-bound to follow the judge's instructions on the law in reaching the general verdict?[24] These issues produced a number of classic exchanges on the freedom and obligations of the criminal jury: in New York, between Judge Kent in favor of the jury's right to determine the law and Chief Judge Lewis against; in Vermont, between Judge Hall in favor and Judge Bennett against; in Massachusetts, between Justice Thomas in favor and Chief Justice Shaw against; and in the United States Supreme Court, between Justice Gray in favor and Justice Harlan against.[25]

For some forty years after the adoption of the Constitution, the view that the criminal jury had the right to determine the law had a widespread vogue.[26] In some measure this was no doubt attributable to the early American view of the relation of law and democracy—that the official organs of state authority should be sharply curtailed, that the application of the law had always been a powerful weapon in oppression, that for the people to govern themselves it was necessary not only that they make the laws but also that they control their administration. As Jefferson wrote, "Were I called upon to decide whether the people had best be omitted in the legislative or judiciary department, I would say it is better to leave them out of the legislature. The execution of the laws is more important than the making of them."[27] Other contributing influences were the small difference in legal training, experience, and intelligence between judges and juries of the time and the reaction both against the participation of judges in the political and religious persecutions under the Stuarts and against the performance of first royal and later federalist judges in some of the colonies.[28]

This early view began to lose its hold in the 1830's, and by the end of the nineteenth century had been substantially repudiated.[29] All that remains of it today are constitutional provisions in the three states—Georgia, Indiana, and Maryland—still asserting the right of the jury to judge the law in criminal cases.[30] But they are by now virtual relics. They have been narrowly interpreted[31] and grudgingly upheld only at the cost of being roundly denounced as "anachronistic," "anomalous," a "blight upon the administration of justice," "archaic, outmoded and atrocious," and "unique and indefensible."[32] Behind this shift in the prevailing view of the jury's duties stands the ideal of the rule of law, with which a jury's freedom to take the law into its own hands is wholly incompatible.[33] According to the rule-of-law model, to recognize such a freedom would risk an intolerable uncertainty as the law shifted from case to case depending on the jury's chance makeup. Moreover, to do so would invite any jury to abrogate a law duly enacted by the legislature on the basis of its own views. Protection against bad laws should not come through the nullification of democratically enacted legislation by any dozen jurors, but through the established democratic processes for changing the law.

In recent years the moral repugnance to the war in Vietnam

and to the laws supporting it, such as the draft law, led lawyers to renew the old argument that the jury should be told they are free to disregard the judge's instructions and that lawyers should be permitted to try to persuade the jury to do so.[34] But the traditional view of the nation's early years is apparently too long dead to be revived. As a United States Court of Appeals recently held, quoting a Supreme Court opinion at the turn of the century: " 'We must hold firmly to the doctrine that in the courts of the United States it is the duty of juries in criminal cases to take the law from the court, and apply that law to the facts as they find them to be from the evidence.' "[35] A standard instruction on the duty of the jury in California is representative of current practice: "It is my duty to instruct you in the law that applies to this case, and you must follow the law as I state it to you."[36]

Ambiguities in the Jury's Role

But the triumph in court decisions of the restrictive view of the jury's role has by no means cleared the air of uncertainty concerning the jury's role in acquittals. Not only the judge's instructions but the context in which they are given must be considered if the conscientious juror is properly to understand what he is truly obliged to do. And that context as it exists today tends in a number of respects to cloud the issue.

Power and Right. As we have seen, the criminal jury has evolved to a point where it exercises what might be called a sovereign power to acquit in criminal cases. The power to return a general verdict cannot be taken from it. It returns its verdict without stated reasons or justifications of any kind. If it finds the defendant not guilty, the acquittal must be given final and binding legal effect, no matter what may be thought or known about the jury's failure to follow the law. And the jury itself is fully insulated from any accountability for its action.

In these circumstances Alexander Hamilton's argument in an early New York case must be squarely faced: "All the cases agree that the jury have the *power* to decide the law as well as the fact;

and if the law gives them the power, it gives them the *right* also. Power and right are convertible terms, when the law authorizes the doing of an act which shall be final, and for the doing of which the agent is not responsible."[37] Hamilton was not arguing that there should be no constraints on the way a jury exercises its power, but that the legal right to decide the law follows from the legal power.[38] Judge Kent accepted Hamilton's argument, stating:

The law must ... have intended, in granting this power to a jury, to grant them a lawful and rightful power, or it would have provided a remedy against the undue exercise of it. The true criterion of a legal power is its capacity to produce a definitive effect, liable neither to censure nor review. And the verdict of not guilty, in a criminal case, is, in every respect, absolutely final. The jury are not liable to punishment, nor the verdict to control.[39]

Courts and Jury. The force of these propositions is enhanced by the way the courts have dealt with specific legal issues concerning the criminal jury. If a judge hears a criminal case without a jury and finds the defendant guilty of one charge and not guilty of another in circumstances where such a finding is illogical and inconsistent, the judgment of guilt is reversible on the ground that there can be no confidence in its correctness.[40] But if a jury returns similar verdicts that are no less illogical and inconsistent, the verdict of guilt is regarded as irreversible. In a leading case so holding,[41] Justice Holmes referred to his own earlier dictum that "the jury has the power to bring in a verdict in the teeth of both law and facts,"[42] and quoted with approval from Learned Hand, who had observed in a comparable situation: "We interpret the acquittal as no more than their assumption of a power which they had no right to exercise, but to which they were disposed through lenity."[43] The nature of their lack of "right" is put into context by a subsequent observation of Judge Hand:

The institution of trial by jury—especially in criminal cases—has its hold upon public favor chiefly for two reasons. The individual can forfeit his liberty—to say nothing of his life—only at the hands of those who, unlike any official, are in no wise accountable, directly or indirectly, for what they do, and who at once separate and melt anonymously in the community from which they came. Moreover, since if they acquit their verdict is final, no one is likely to suffer of whose conduct they do not morally disapprove; and this introduces a slack into the enforcement of law, tempering its rigor by the mollifying influence of current ethical conventions.[44]

In civil cases tried before a jury the use of special interrogatories formulated by the court to assist the jury in arriving at their general verdict logically and according to the judge's instructions is a generally authorized practice. So is the special verdict, in which the jury is instructed to return only a special written finding on each issue of fact, leaving it for the court to enter judgment in accordance with the law as applied to the jury-found facts.[45] Both devices serve as controls on the jury, functioning to ensure judgments in accordance with the law.

At the common law there is authority for the use of such devices in criminal cases as well, though the jury can always insist on returning a general verdict.[46] Such devices have been even more rarely used in this country than in England, however, and current authority finds them in violation of the right to trial by jury. An instructive case is *United States v. Spock*, in which the court reversed a conviction of conspiracy to counsel evasion of the draft.[47] The trial court had put to the jury, in addition to the general issue of guilty or not guilty, ten special questions calling for a yes or no answer. The use of this procedure was enough to require reversal of the conviction, even assuming the correctness of the questions proposed. The right to jury trial, the appellate court reasoned, would be meaningless if the jury were not free from judicial pressure. Of course, the directed verdict of guilty is the most direct of such pressures, and it is accordingly prohibited. But lesser and more indirect pressures, such as the requirement of a special verdict or the use of special interrogatories, are impermissible for the same reason. In explanation, the court quoted the following excerpt from an earlier decision:

To ask the jury special questions might be said to infringe on its power to deliberate free from legal fetters; on its power to arrive at a general verdict without having to support it by reasons or by a report of its deliberations; and on its power to follow or not to follow the instructions of the court. Moreover, any abridgement or modification of this institution would partly restrict its historic function, that of tempering rules of law by common sense brought to bear upon the facts of the case.[48]

Moreover, the fact that the questions were proper in substance and therefore helpful in producing a logical and consistent application of the law could not be considered sufficient reason for condoning the practice. In this connection the court quoted a statement of Learned Hand:

I should like to subject a verdict, as narrowly as was practical, to a review which should make it in fact, what we very elaborately pretend that it should be: a decision based upon the law. In criminal prosecutions there may be, and in my judgment there are, other considerations which intervene to make such an attempt undesirable.[49]

"Uppermost of these considerations," continued the court, "is the principle that the jury, as the conscience of the community, must be permitted to look at more than logic."[50]

Also of substantial relevance in understanding the jury's role is the basis on which the Supreme Court has held the right to trial by jury protected by the due process clause of the Fourteenth Amendment. In doing so recently the Court recognized the jury's power to displace law by appeal to conscience as one of the characteristics that makes the right to a jury trial "fundamental to our system of justice."[51] Not only are juries the historical "safeguard against the corrupt or overzealous prosecutor and against the compliant, biased or eccentric judge," said the Court, but in differing from the law-bound conclusions judges would reach, they serve "some of the very purposes for which they were created and for which they are now employed."[52] In other words, the jury's fundamental function is not only to guard against official departures from the rules of law, but on proper occasions themselves to depart from unjust rules or their unjust application. Even Justice Harlan, in dissent, conceded that the criminal jury "eases the burden on judges by enabling them to share a part of their sometimes awesome responsibility."[53] Whatever doubt there might be about what he had in mind is resolved by his footnote reference to Benjamin Curtis's observation: "Juries relieve the judge of the embarrassment of making the necessary exceptions. They do this, it is true, by violating their oaths, but this is better than tempting the judge to violate his oath of office."*

Jury Tradition. The jury's obligations and freedoms are determined by tradition as well as by law. The landmark cases, particularly those involving criminal libel and sedition, in which the jury invoked its power to nullify what were widely regarded as unjust laws, are regarded not as regrettable departures from the rule of law but as historic and seminal assertions, like the Magna Carta and the Bill of Rights, of man's right to be free of unjust laws. Arguments in support of the jury's fundamental value almost always rest on the nullifying function of criminal juries. Roscoe Pound, for example, observed: "Jury lawlessness is the great corrective of law in its actual administration. The will of the state at large imposed on a reluctant community, the will of a majority imposed on a vigorous and determined minority, find the same obstacle in the local jury that formerly confronted kings and ministers."[54] Lord Devlin remarked:

In most systems the just decision is tied pretty closely to the law; the law may be made as flexible as possible, but the justice of the case cannot go beyond the furthest point to which the law can be stretched. Trial by jury is a unique institution, devised deliberately or accidentally—that is, its origin is accidental and its retention deliberate—to enable justice to go beyond that point.[55]

---

* Curtis, "The Trial Judge and the Jury," 5 *Vand. L. Rev.* 150, 157 (1952). Unlike the majority, however, Justice Harlan had some reservations: "A jury may, at times, afford a higher justice by refusing to enforce harsh laws (although it necessarily does so haphazardly, raising the questions whether arbitrary enforcement of harsh laws is better than total enforcement, and whether the jury system is to be defended on the grounds that jurors sometimes disobey their oaths)." 391 U.S. at 187.

Nor is trial by jury only "a protection against tyranny," he added. "It is that: but it is also an insurance that the criminal law will conform to the ordinary man's idea of what is fair and just. If it does not, the jury will not be a party to its enforcement."[56]

Jury Behavior. Jury nullification of unjust laws is a continuing tradition. The classic historical instances include the jury's refusal to convict in a number of famous criminal libel cases until the law was changed to give juries the authority to acquit through general verdicts.[57] Early English juries employed various strategies to avoid capital punishment, such as finding against the evidence that only 39 shillings had been stolen when to find 40 shillings or more would mean a mandatory death sentence.[58] Later, in this country, we have witnessed the American jury's systematic nullification of the Prohibition laws during the 1920's—"the most intense example of jury revolt in recent history."[59] More recent data collected in a study by Professors Harry Kalven and Hans Zeisel show a subtler use of the nullification power by contemporary American juries. Of 3,500 sample trials reported on, about 19 percent were cases in which the jury acquitted but the judge convicted. Kalven and Zeisel determined that "jury sentiments on the law" accounted for or contributed to half of all the judge-jury disagreements. Of that half, twice as many disagreements were attributable to a combination of "facts and values" as were attributable to values (jury sentiments on the law) alone. The authors conclude that their findings reveal "the salient role played by jury sentiments on the law in causing disagreements; jury equity looms as a significant factor."[60] They further identify evidentiary determinations as the principal vehicle by which contemporary juries infuse their own values into their verdicts. "We know . . . that the jury does not often consciously and explicitly yield to sentiment in the teeth of the law. Rather it yields to sentiment in the apparent process of resolving doubts as to evidence. The jury, therefore, is able to conduct its revolt from the law within the etiquette of resolving issues of fact."[61]

The jury's "revolt from the law," Kalven and Zeisel note, is a modest one at present, reflecting a general acceptance of the substantive criminal law. They see it manifested "as a moderate corrective against undue prosecutions for gambling, game, and liquor violations and, to some extent, drunken driving."[62] They also see it revealed in juries' rejection of particular rules of the criminal law, such as the "nice" legal obstacles to the privilege of self-defense, the legal irrelevancy of the contributory fault of the victim, and the legal irrelevancy of the extent to which the defendant has already suffered.[63]

Interpreting the Jury's Role

If, now, the juror is obliged to do as he is instructed by the judge and if he may, nevertheless, do as he thinks best; if, in fact, he is afforded every protection that will make it possible for him to do as he thinks best and his function as a juror is extolled because jurors sometimes do, how is the conscientious juror to understand his role? What is he to do in his jural role if it seems to him that to follow the judge's instruction would lead to a verdict he is convinced ought to go otherwise?

The question appears puzzling on the common and not implausible assumption that the law must present itself to an agent in a univocal sense, revealing a single, consistent directive fixing the agent's duty and, so far as the law extends, leaving nothing up to him. We shall comment on each of two possible interpretations of the jury's role that make this assumption and thus hold the juror's duty to comply with the judge's instructions to be logically incompatible with the juror's liberty to do as he thinks best. Then we shall try to reinterpret the jury's role in acquittals on the hypothesis that the dilemma between duty and liberty is a false one for the legal system.

The Conventional Interpretations. The first interpretation (Interpretation I) holds that the jury's role is to follow the judge's instructions. According to this way of understanding the situation, official formulations fully state the jury's proper role, which is strictly that of a fact-finding agency. A jury reaches its general verdict by deciding the facts of the case and applying the law as given by the judge. Of no consequence are its own sentiments concerning the law's justness, either generally or as applied to a specific case; its own conception of the law's meaning; or its own estimate of the force of any mitigating circumstances not comprehended in the law. The vaunted "sovereignty" of the jury, therefore, is a matter of power, not of right. The jury can reach a perverse verdict of acquittal and get away with it, but that does not imply the right to reach such a verdict. When juries reach verdicts that run counter to the judge's instructions, they usurp a discretion not theirs to exercise. That jury nullification has sometimes produced good results does not show that nullification is within the jury's legal role.

Such is one way of construing the jury's role. The technique is to acknowledge an inconsistency between jury power and jury duty in cases of acquittal, assume that the inconsistency cannot be, and then explain away the class of evidence that points to a jury liberty. But in fact the decision to choose jury duty over the competing value of jury liberty is arbitrary. One might equally well follow Alexander Hamilton and discover in the scrupulous protection of jury power the institution of a sovereign right. Even in ordinary matters, when people are systematically protected not only against incursions into their power to act as they think best but also against any attempt to hold them accountable for their use of the power, they assume they have the right to act as they think best.

The second interpretation (Interpretation II) holds that the jury's role is to do as it thinks best. Pound's famous distinction between the law in action and the law in books[64] makes plausible a single, consistent interpretation of the jury's role that is precisely the reverse of Interpretation I. Instead of arguing that the jury's role demands following the judge's instructions, one may argue that the judge's instructions constitute only the formal law, whereas the real law, the law in action, leaves it to the jury to follow the judge's instructions only when so inclined. To be sure, there is the difficult question of what Pound and others who have adopted the distinction mean by the law in action. Sometimes they seem to mean that the law in action is, flatly, what people in authority do, independent of any rule. In that sense, of course, the law in action makes no requirement on juries at all: whatever they succeed in getting away with is the law in action. At other times the law in action means the actual norms of the political-legal community as opposed to the norms announced in the books. It is in this sense that the realist distinction shores up a rule of competence for the jury: "Do as you think best. Take or leave the judge's instructions." Any jury that thought itself bound to the judge's instructions would then have misunderstood its own role. The inconsistency between duty and liberty has been overcome: the duty is merely formal; the liberty is real in the law.

But even if Interpretation II should rest on the law in action in this latter sense—that is, on the basis of a determination of what the real, rather than the apparent norms of the law may be—the question of how to determine the real norm remains. We propose that there is no direct inference from the law in action to the real norm of jury sovereignty postulated in Interpretation II without the addition of an independent preference for that condition. In the face of the history of jury acquittal, Interpretation II, like Interpretation I, needs a normative principle to select one part of the evidence rather than the other as determinative.

Such a principle is necessary because for the law in action to be law, it must define some behavior as a transgression, even if the transgressor is an official. What actual behavior cannot violate constitutes no rule. How, then, in view of the all but unpredictable course of human actions, are we to argue to the real, binding rule? Which class of behavior represents compliance with the actual norm, and which a misguided attempt to follow merely fictitious ones: the behavior of deferring to the judge's instructions or the behavior of defying them? When, in effect, does the jury deviate from the law in action, and when does it not? To ascribe to the jury a determinate role at all implies that the jury *might* deviate from the law in action. Why should the statistically far more numerous instances of compliance with court instructions carry so much less weight in determining the law in action than the far fewer instances of departure? Why should the fact of jury impunity be granted all possible weight? Such questions seem readily answerable only if one asserts a preference for one sort of jury behavior over another as a basis for determining what the law in action actually is. Then behavior that fulfills presumably valuable functions will satisfy the law in action, while behavior that fulfills no such functions but is grounded only on formal obligations becomes a misguided attempt to satisfy the law in books.

But even if the jury's role is to carry out the law in action, and even if that law can be determined by a value judgment, much that the practitioners of the legal profession consider law remains to be accounted for. Jurors are still obliged to take an oath to decide the case according to the law and the evidence. The judge does instruct the jurors in the applicable law and direct them to arrive at their verdict in accordance with it. The lawyer for the defendant typically is not permitted to argue to the jury that the law is otherwise than as stated by the judge or that it should be disregarded in any event. In these respects the jury cannot be said to have the right to act according to its own judgment in the sense that an official has the right to act according to his own judgment when the law grants him explicit discretionary authority to do so.

In short, the logical source of the notion that the jury's duty is either to follow the judge's instructions or to do as it thinks best is the commitment to the rule-of-law model for official roles. Both interpretations of the jury's role are single and consistent: in the first case, a juror must do what he is told; and in the second, he must do as he thinks best. Neither leaves room for the notion of departure from a rule.

The Jury's Role as Recourse Role. Whatever the rule-of-law model may require, logic does not prohibit an interpretation of the jury's role under the law as both requiring conformity to the judge's instructions and extending the liberty to return a general verdict of acquittal counter to those instructions. That liberty may be seen as merely reflecting the fact that the system of law extends recourse to the juror where a conflict exists within the jury's context of evaluation. A liberty does not necessarily contradict an obligation, so long as a significant surcharge is placed on the denial of the obligation; not all obligations need be unremitting, as we tried to show in Chapter One. Of course, an obligation ceases to be an obligation if a person can be said to have a right not to comply with it. If a jury had a right to ignore the judge's instructions for whatever reason, as Interpretation II claims, there could be no question of its being under an obligation to accept the judge's instructions. But we claim only that the jury is at liberty to depart from the judge's instructions, not that it has a right to do so at will.

In brief, the confusions in Interpretations I and II arise because the role of juror is a recourse role, while it is customary to think of official roles exclusively as either clerklike or discretionary. Under this customary assumption the role of the jury must be either to do as the court instructs or to exert a right to do as it thinks best. To be sure, this assumption of a single, consistent directive has a prima facie plausibility. To deny it seems to demand that we imagine a judge saying simultaneously, "Follow my instructions; it is your duty!" and "Use your own judgment!" One could fairly conclude that such a judge did not know what he wanted and had provided no guidance whatsoever. And such would be the case if one conceived the judge to be simultaneously placing an obligation on the jury and granting it the right not to comply with the obligation. But in fact, as we have suggested, while it can be said that the judge places an obligation on the jury, it cannot be said that he grants it the right not to comply. For one thing, the liberty to depart from the judge's instructions comes from other sources than the instructions themselves; for another, it is a liberty to depart from the instructions that those other sources extend and not a right to do so at will.

Thus the juror is the focus of a variety of claims and dispensations. He is told what he must do, but he is not forced to do it and neither he personally nor his verdict may be called to account. He is told what the law is, authoritatively; he is sworn to uphold it; and then he is left alone to reach his decision. He must judge not merely the defendant's guilt or innocence but the merit of the judge's instructions for the particular case. He has become the final judge of whether or not to fulfill his legally defined obligation as a juror. He is, in effect, the agent of a recourse role. Let us review the principal reasons why we think this is so, and then consider some likely objections.

The first reason depends on the assumption that all official roles are created to carry out certain activities according to certain prescribed procedures and constraints to achieve certain ends. So the jury has been set up to reach judgments of guilt or innocence according to certain procedures and constraints, among which are the judge's instructions, in order to achieve the ends of criminal justice. From this assumption arises both the critical problem of acting in a role and the possibility of a solution. As we noted in Chapter One, though the prescribed means for securing a role's ends are binding on the role agent, those means may from time to time prevent the role agent from achieving the role's prescribed ends. But the problem is solved if the role is structured, as the jury role is, to allow the role agent to evaluate the consequences of adhering to the role's prescribed means in terms of the role's prescribed ends—that is, if the role is structured as a recourse role. Thus the jury considers whether literal adherence to the judge's instructions will advance or impede the goals of criminal justice as well as the institutional and background ends of the society more generally. In contrast to roles that extend no liberty, the recourse role allows the agent recourse to a system of role ends that enables him to judge the applicability of his obligations and to act on that judgment. If the conflict occurs among different ends of the role itself rather than simply between some prescribed means and ends, the solution is similar. The agent may consider the role's entire structure of means and ends before making a judgment on which end or ends shall prevail and which yield.

Second, judgment by a role agent of any of his obligations is made possible, and the transition from a role that extends no liberty to a recourse role is achieved, because the reality of an obligation is not necessarily denied when the obligation is held as something less than absolute. It is on this ground that we say that the judge's instructions are binding on the jury and at the same time that the criminal jury in considering an acquittal may judge its obligation in relation to the particular case. Because the jury system requires the conscientious juror to distinguish between departing from an instruction at will and departing from an instruction because he has "damn good reason" for doing so as determined by the role ends he is committed to serve, the jury role retains the obligatory status of the judge's instructions while permitting departures from them. For in general, we regard a constraint as obligatory when we require not merely reason to deny it but overriding reason—which, of course, is the meaning of placing an extra surcharge on reasons for departing from a rule.

It may be objected that we can rid ourselves of the notion of a recourse role and preserve a single, consistent directive to act in a certain way simply by recognizing the actual definition of the role to be conditional: "If you don't have overriding reason —damn good reason—to do otherwise, then do as the judge tells you." According to this argument the current formulation of the judge's instructions to the jury is misleading. The proposed conditional formulation properly expresses the relationship between jury liberty and jury duty, without the need to introduce the concept of rule departure at all.

But this argument falls short for several reasons. The conditional formulation is spurious if its intent is really to restate the conditions met by the idea of a recourse role as a single, consistent directive that in itself generates no conflict. Liberties can always be stated to qualify obligations, but to do so does not diminish either the liberty or the obligation. Any juror hearing the above conditional would know immediately that his legal obligation weighed no less heavily simply because it was not universally compelling; the weight of his obligation, he would understand, was precisely the point of the demand for overriding reason not to carry it out. Regardless of whether the juror translated the conditional message into the language of liberty and obligation, he would face the same consequences as before: that the choice whether to obey the judge's instructions had been thrown back on him; that he would, finally, not escape making a judgment on what obligations would bind him in the instant case and what would not; that he would need to find reasons of overriding weight if he decided not to meet his obligations.

Further, the "overriding reason" condition in the above conditional requires the jury to invoke some ultimate moral or legal norm, and is only poorly understood when assimilated with simpler, more concrete conditions. "Do as the judge tells you unless the consequence is serious injustice" differs in important respects from "Assign applicants to windows according to their last names unless the line exceeds ten persons." First, there exists no routine for determining what "serious injustice" means, as there does for determining the number of people in a line. The rules of law have presumably been formulated to achieve justice. The jury liberty is extended because in some unknown and hence unstatable circumstances they may not, and the determination of those circumstances is left at large to the jury. Second, there can be no question of conflict in determining the number of people in a line, as there can be in deciding to apply some higher legal or moral norm in reaching a just verdict rather than to obey the judge. So it simply will not do to treat the introduction of an ultimate end into the deliberations as though one had merely introduced another condition in a conditional directive for attaining some end, thereby producing a consistent directive requiring the juror to decide only whether to comply or not. To mask the conflict by a conditional statement does not resolve it.

We have been arguing that one cannot rid oneself of the concept of the jury's role as a recourse role simply by recognizing the actual definition of the rule binding the jury to be conditional. We did not deny that the net effect of the constraints and powers through which the jury defines itself is to obligate the jury to follow the instructions of the judge except in the truly exceptional case where the jury finds that to follow those instructions would work a substantial disservice to the fundamental values of justice and fairness. We denied merely that the conditional formulation eliminated the recourse role as a logical possibility and assimilated the jury role into an ordinary discretionary role. Now, as a third point, we wish to observe that an explicit articulation of the jury's privilege to nullify the law where they think that to do so would serve the interests of justice constitutes one special way of engineering the legal system—a way that leads away from the preservation of the jury's role as a recourse role—while the way of engineering the jury system that has been described as the case in these pages constitutes another way. Not only are these two separate legal strategies, but there are consequences of import in the choice of which one to employ.

The different consequences underlie the debate, recently revived in prosecutions of Vietnam War resisters and protesters, over whether the judge should inform the jury of their liberty to disregard the judge's legal instructions if they find that to follow the instructions would produce an unjust conviction of the defendant.[65] The advantages of this instruction are plain enough. First, it would ensure that all juries would understand their role in the same way, and consequently that the benefit of their liberty to acquit despite the judge's instructions would be available equally to defendants in every case. Second, it would provide for fuller participation by the defendant in the processes of adjudication by allowing him to present evidence and argue his case to the jury more fully in terms of the grounds on which the jury might properly choose to decide it.

But there would be disadvantages to such an instruction as well, disadvantages that have motivated some courts in recent years to reject the proposal.[66] The very technique of explicitly instructing the jury, without qualification, that they are obliged to apply the law given by the judge helps ensure that they will impose the required extra surcharge on any decision to depart from the rule. One of the interesting conclusions reached by Kalven and Zeisel in their study of the behavior of the criminal jury was that while the jury does in fact make use of its power to follow its own conscience, it does not deviate from the judge's instructions very often; the jury is not, as they say, "a wildcat operation." This is so, they observe, not only because there is presently no great gap between official and popular values in criminal cases but also because the jury "has been invested with a public task, brought under the influence of a judge, and put to work in solemn surroundings." And, they conclude, "Perhaps one reason why the jury exercises its very real power so sparingly is because it is officially told that it has none."[67]

To the extent this is so, an explicit statement that the jury may invoke their own values, even if put in terms of the highly exceptional case, would reduce the impact of the judge's instructions on the law and invite jury nullification on a greater scale. Whether this result is desirable or not is another matter. The choice turns on the value placed on jury nullification in particular stages of a legal system's development as opposed to the increased danger of arbitrary verdicts and of removing the criminal law still further from the control of court and legislature. Our task here is not to argue the issue but simply to show that there is one.

In sum, the case for characterizing the jury's role as a recourse role turns on the following propositions. First, logic does not prohibit such a role, nor does an easy reformulation make such a role dispensable. Second, recourse roles like that of the jury are functional; they serve distinct purposes in the administration of justice. Third, this characterization of the jury's role accommodates the apparently divergent themes presented by the evidence. It does not require, as alternative interpretations do, that portions of the evidence be oversimplified or explained away.

We can now answer the question posed at the beginning of this section: how is the conscientious juror to understand his role? The duty of the jury is indeed to find the facts on the basis of the evidence presented and to return a general verdict by applying those facts to the law as given by the judge. This is the rule, and it imposes an obligation to comply. But the obligation is not absolute. Sometimes considerations of common sense, or considerations of fairness to the defendant, or the jury's appraisal of the law in contrast to the judge's statement of it may weigh so heavily that the jury may justifiably depart from the rule requiring it to defer to the judge's instructions.

The Concept of Legitimated Interposition

We may now generalize from our analysis of the jury's role to show what happens when official roles provide for the possibility of justifying, under the law, departures from rules of competence. When, in virtue of the institutionalization of a liberty, officials may justify departing from the rules of competence pertaining to their office, we shall say that we have encountered instances of legitimated interposition. In contrast to the concept of delegated discretion, which denotes an explicitly delegated legal power to act according to an agent's best judgment within defined limits, and in contrast also to the concept of usurpation, which denotes an exercise of power in outright defiance of the legal system, the concept of legitimated interposition denotes instances where deviational discretion—power to act according to the agent's best judgment in ways that are unauthorized or even prohibited by rules of competence—has become embedded in legal arrangements. "The essential feature of a jury," wrote Justice White for the Supreme Court, "obviously lies in the interposition between the accused and his accuser of the common sense judgment of a group of laymen, and in the community participation and shared responsibility which results from that group's determination of guilt or innocence."[68] The concept of legitimated interposition generalizes the phenomenon Justice White has pointed out. Actions are legitimated for a role agent insofar as the role justifies an argument to appropriateness for the action. When a legal system presents an official with the liberty to depart from a rule that might work against his achieving the ends of his role, it legitimates his departure from the rule; that is, it legitimates the interposition between the rule and his action of his own judgment that departure from the rule best serves the prescribed end.

Conditions for Legitimated Interposition

What characteristics of the legal system tend to support the interpretation of a particular official role as a recourse role—that is, as a role that provides for legitimated interposition? Legitimated interposition requires that the constraining rule of competence not be constitutive and hence that it not deprive the official's action of legal or practical effectiveness when it is departed from. In addition, it requires that the system provide no means for holding the official himself accountable for his disregard of the rule.

Yet these conditions are not sufficient for a rule departure to have the force of a justified act, as it does in the case of legitimated interposition. That an act and the agent who undertakes it are both unchallengeable may only demonstrate the lamentable shortcomings of the system and confirm the truth of Lord Acton's dictum that all power tends to corrupt and absolute power corrupts absolutely. If there is to be legitimation at all, therefore, the system must establish and make available to the agent who proposes to depart from a rule some body of policies, principles, and ends in virtue of which the departure may be justified. But precisely when this second condition obtains, and a class of rule departures is thereby legitimated within the system rather than acts of arbitrary power facilitated and protected, is hardly self-evident. The determining consideration is whether the class of rule departures has become institutionalized, in the sense that it has become a domesticated and integrally functioning instrument for achieving the ends of the legal system. Determining when this is so for any class of actions demands a reading of a complex and subtle interplay of rules, practices, and arrangements, and of their underlying purposes. It demands a determination of the context of evaluation of the role, in all the ways explored in Chapter One. The example of legitimated interposition by a jury has shown what this might mean concretely.

We have spoken in terms of classes of rule departures. But what of any particular rule departure within a class? Because the jury's role is a recourse role extending a liberty to depart from the judge's instructions, does it follow that every jury verdict contrary to those instructions is necessarily legitimated? Certainly in at least one case it does not follow. This is the case where the decision to depart is grounded on considerations that do not even purport to be part of the accepted ends of the role. A bribed juror, or one who responds to a familial relationship with the defendant or to personal fear, cannot be regarded as acting legitimately in his role. Such a juror abuses his authority in order to serve a personal interest. Yet what should we say of a jury that seeks to serve the ends of its role but grossly misinterprets them? For example, consider a Southern jury that acquits a white segregationist of killing a civil rights worker, on the grounds that in the public interest carpetbag troublemakers must be discouraged from venturing into their community, and that in any event the defendant's act was a political act that should not be punished as a common crime. Is this an instance of legitimated rule departure? The answer, we think, has to be yes. One is entitled to say that this jury is egregiously wrong in its interpretation of the ends of its role, both institutional and background; that its ventured justification rests on premises that contravene the basic ethos of the Constitution and the legal system founded on it; even that it has violated the law insofar as one may regard policies and ends of this kind as part of the law, as we do. But if our argument is correct, one cannot say that this jury has acted lawlessly, in the sense of usurping an authority it did not have, any more than one could say of a judge that he acted lawlessly when in good conscience he grossly misread the law. The liberty to make a judgment on role ends is precisely what is entailed in recourse roles; so long as the agent's judgment is conscientiously made on his view of those ends, his rule departure is legitimated. Of course, there is always the grave danger in recourse roles that the agent will act in crass and damaging ignorance, with no possibility of check or control. Any liberty may be misused. But if our interpretation is right, the law has chosen to take that chance in the case of the jury.

The Possibility of a Lawful Rule Departure

The concept of legitimated interposition plainly rests on the logical coherence of lawful departures from mandatory rules. But how, it might be argued, could a departure from a legal rule be legally justified unless the rule in question was not actually a legal rule of the system? If a citizen breaks a law, appeals his conviction, and persuades a court to hold the law invalid, do we not commonly say that since the law was unconstitutional it was never law?[69] If an official disregards a rule of competence pertaining to his role in undertaking an action that turns out to be legally justified, should we not say that the rule of competence has been shown not to have been a rule? In short, "lawful rule departure" is not simply a paradox, it is an inconsistency; to say the action is lawful is to say no rule was departed from.

At issue is the desirability of retroactive explanations of legal phenomena. Such explanations are hardly logical necessities. They are dictated rather by a need to maintain appearances, a need that other institutions manifest as well: the Church never changes; the truth is merely recognized. The basic trouble with such explanations is that they obscure the conditions under which the agent confronts the rules in the process of deciding on his course of action. To be sure, we might say that the rule in question really allowed for the departure in the first place. But that is a manner of speaking. If it is offered as an accurate description of a given rule, what is there to make anyone believe it except that after the process of decision is over a rule might be formulated to allow for action that was not allowed when the agent had to decide whether to comply or not? This mode of reasoning represents the same "retrospective fallacy"[70] that Prof. Grant Gilmore pointed to as one of the vices of historicism:

> At any given moment in time, there exists an indefinite number of possibilities for future development. We know that this is true when we look around us. But when we look backward in time, we can see that, of all the things that might have happened, only a few were made flesh. In the historicist reconstruction, only the things that actually happened count; the things that might have happened, but did not, are cast out of the equation. Under the historicist hypothesis that the course of history is predetermined and inevitable, the only relevant facts about the past are those which can be made to fit what later turned out to be the actual course of events.[71]

In the case of departures from rules, not only does the retrospective fallacy misdescribe the past by misdescribing the decision the agent faced—specifically his choice of confrontation with some legal authority—it also obscures a very special way in which legal systems accommodate change. The usual way in which legal systems are thought to do so is through the exercise of delegated authority within established channels. The system expands and contracts through processes that are part of its formal structure, such as the passage or repeal of statutes. But most people will acknowledge that there are also nonformal processes of change at work; our point is that retroactive ways of explaining the law obscure them. As the jury's role in acquittals illustrates, systems also change when different lines of development in a complex institution, each representing different values, come into conflict under the pressure of circumstances. In such a case the decision of which line of development shall be given precedence, and which value served, is remitted to individuals who by the nature of the situation receive only incomplete systematic guidance. The concept of legitimated interposition offers a partial explanation of how, short of revolution but beyond the system's formal structure, the legal system accommodates change.

There is another way of challenging the conception of legitimated rule departures in the law. It might be said that the conduct characterized here as legitimated interposition constitutes an instance of the usual way one manages principles and policies, rather than an instance of departures from rules. As Professor Dworkin has argued, legal rules are distinguishable from legal principles and policies. A legal principle "states a reason that argues in one direction, but does not necessitate a particular decision," as a rule does. Moreover, "principles have a dimension that rules do not—the dimension of weight or importance."[72] On this basis it might be argued that juries do not legitimately depart from a rule of competence when they defy the judge's instructions, since the requirement that they follow those instructions is not a rule at all but a principle or policy of the role. If the jury gives the court's instructions some weight, then even though it departs from those instructions it has not failed to carry out its obligation.

The differences in the way policies and principles, in contrast to rules, function in decision making were significant for Professor Dworkin's argument. But the differences do not imply the falseness of the concept of legitimated interposition. First, principles and policies may be departed from as well as rules, as we observed in Chapter One. Even though all that principles and policies require is that due weight be given to them, an official in some instances might find it impossible to give them all their due in a given case and still properly serve the ends of his role. In such instances he would face the predicament of departing from the constraint of some principle or policy. Second, and of fundamental importance, to absorb all instances of legitimated interposition into cases of the application of principles and policies seems once again to employ the retroactive way of regarding legal phenomena. We suggest that there are no principles or policies in themselves, but that directives of the legal system become rules, policies, or principles according to the manner of their use. Their use does not follow from their nature, but their nature from their use. Degrees of generality and precision do not determine whether directives function as principles, policies, or rules. The critical determinant, we propose, is the way such directives function in a context of directives: when they function in such a way that departures from them may be legitimated in that context, then they tend to be adjudged principles or policies rather than rules.* Whether a "Keep off the grass" sign states a policy or a rule depends on whether the obligation to keep off the grass can be maintained simultaneously in the instant case with other legally recognized obligations. If it cannot, it becomes a policy or principle to which one gives a certain weight in deciding whether or not to walk on the grass. Similarly the status of *stare decisis* as a legal obligation depends on whether other legal obligations conflict with it or not. If they do not, *stare decisis* functions as a rule; if they never did, we would without much hesitation call it, precisely, a rule. But if they do, we speak of the principle or policy of *stare decisis*. Only when we determine that a rule may legitimately be departed from within its own legal context are we in a position to say that the rule was really a principle or policy all along. Until that happens the role agent confronts the predicament whether to comply with a constraint. He does not know that it is a principle or a rule. It may be useful for some purposes to call the constraint a principle or policy if departure from it is legally acceptable, but it is no help at the point of action. The agent's dilemma remains whether to depart from the constraint or to comply with it. In a word, calling a rule a principle or a policy may be a way of saying the agent's departure from it was legitimated.

Legitimated Interposition in Other Roles

Our purpose is not to present a systematic canvass of the occurrence of legitimated interposition in our legal system. To stop with the criminal jury, however, would leave open the pos-

---

* Of course, they may be considered principles or policies for other reasons, too, as in the express announcement that an agency is to be bound by certain principles or policies.

sibility that we have perhaps made too much of a singular and anomalous legal phenomenon. We shall therefore try to show that justified rule departures by officials are a familiar feature of the legal terrain by describing some of the circumstances under which the roles of the police, the prosecutor, and the judge may also be recourse roles.

The Police. By and large, American statutes and municipal ordinances do not explicitly grant the police discretion to decide which laws they should enforce, under what circumstances they should enforce the laws, or whom they should enforce the laws against.[73] The criminal laws of a state represent the legislature's determination of which conduct is forbidden on pain of punishment, subject only to those exceptions and qualifications the legislature itself provides. Those laws themselves delegate to the police no dispensing power or power to make further exceptions. The duty of the police is to enforce the laws not just when they think the laws are just, or when enforcement is not inconvenient, or when they think enforcement is not unduly costly, but all the time. Sometimes this obligation is explicit in state laws and local ordinances.[74] But even in the absence of an explicit statute it follows from the traditional conception of the policing function.[75]

It is well known, however, that despite this formal rule of competence the police in fact exercise a broad power of choice in deciding whether to arrest, even in cases where probable cause is manifest.[76] Sometimes the basis for nonenforcement is the police perception that the legislative purpose in making certain conduct criminal would not be served by arresting all persons who engage in the prohibited conduct. Instances include the deliberate nonenforcement of gambling laws against social gamblers, even though the laws make no such exception, on the ground that the inclusiveness of the laws is designed only to prevent professional gamblers from escaping prosecution; the nonenforcement of legislation prohibiting extramarital or deviant sexual behavior between adults, on the ground that the laws do not really reflect a community judgment that this conduct should be criminally punished; and the nonenforcement of laws considered obsolete. At other times the basis for nonenforcement is the need to conserve police resources, which may lead to judgments that certain violations (e.g., traffic, juvenile, drunkenness violations) are too trivial to warrant arrest; or that what are generally regarded as serious violations are not regarded as serious by the cultural subgroup in which they occur (e.g., an intrafamily knifing in a Black slum, where the victim does not insist on prosecution); or that in some minor offenses the victim chiefly desires restitution (e.g., shoplifting or passing bad checks); or that in others the victim has brought the crime on himself (e.g., a case in which a patron is defrauded by a defaulting prostitute). Then there are nonenforcement situations that do not fit into any discrete category. We learn that the police often respond to local community preferences, for example, by permitting gambling to continue in local taverns where local citizens want it to; that they may decline to arrest an informant (e.g., a narcotics user) because of his usefulness in apprehending more serious offenders; and that, as might be expected, they often do not arrest in a wide range of cases where they judge that the personal harm the offender would suffer on being arrested outweighs the law enforcement gains that would be achieved by arresting.

It is plain, therefore, that the police in their day-to-day work are in fact acting on their own judgments of whether or not to enforce the criminal law. Sometimes the judgments are made by the police department; more often they are made by the individual officer himself. Yet the rules themselves do not vest this dispensing power in the policeman. Is he, then, a usurper of authority when he makes and acts on these judgments? Those familiar with criminal justice would surely not say so, for the system in a number of ways shapes a role for the policeman that allows for his self-determined decision not to enforce the criminal laws.

That the police make decisions of this sort is widely understood. Professor Davis observed that "the strongest argument" for policy making by the police "rests upon legislative inaction in the face of long-continued police practices."[77] To a substantial extent the exercise of such authority is invited both by the existence of statutes that overreach their real target, thereby inviting law enforcement officials to make discretionary enforcement decisions, and by the retention of laws that few expect the police to enforce at all. Moreover, this police authority is widely regarded by responsible sources as both inevitable and desirable. So, for example, a presidential commission has identified as the most important factor accounting for nonenforcement decisions "an entirely proper conviction by policemen that the invocation of criminal sanctions is too drastic a response to many offenses."[78] Judge Breitel has stated: "If every policeman ... performed his ... responsibility in strict accordance with rules of law, precisely and narrowly laid down, the criminal law would be ordered but intolerable."[79] The arguments of Professor Davis, a severe critic of unchecked policy making by the police, are apt for our purposes. He writes:

Legislative bodies have long acquiesced in the assumption of power by the police, legislation has long been written in reliance on the expectation that law enforcement officers will correct its excesses through administration, the legislation often reflects unrealistically high aspirations of the community and hence compels the law enforcers to temper the ideals with realism, and the system we have is the product of natural evolution through responses to the multiplicity of community needs.[80]

In addition to the evidence of public and legislative acceptance of and reliance on interpositional decisions by the police, the absence of any substantial legal sanctions against such decisions serves, as in the case of the jury, to reinforce the liberty of the police to make them. To be sure, the individual policeman is subject to administrative sanction if he is caught contravening department policy. But the police as a whole are substantially immune to legal recourse.

Equally significant is the power of the police, again like the jury, to determine final legal consequences beyond their authority as expressed in the rules of competence pertaining to their role. Although not on a par with a jury's decision to acquit, which is always final and absolute, a police decision not to arrest a violator generally ends the matter. Of course, a police decision does not affect the legal status of the violator, who may subsequently be arrested for the same offense—perhaps by another officer, by a citizen, or pursuant to the complaint of an aggrieved party. But in the overwhelming majority of cases a police decision not to invoke the criminal process is, as a practical matter, dispositive.

A police department decision not to invoke the criminal process at all against certain defendants in certain kinds of circumstances is almost as immune to judicial recourse as a jury decision to acquit. The proof of this point is largely negative: the absence of legal provisions for recourse in the face of the widespread and generally known practice of police nonenforcement. One recent case in England—a rare instance of an attempt to invoke judicial review of police nonenforcement—is informative.[81] A private citizen sought mandamus to compel the London police commissioner to abandon his policy of not enforcing the gambling laws against London casinos except on complaint. The court's analysis reveals the amplitude of police nonenforcement authority. It is the police commissioner's duty to enforce the laws, said the court, but no government official has the power to compel him to discharge that duty. "The responsibility for law enforcement lies on him. He is answerable to the law and to the law alone."[82] In many areas, said the court, there could be no interference with the commissioner's judgment: in deciding in any particular case whether to make inquiries or to arrest; in deciding on the disposition of the force; and even in deciding on a policy of not enforcing certain laws, such as that against attempted suicide. The court suggested that the police are judicially answerable only in the exceptional case, perhaps like the one before the court, where without basis in legislative intent or social policy, they adopt a deliberate policy of nullifying a law.* But, of course, this is plainly to say that the police are at liberty to establish and carry out such nonenforcement policies in other kinds of cases.

In discussing the jury we found that another condition was necessary to support the conclusion that an official's power to depart from a rule of competence was an instance of legitimated interposition: the legal system must make available to the official some set of ends in virtue of which his departure from the rule may be justified. We argued that this condition exists to the extent that rule departures become an accepted pattern of the official's exercise of power and generally serve purposes consonant with those of the legal system. It is plainly present in the case of the police official who declines to arrest. The legislature necessarily writes the rules with a broad brush. It cannot for a variety of reasons set out all the appropriate exceptions and qualifications. Nonenforcement decisions by the police serve in some measure to compensate for this inability. Delegated discretion, of course, would achieve the same result, and in very many respects in a far better way, principally because it would make decision making by the police more visible and hence more amenable to controls. But the interpositional strategy has the advantage of allowing the official rule of full enforcement to be maintained. This is not idle ceremony. A criminal code has symbolic offices to fill. The unequivocality of the criminal prohibition and of the threat of punishment for transgressors contribute something—how much is problematical—to the deterrent and moralizing force of the criminal law. Relying on police interposition avoids proclaiming outwardly that the law is not meant to be taken literally. Furthermore, it avoids acknowledgment of the extent to which important matters, even those directly

---

* Regina v. Commissioner of Police, [1968] 2 W.L.R. 903-4 (C.A.). The court did not have to consider this question in the instant case because it had become moot: the commissioner had already revoked his policy of nonenforcement with respect to the gambling laws. *Id.* at 904. It is relevant to note that since English police exercise the prosecutorial as well as the police function with respect to gambling laws, the discussion of the commissioner's nonenforcement policy applied to prosecuting as well as policing.

affecting the citizen's liberty, are left to the official's discretion—
an acknowledgment that would undoubtedly be an affront to
the rule-of-law tradition.* We are not arguing that it is better
to permit the police to operate outside the rules than to recognize their discretionary authority and seek to control it within
a rational structure, thereby ensuring equal treatment of citizens before the law. Our point is rather that the device of not
formally delegating discretionary authority and relying on the
police to make—hopefully—sensible and sensitive judgments
outside the stated rules of their competence is an alternative
strategy that serves identifiable social purposes.

It is instructive to observe now that the roles of police and
jury differ in ways that cast further light on legitimated interposition as a socially conditioned phenomenon. We have observed that whereas the jury has a de jure power to render determinate and unchallengeable consequences even though it
departs from the rules that bind it, the policeman has only a de
facto power to do so. Now let us note a more interesting difference. In the case of the jury we concluded that the rules of the
legal system do oblige juries to apply the court's legal instructions to the facts found. It is not so clear, however, that the rules

---

* A similar point was recently made by Louis Jaffe in commenting on
Professor Davis's argument that the grounds of police discretion should
be explicit and public. Davis illustrated his point by drafting a formal
statement of policy on the use of informers describing the actual but covert
practices of the police in order to show how explicit delegated discretion
and the requirement of open policy formulations would reveal the inde-
fensibility of those practices. Jaffe's comment takes note of the social uses
of interpositional rule departures: "His drafting does point up all that is
questionable about these practices but it is not easy to imagine a draft which
would be acceptable. What is the alternative? That depends on whether
there is or is not general approval of the use of informers. I believe that
there *is* approval in a kind of covert, perhaps shame-faced way. If there is
such approval, it involves inevitably the acceptance of the arbitrary discretion embodied in Davis's regulation. Little would be gained by the regulation other than making public what the society prefers not to make public. This under-the-counter approach may offend the Puritan, it may offend
the legal theorist, but I am sure that those who are offended are in the
rather small minority, and if a society—a democracy if you will—chooses
to operate that way, the appeal to general principles of equal protection
and formal legality does not seem to me to be sufficient." Jaffe, Book Review, 14 *Vill. L. Rev.* 773, 777 (1969).

still oblige a policeman to arrest all persons he reasonably believes have committed a crime. The conventional principle of nonselective police enforcement has undergone extensive public examination, particularly in the past decade. Public reports have dwelled at length and in detail on the regularity and frequency with which policemen depart from that principle in their daily work, and there are increasing pressures to recognize a different operating rule that would rationalize and improve the quality of arrest decisions by explicitly recognizing the discretionary authority of the policeman.[83] Moreover, the policeman's decision not to arrest the guilty, unlike the jury's decision not to convict the guilty, is both frequent and visible to large numbers of observers. As a result selective nonarrest decisions have become so widely accepted that the question arises whether there is really a rule of competence denying the policeman authority to make such decisions. If the official may depart from the rule whenever he believes it better to do so, rather than only when he is persuaded by reasons that override the heavy presumption against doing so, we may not properly speak of the rule as binding at all.

Whether, in light of all the evidence, one should conclude that police are indeed departing from an authoritative rule of competence in declining to arrest apparently guilty persons, or on the other hand, that the rule of competence has by now so lost its vitality that it is improper to speak of rule departures in these cases, we need seek no further to determine. Still, the complexity of the evidence for the police situation illustrates a feature of some importance affecting the historical nature of role adjustments and legitimated interposition, namely, that those adjustments are neither final at any period nor, necessarily, even clearly defined. For it would, after all, be surprising to find all official roles as they actually exist so neatly defined that one could always say that any given exercise of authority fell outside the agent's delegated discretion, rather than within it, and hence that it constituted a rule departure, either legitimated or not. Role authority is a matter of law, and there is no reason to expect the law to be any clearer in questions of interposition than in other questions. Arguments over the existence and limits of discretion inevitably vary in degree of persuasiveness. For the policeman's role the argument justifying selective enforcement is strong. Whether the role is persuasively cast in terms of legitimated interposition or in terms of the absence of a mandatory rule is arguable. Still it remains true that the inconclusiveness of the argument for legitimated interposition for a given role at a given time scarcely detracts from the form and identity of legitimated interposition and the recourse roles shaped to exercise it.

The policeman's role sharply illustrates another characteristic of definitions of role authority. Not only are they sometimes indistinct, but they may be changing. In any dynamic society the amount and kind of authority extended to officials by the legal system constantly varies. Thus an official's assumption of authority to undertake a given act may constitute at one stage in the legal system's development an ordinary usurpation of power; at another stage, an instance of legitimated interposition; and at still another stage, the formally justifiable exercise of an explicitly delegated discretion. Something of that evolution may be represented in the police role, which seems to have reached a point somewhere between the second and the third stage, if it has not already reached the third. There is nothing inevitable about this line of development, however. In the case of the jury, as we have seen, the progression was different. In the early stages of the law's formalization a rule emerged requiring the jury's adherence to the judge's instructions with no interpositional liberty to depart. There then followed a variety of developments establishing a firm case for legitimated interposition. But the further movement toward an explicit, delegated discretion failed, although it was strongly argued, and legitimated interposition became characteristic of the role's function.

The Prosecutor. A settled legal tradition surrounds the prosecutor's role with substantial restraining norms. Writing in the early 1930's, Thurman Arnold listed among the basic assumptions of the law enforcement creed: "It is the duty of the prosecuting attorney to enforce all criminal laws regardless of his own judgment of public convenience or safety."[84] A leading state decision[85] rests on the proposition that the law forbids "the injection of the prosecutor's private notion of criminal policy into the public policy of the state."[86] Statutes speak of the prosecutor's duty to initiate and carry out prosecutions of the criminal laws, with no qualification that the prosecutor may do otherwise if he deems prosecution to be inopportune or unjust in a particular instance. As Prof. Baker observed in his classic study:

The duties of the prosecutor, as set forth in the statutes, say nothing about compromise or adjustment, bargaining with defendants, mediation in quarrels, or crime prevention. On paper, the rules for the administration of the criminal law provide that all offenders should be treated equally—no defendant should receive more or less punishment than another who committed a similar offense.[87]

Sometimes courts flatly assert that the duty to prosecute imposed by such statutes is "mandatory and not discretionary."[88] Moreover, numerous statutes expressly require the prosecutor to prosecute those who commit specified offenses—usually offenses having to do with liquor and gambling, but also others that have given rise to particular public alarm.[89]

Even so, the prosecutor's accountability is sharply limited. Laws in various states do provide some remedies against prosecutorial nonenforcement decisions. There are provisions authorizing the prosecutor's removal and even his criminal prosecution. In addition state attorneys general often are empowered to supersede the prosecutor and initiate prosecutions themselves.[90] These remedies, however, tend to be limited to cases of manifest bad faith and scarcely touch the vast majority of prosecutorial judgments.[91] Though other remedies against a prosecutor's inaction may also be occasionally available,[92] the prosecutor's self-determined power not to prosecute, if legally not as broad as the policeman's power not to arrest, is nonetheless substantially uncontrolled.[93] Whether the rationalization for this state of affairs is found in the role of the prosecutor as attorney for the state,[94] or in the exclusive nature of the prosecuting function,[95] or in the principle of separation of powers between executive and judicial functions,[96] the prosecutor is in practice substantially immune to judicial accountability for the noncorrupt exercise of his power not to initiate criminal prosecutions.[97]

Nonetheless, the argument for legitimated interposition based on the absence of effective means for enforcing the prosecutor's legal duty to prosecute cannot be pushed too far. In practice prosecutors make judgments not to enforce on a vast scale,[98] and the legitimacy of their doing so is so pervasively and authoritatively recognized that full enforcement, even more than in the case of the police, probably cannot be regarded as a rule at all. In our terms, deviational discretion in the prosecutor's role has been substantially converted into delegated discretion. One finds this explicitly recognized in judicial opinions. A state court has written: "It is undoubtedly part of the prosecutor's job to individualize justice."[99] Chief Justice Burger, while a judge on the District of Columbia Circuit Court, observed: "Myriad factors can enter into the prosecutor's decision. . . . He is expected to exercise discretion and common sense."[100] Judge Burger was not making new law. An earlier court had stated: "The discretionary power of the attorney for the United States in determining whether a prosecution should be commenced or maintained may well depend upon matters of policy wholly apart from any question of probable cause."[101]

Indeed, it is widely accepted that a vital part of the prosecutor's official role is to "determine what offenses, and whom, to prosecute," even among provably guilty offenders, and that in so doing the prosecutor must "consider the public impact of criminal proceedings [and] balance the admonitory value of invariable and inflexible punishment against the greater impulse of the quality of mercy."[102] That discretion is an explicit part of the prosecutor's role is further evidenced by the fact that law reform issues currently center on devising administrative, legislative, and judicial means to rationalize the standards the prosecutor employs in making discretionary judgments.[103]

Still, to say that an official has a delegated discretionary authority to act on his best judgment is not to say that the law imposes no constraints on action in his role, and hence that there is no occasion for limited interposition in his role.[104] Though not all instances of prosecutorial discretion constitute interposition, there are some that do. A notable and widely recognized instance of prosecutorial rule departure involves statutes that mandate severe sentences and leave no option to the sentencing judge. For example, some laws set a high mandatory punishment or deny the possibility of probation to offenders with prior convictions and often impose a duty on the prosecutor to charge offenders with all known prior offenses. It would be difficult to construe these laws as empowering the prosecutor to prosecute at his discretion. Yet it is well known that prosecutors do so, and often with the help of the court. As the President's Crime Commission reported, "There is persuasive evidence of nonenforcement of these mandatory sentencing provisions by the courts and the prosecutors."[105] In fact, these provisions are invoked in only a small fraction of the cases in which they obtain. This pattern also prevails in states where the prosecutor is statutorily obliged to charge multiple offender counts, thus producing a substantial prosecutorial nullification.[106] For the same reasons as those advanced earlier in connection with rule departures by juries and police, these rule departures seem to represent instances of legitimated interposition—instances in which the legal system has recourse to the judgment of its officials to resolve the tension between the prescribed means and ends of their roles.

A comparable instance of a more general deviational discretion is the institution of prosecutorial plea bargaining. Until quite recently the universal phenomenon of bargaining between the prosecutor and the defendant over prosecutorial concessions (such as noninclusion or dismissal of counts, reduction of charges, and sentencing recommendations) in return for a plea of guilty operated as a shadow procedure, "in the limbo of dubious legality."[107] It grew up outside the law as a device both to mitigate excessively harsh penalties and to prevent a breakdown of the system from congestion and delay.[108]

The incompatibility of this process with traditional models of the proper exercise of discretionary authority has long been noted: bargaining has no place in the criminal law. Civil cases may properly be compromised, but justice and the public interest in crime prevention as reflected in the criminal law may not be.[109] That public interest is served by the criminal law as modified by the prosecutor's conscientious exercise of discretion in assessing the merits of the case in view of the circumstances surrounding it. "However, when he goes beyond those factors and weighs the state of his or the court's backlog in the balance, he employs that discretion in a manner unrelated to the policy underlying delegation of that discretion to him."[110] Penalties may be reduced or not exacted because to inflict the penalty prescribed by law seems either unfair to the defendant, under the circumstances, or inappropriate to the social interest. But to reduce or fail to exact a penalty in order to save time or money, or to avoid court congestion, distorts the process and tends to produce "de facto invalidation of extant laws."[111]

Certainly there are countervailing considerations and arguments. But it is more relevant to our argument that for generations these views of the inconsistency of plea bargaining with the proper role of the prosecutor were part of the accepted jurisprudence.[112] Of course, bargaining continued on a vast scale nevertheless. But the courts adjusted to the situation by acting as though it did not exist; to do otherwise would have required them either to oppose it, which practical considerations would scarcely permit, or to admit that the system was not operating wholly lawfully. Hence the oft-noted charade in which the court asked the pleading defendant whether he had received any promises or inducements in exchange for his plea, and the defendant, properly coached, responded that he had not, though all present, including the judge, knew very well that the opposite was the case.[113]

In recent years all this has changed. Influential commissions have publicly supported plea bargaining as producing better results than the "straight application" of the law would permit.[114] The United States Supreme Court recently recognized the lawful status of plea bargaining, substantially on the ground that considerations of expediency, expense, and court congestion may legitimately be taken into account.[115] The California Supreme Court followed suit, concluding that "plea bargaining has become an accepted practice in American criminal procedure, 'an integral part of the administration of justice,' "[116] and requiring that the terms of the agreement be made part of the record. In short, the institution of plea bargaining has been formally recognized and the prosecutor's role expressly redefined to accommodate it. But this development only serves to dramatize the antecedent status of plea bargaining as a widespread departure from prevailing rules of competence that was informally legitimated within the context of the legal system.

As these examples tend to show, therefore, the prosecutor sometimes, though not always, may fairly read his role as a recourse role, a role providing recourse against the inevitable limitations of a delegated discretion. The prosecutor may consider himself justified, as a prosecutor, in taking an action on himself contrary to his rule of competence. He has the liberty to interpose.

The Judge. In determining whether the judge's role provides for instances of legitimated interposition it is necessary first to distinguish situations in which judges act in essentially administrative ways from those in which they act in essentially judicial ways.

Often a judge is called upon to perform functions that are administrative in character. At these times the fact that he is a judge rather than a juror, a policeman, or a prosecutor is plainly irrelevant. Rules are established to control the exercise of his delegated authority—rules of the same kind that constrain these other officials. For example, the judge's discretion in sentencing convicted offenders is often subject to defined constraints, such as a rule that he may not grant probation to prior offenders. If the judge departs from this rule because he thinks it unjust, and if the context in which he makes such judgments suggests that he does not violate his role obligation by doing so in certain cases, we may properly speak of legitimated interposition by the judge. If a judge departed from a rule forbidding him to grant probation to prior offenders, it would soon be discovered that there is no appeal or other remedy available to the prosecutor; that no subsequent challenge is possible; that disregard of the rule in particular cases where the judge deems it improper is widespread; that the other participants in the process rely on the judge's doing so in certain cases; even that legislators may have expected the judge to be sensible enough occasionally to depart from the rule when they adopted it. Therefore, consistent with our previous analysis, we may say that the legal system extends to the judge a liberty to interpose his own judgment in place of the rule. The following observation by a judge concerning a severe mandatory sentencing provision is not at all untypical:

This is ridiculous law, passed in the heat of passion without any thought of its real consequences. I absolutely refuse to send to prison for twenty years a young boy who has done nothing more than sell a single marijuana cigarette to a buddy. The law was not intended for such cases. I have been accused of usurping commutation and pardon powers. This is not true. I simply will not give excessive sentences and where the legislature leaves me no alternative, I will lower the charge or dismiss altogether.[117]

In analyzing the more difficult situations in which a judge acts adjudicatively, rather than administratively, and applies the methodology and precepts of common-law reasoning to the cases brought before him for decision,* it is helpful to consider first the factors of finality and absence of recourse as they pertain to the judicial process. We argued earlier that a legal power to bring about determinative legal consequences combined with the absence of any legal recourse for testing the exercise of that power against rules of competence constitutes evidence of a liberty to interpose. A similar phenomenon occurs in the exercise of the judicial function by courts of last resort. Must we

---

* Here, of course, we are thinking particularly of judges in appellate courts.

conclude, then, that judges of these courts are at liberty to depart from the rules that constrain them precisely because they are in courts of last resort?

Not only is this conclusion implausible as a description of the role and functions of judges in supreme courts in our legal system, but as Professor Hart has shown, using the instance of an umpire in a game who has final authority to interpret and apply the rules during the course of play, so much cannot be drawn from finality. Even though there is no appeal from his rulings, we would never say that the umpire is free to change the rules when he thinks it right to do so. That would imply a very different game. We would quite properly insist, first, that finality does not import infallibility, and second, that an umpire has an obligation, not diminished by the finality of his decisions, to call the plays according to the rules—an obligation imposed by the very nature of the game and by the common understanding by all the players of what playing the game means.[118]

In the case of umpires in games and judges in courts of last resort in legal systems, therefore, finality and the absence of recourse do not themselves import a liberty to depart from the rules. How is it, then, that these same factors do produce this effect in the case of the jury? The answer, we suggest, lies in the nature of the legal roles involved. Juries, unlike umpires and judges in courts of last resort, are not the ultimate and essential custodians of the rules. The final and unchallengeable authority juries and some officials enjoy in certain circumstances leads to the inference that their obligation to follow the rules has been qualified precisely because their actions have been insulated from the checks and controls normally applied by those custodians of the law. In the case of judges in courts of last resort, on the other hand, we may not infer a liberty to interpose simply from the fact that their decisions are final, given that the system has no alternative but to make their decisions final. As Justice Cardozo observed,

Judges have, of course, the power, though not the right, to ignore the mandate of a statute, and render judgment in despite of it. They have the power, though not the right, to travel beyond the walls of the interstices, the bounds set to judicial innovation by precedent and custom. Nonetheless, by that abuse of power, they violate the law.[119]

Putting aside the circumstances of finality and absence of recourse, then, we confront the central difficulty (not present in cases in which the judge acts administratively) of determining the rules of competence for judges in the judicial process. We can hardly expect to determine when judges may legitimately depart from the constraining rules of their role without first determining what those rules are. Any full-scale treatment of legitimated rule departures in the judicial process, therefore, invites an equally full-scale treatment of the nature of judicial reasoning, a subject clearly beyond the bounds of this book. Nevertheless, we may make some progress toward identifying the possibilities of judicial interposition by using as a starting point what the judicial rules of competence have been taken to be.

With the exception of extreme advocates of the realist school,[120] most observers agree that the judge's role is not free from constraints. At a minimum they would accept Justice Cardozo's statements that the "power . . . to shape the law in conformity with the customary morality is something far removed from the destruction of all rules and the substitution in every instance of the individual sense of justice, the *arbitrium boni viri*," and that one must distinguish between "the command embodied in a judgment and the jural principle to which the obedience of the judge is due."[121] The content of that "jural principle" (the rule of competence, in our terminology) is subject to widely differing interpretations. But what is striking is the extent to which courts in their judicial opinions proclaim obedience to a principle far more restrictive than the principle they employ in practice.

This was one of the central observations of the realists. Much opinion writing proceeds on the principle that the judge simply finds the law and that the conclusions reached are its ineluctable result. And yet, at least in the hard cases, it could be shown that the governing considerations were not the logical inevitabilities of preexisting legal principles, but assessments of social policy, expediency, national priorities, and a vast array of other imponderables quite outside the formal law, if not wholly inside the judge. The thrust of realist criticism was that much opinion writing should be recognized for what it is, namely hyprocrisy and self-deception; that judges and the public should face squarely the fact that the judicial process inevitably entails a far-ranging discretion to invoke values and policies outside the law; and that assumptions of certainty and inevitability should be discarded. As Jerome Frank observed:

> The task of judging calls for a clear head. But our judges, so far as they heed the basic myth, can exercise their power with only a fuzzy comprehension of what they are doing. When they make "new rules," they often sneak them into the *corpus juris*; when they individualize their treatment of a controversy, they must act as if engaged in something disreputable and of which they themselves can not afford to be aware. But the power to individualize and to legislate judicially is of the very essence of their function. To treat judicial free adaptation and lawmaking as if they were bootlegging operations, renders the product unnecessarily impure and harmful.[122]

It is instructive to compare Frank's views with Jeremy Bentham's much earlier criticism of judicial decision making, centering around the use of fictions. Legal fictions are devices long used by common-law judges to support a conclusion at variance with some rule of law. For example, the fiction that "attractive nuisances" *invite* a person onto the defendant's property serves to avoid the rule that no duty of care is owed to trespassers.[123] Bentham excoriated judges for employing these devices. To him a fiction was a transparent cover for shameless usurpation, "a willful falsehood, having for its object the stealing of legislative power, by and for hands which could not, or durst not, openly claim it, and but for the delusion thus produced could not exercise it."[124]

For Frank, then, the judicial rhetoric was irrational. Since judges had every right to mold the law as they thought right, they should assert as much and get on with the task. For Bentham the judicial rhetoric was duplicitous. Since judges had no right at all to fall back on their own assessment of what the law

should be in deciding cases, they should be deprived of the use
of such devices as fictions that mask their usurpation. Yet neither
criticism captures what is entailed in the observed judicial
tendency generally to cast results in terms of logical inevitability
or in the use of fictions in particular. Frank misread the legal
tradition in arguing that the judge is free of the obligation to
follow the rules of law in administering justice. Bentham also
misread it in arguing that the judge must always follow the
rules, however unjust the result may seem. There is a third possibility, one that is concealed by the premise that rules of competence, to be such, must be single, consistent directives. This
same premise, it will be recalled, underlies the two alternative
interpretations, discussed earlier, of the clash between the jury's
obligation to defer to the instructions of the judge and its prerogative not to do so. On this premise one is forced either to deny
the incurred obligation or to deny the reality of the prerogative.
So for Frank there is no obligation: the role of the judge is to
engage in "free adaptation and lawmaking." For Bentham there
is no prerogative: the role of the judge is to comply with the
rules. But neither interpretation comports with the evidence of
the role of the judge as it is experienced in the legal system. Each
seizes on the evidence that supports it and rejects the rest. The
third possibility, which does account for the conflicting evidence, is comparable to that developed for the jury's role: the
judge is indeed bound by the rules of law, and he is bound to
administer justice through those rules. But sometimes the ends
of justice may be disserved by following those rules. In those
cases the judge's role, unlike the clerk's, extends him a liberty
to make this judgment and to depart from the rules to achieve
results consistent with the ends for which his role is set up. In
sum, the judicial role is a recourse role.

We should have to marshal more evidence than we have to
make this claim stick; and this book is not the place to try. But
we suggest that the observed role behavior of officials is one of
the important places one looks when seeking to interpret a role.
And the judicial behavior that Frank and Bentham observed

and criticized in their different ways tends to support the interpretation we are suggesting—an interpretation supported by other evidence as well. For judicial departures from the obligation to decide in accordance with the established rules has become a deeply ingrained and characteristic feature of the judicial process, a feature sustained by the milieu in which judges operate. So government officials take judicial lawmaking into account when acting in their own roles; legal analysis and argumentation rest on it; initiates into the legal system encounter the tension between analytical and result-oriented thinking as one of the central features of a process they are expected to master.

It is, of course, strongly arguable that however it may have been in the last century, in more recent times the judge's authority to depart from what once were regarded as rigorous restraints on judicial decision making has become accepted as a delegated discretionary power. Earlier sections of this chapter noted a comparable transformation in the role of the prosecutor with respect to the duty of prosecution. We have no quarrel with this interpretation, since it leaves the principal thesis intact—that recourse roles constitute a discrete type of legal role that our legal system gives evidence of incorporating at some points in its history.

Other Roles. Apart from the judicial process, the instances of legitimated interposition so far discussed have been confined to the criminal law. That has been so partly because those instances are at once more obvious than others and tend to unsettle the more traditional conceptions of legal systems, and partly because interposition by law enforcement officials bears directly on an analogous liberty of citizens with respect to the rules those officials enforce against them, as will be shown in the next chapter. For the sake of a more complete assessment of the place of legitimated interposition in the legal system, therefore, it will be useful to draw attention at least to the possibilities of the concept of legitimated interposition for analyzing issues removed from those of the criminal law and the courts. The most dramatic of these issues are those raised by the confrontation between the legal power of the President and that of Congress. We will mention here just two of the contexts in which this issue has arisen—the power of the President to initiate military actions without congressional authority and to refuse to expend funds despite congressional authorization.

Though both of these questions have recurred periodically in American history, no definitive articulation of the respective authority of the President and of Congress has emerged.[125] The President's case for his liberty to initiate military actions without congressional authorization rests preeminently on his role as commander-in-chief of the armed forces and as chief executive with a "duty to take care that the laws are faithfully executed." These powers entail an inevitable discretion to employ troops in the protection of national interests, which may lead—and has led—to open war. Yet the Constitution grants Congress alone the power to declare war, and the President is sworn to uphold the Constitution. Shall the President acknowledge congressional privilege and stifle the powers constitutionally delegated to him, or shall he exert those powers and infringe on congressional right?[126] President Nixon has most recently faced a similar dilemma through his determination to combat inflation by impounding funds authorized by Congress in support of a broad program of social legislation.[127] Some have argued that in impounding those funds he acts directly counter to the constitutionally delegated power of Congress to raise revenues to provide for the general welfare and to make all laws necessary and proper to carry into effect its enumerated powers over interstate and foreign commerce; and that the presidential duty to "take care that the laws are faithfully executed" generates an obligation to implement congressional action rather than impede it. On the other hand, executive power has been vested in the President, with implicit authority to make judgments on how authorized expenditures should be made.

Now it is not our purpose to enter the discussion of the specific constitutional rights and duties that appear in the dispute between the President and Congress. No doubt some of the constituent issues will in time be settled by the Supreme Court. But it is pertinent here to observe that prima facie, at least, the presidential office faces the kind of conflict between duties and rights, between legal means and legal ends, that constitutes the essential basis and provocation for an official role in which interposition is legitimated—a recourse role. We do not argue that the presidency does or ought to constitute such a role, but merely that the President's responsibility for ultimate national ends strongly suggests that such is the case. Accordingly, to interpret the dispute between the President and Congress as a dispute over usurpation may be to cast the issue in too narrow terms. If legitimated interposition is a possibility, it may not be assumed that the President either has the necessary delegated authority or is simply usurping powers not his in flat violation of his oath, and nothing else. For to make that assumption, to assume that the conflict of presidential obligations *cannot* be genuine, is to read the Constitution on that assumption of the single, consistent voice we found wanting in other contexts. The possibility remains that the conflict in presidential obligations is indeed genuine. Under this view it remains to examine whether the role of the President can be construed as a recourse role analogous to the jury's role and the other roles we have touched on.

In a word, the implication of our analysis is that in the current debate the President has another move: to claim an entitlement to act not on the basis of what the rules are but on the liberty of the chief executive of a nation to depart from the rules when his assessment of national ends exigently requires it. We do not argue that the move could not or should not be countered. The determination of the nature and extent of a recourse role has to be hammered out in terms of social and political circumstances and prospects; it cannot be settled a priori. Considerations of social utility, of success or failure in securing legal effect for interpositional acts, of effective and continuous immunity to impeachment, and many other considerations, the analogues of which were examined earlier in this chapter, will settle the issue. It remains for us here only to point out that presidential claims to action such as President Nixon has undertaken have at times been defended in the terms we are suggesting. Legitimated interposition was essentially President Lincoln's justification for suspending habeas corpus: "Would not the official oath be broken," he wrote, "if the government should be overthrown when it was believed that disregarding the single law would tend to preserve it?" And President Jefferson earlier had occasion to observe:

To lose our country by a scrupulous adherence to written law, would be to lose the law itself, with life, liberty, property, and all those who are enjoying them with us; thus absurdly sacrificing the end to the means. . . . The line of discrimination between cases may be difficult; but the good officer is bound to draw it at his own peril, and throw himself on the justice of his country and the rectitude of his motives.[128]

That last is precisely the point. Even if President Nixon's conduct of foreign affairs and domestic spending prove in the end to be legitimated by the nature of his role, he is compelled to take his actions upon himself at his own peril and throw himself on the justice of his country and the rectitude of his motives. No one can tell in advance how the judgment will come out.

CHAPTER THREE

Justified Rule Departures by Citizens

H AVING ARGUED that legal officials in our system may at times legitimately depart from the rules of competence that constrain them in their role, we now consider whether citizens may legitimately depart from the mandatory rules—peremptory rules, we called them earlier—that constrain them. These are the rules, whether deriving from the criminal law, administrative or judicial tribunals, or individual officials, that carry a penal sanction for noncompliance. The sanction functions to make their mandatory import explicit—mandatory in the sense that they purport to impose a legal obligation on the citizen to comply.

Prima facie, suggestions that peremptory rules merely offer the citizen an option to comply or to suffer the consequences of noncompliance misconceive the law's intent.[1] Punishment exists to prevent and condemn violations, not to offer citizens the option of committing them at the cost of imprisonment. It is precisely the point at which the punishment has come to be considered an acceptable option that it loses its character as punishment.[2] Conviction constitutes not merely a basis for the imposition of painful consequences; it stigmatizes the violator as a blameworthy person who has breached his duty.[3] The threat of punishment, therefore, not only obliges the citizen to comply in the sense of warning him that he had better do so, but also serves to lay an obligation on him as a proper citizen to comply. This is not to say, of course, that therefore people have a moral obligation always to obey peremptory rules or that they have any obligation at all to assume the citizen's role. These are different matters. The point is only that one way peremptory rules purport to constrain the citizen is by appealing to his legal obligation as a citizen to comply.

As seen in the case of officials, however, to find a legal obligation to comply with rules raises rather than disposes of the question of justified rule departures. This chapter will develop a concept of legitimated rule departure by citizens analogous to legitimated interposition by officials and explore the American legal system for confirmatory evidence of its acceptance.

The Law-and-Order Model and the Citizen's Role

In pursuing a related inquiry with respect to legal officials, the last chapter began by presenting the rule-of-law model, the conventional model for the official's obligation under the law. It happens that an analogous model exists for the citizen's obligation, which we shall refer to here, though at some risk, as the law-and-order model. "Law and order" has become a rallying cry in recent years for those who urge the rigorous and forceful suppression of crime, political and nonpolitical, with single-minded disregard of countervailing considerations. But this connotation is not the one invoked here. The phrase also has a long-standing and very different usage conveying a sense of the citizen's obligation before the law comparable to the sense of the official's obligation conveyed by "rule of law." Indeed, "rule of law" and "law and order" are intertwined in usage and in history.

According to the law-and-order model, the citizen's obligation consists of unqualified compliance with the mandatory rules of the state. That those rules do or do not accord with the citizen's own sense of justice is immaterial: he is not to judge the law but to obey it. In effect, the law-and-order model denies the possibility that the law itself might make provisions for a citizen to judge whether or not he should be bound by the law under certain circumstances.

This model is not necessarily more appropriate to a dictatorship than to a democracy. The critical differences between a dictatorship and a democracy lie in the method of making laws and the freedom-preserving character of the laws made, not in the nature of the citizen's obligation before the law. However the laws are made and whatever they provide, the law-and-order model requires the citizen always to comply: thus a citizen in a democracy may be free to denounce a law and to seek changes in it through the political process, but until the law is changed it commands obedience of him. While the law stands the citizen complies. The rule provides all that is necessary to guide action. There is no place for his own judgments, however persuasive the grounds. To depart from the rule amounts in principle to an act of rebellion, and though such an act might at times be justified morally, it can never be justified by the legal system being rebelled against.

This model offers a coherent conception of the citizen's obligations before the peremptory rules, just as the rule-of-law model offered a coherent conception of the official's obligations before the mandatory rules addressed to him. And no doubt in many respects the workings of our own legal system reflect its premises. We propose to show, however, that the law-and-order model is not the only possible model of a citizen's obligations in a community ordered by law. Nor is it necessarily the best model. Moreover, in a number of significant instances it fails to describe accurately the nature of the obligations imposed on the citizen by our legal system—instances in which the legal system legitimates rule departures by citizens, just as it sometimes legitimates rule departures by officials. In sum, we propose to show that the citizen's role is at many critical points a recourse role, totally incompatible with the law-and-order model. In the pages that follow we shall identify instances of legitimated rule departure by citizens and indicate the source and force of the propositions of appropriateness that furnish a basis for them.

The Concept of Legitimated Disobedience

The last chapter developed the concept of legitimated interposition to account for instances in which departures by officials from binding rules of competence are made justifiable within the official's role in the legal system. The differences between the official's role and the citizen's role require a different, though related, concept to account for justifiable rule departures by citizens. This is the concept of legitimated disobedience.

A rule departure is justifiable in the same sense in both legitimated interposition and legitimated disobedience. The obligatory force of the rule remains, but it is overcome in the particular instance by considerations of merit measured by role ends. Moreover, the system grants the role agent, whether citizen or official, the liberty to make the decision that a rule's obligatory force has been overcome. But legitimated interposition and legitimated disobedience inevitably differ in the way the liberty to make that decision is granted and hence in how one may determine that it is granted. To use the terminology of Chapter One, different roles require different propositions of appropriateness to justify undertaking a departure from a mandatory rule.

So much is apparent from the kinds of considerations already advanced for inferring the existence of justified departures by officials from rules of competence: namely, that those rules grant the official power to effect legal consequences in excess of his right to do so; that the legal system provides no recourse against either the action or the official; and that the system makes available socially approved job, institutional, and background ends on which the official may base his decision to depart from the rules. The rules of competence constraining the official derive ultimately from the nature of his role as an instrument of government authority. But a person as citizen exercises no government authority; hence how the system extends authority and what conditions it establishes for the exercise of authority are not directly relevant to the justification of his action with respect to the mandatory rules constraining him.

Where the rule is not a prescription for how the individual is to perform his legally delegated functions but an authoritative command directing him to perform or abstain from performing some act on pain of punishment, what kinds of considerations does our legal system recognize as a basis for arguments to the appropriateness of his undertaking to disobey? To establish a context for answering this question in a variety of legal circumstances, we suggest at the outset that four general conditions must be met for the legal system to legitimate a citizen's disobedience. First, the legal system must recognize what we shall call a legitimating norm, the applicability of which falls within the final authority of a legal official, usually but not necessarily a court of law, to determine. Second, the norm must have the effect, when found to apply, of relieving the citizen of the usual liability to punishment for disobedience. Third, the norm must function not as a qualification of the rule but as a justification for the citizen's disobeying the rule. And fourth, the citizen must make a colorable appeal to the norm as the justification for departing from the rule.

The import of the first two conditions is as follows. It is true that the citizen may be punished for his disobedience if the official body in due course determines that the norm appealed to is inapplicable or has a different meaning than the citizen claims. Yet since the citizen would have been discharged of accountability if he had turned out to be right, he cannot fairly be said to have failed to meet his obligation as a citizen to comply merely because he turned out to be wrong. His action was wrong on the merits, but it was appropriate for him to undertake the action. In these circumstances it seems proper to say that his obligation to comply has been overridden, and that he is afforded not a freedom to depart from the rule with impunity (he may, in the end, be punished for the departure), but a liberty to make and act on his own judgment of the norm's meaning and applicability.

The third condition requires that the norm be invoked to justify an act of genuine disobedience to a rule rather than merely to support a case for qualifying the rule itself in order to classify the act as legal. In other words, it is necessary to distinguish the situation in which the undertaking to depart from the rule is legitimated from that in which it is found that the rule, as qualified, was not departed from at all. This distinction will be more fully developed later.

The fourth condition requires that the argument to the norm be colorable, by which we mean only that the argument be a genuine argument within the framework of legal controversy. This requirement follows from the nature of legitimated disobedience as a rule departure whose justifiability is found within the legal system. Without the requirement of colorability, any reason at all—so long as it was claimed to be founded on a legitimating norm—would suffice to justify undertaking the act of disobedience. Hence the legitimating norm would cease to function as a legal standard for guiding conduct and as a legal basis for justifying a rule departure.

We suggest that these conditions for legitimated disobedience occur in our legal system with respect to three kinds of legitimating norms: the norm of validity; the norm of the lesser evil; and the norm of justifiable nonenforcement. With that classification as an organizational framework, we may proceed to examine how a citizen's disobedience may be legitimated in a variety of legal contexts within our legal system.

Legitimated Disobedience and the Norm of Validity

Not every action by a government official or agency carries with it the force of law. The Constitution sets forth the powers that may be exercised, the way they must be exercised to have legal force, and specific restraints on the scope of those powers. Moreover, subject to its overall provisions, legislatures and courts establish standards for determining the validity of actions by officials. When a government action takes the form of a peremptory rule, what should a citizen do if he concludes that some governing standard of validity renders the action invalid? In a number of situations the legal system leaves it to the citizen to make and act on his own judgment, creating the conditions for legitimated disobedience.

Unconstitutional Statutes

In American law the most obvious instance of the use of an appeal to the norm of validity to generate legitimated disobedience is judicial review of the constitutionality of government action. The presence of a constitution alone does not suffice. It would have been possible, after all, for constitutional restraints to be self-enforcing within each agency of government, so that the final authority to interpret the Constitution would not rest with the courts at all.[4] It would also have been possible for the courts to be granted authority to rule on the constitutionality of a statute before it comes into effect rather than afterward, much as the President in our present system may veto a law after it is passed by Congress.[5] Another possibility would require the courts to rule on the constitutionality of a statute in settings other than a prosecution for its violation. But none of these possibilities, any of which would obviate legitimated disobedience, have been realized in American law. Instead, as the institution of judicial review under the Constitution has emerged, it has created the essential conditions for legitimated disobedience. The ultimate authority to decide whether government agencies have complied with the Constitution has come to be vested in courts that assert this authority in the course of adjudicating disputes between litigants. Indeed, the Supreme Court originally inferred its power of judicial review from its delegated authority to adjudicate under the law, on the view that the Constitution was a part of the law it was obliged to interpret and apply in deciding cases.[6] Moreover, on this view, a conclusion that the higher law of the Constitution prevailed over a lesser law in conflict with it required that the rights of the parties under the Constitution be given the same retroactive application conventionally accorded to other laws by courts adjudicating legal disputes. Thus it followed that a defense of unconstitutionality to a criminal prosecution functions like any other defense: if the defendant can persuade the court that the law he violated is unconstitutional, the law is given no effect and the defendant is therefore not legally punishable; otherwise the law remains in force and the defendant is punishable. Hence an essential condition for legitimated disobedience is established.

Moreover, in usual circumstances a citizen can obtain judicial review of a law's constitutionality only by breaking the law and invoking the Constitution as a defense when prosecuted. This situation is principally the product of several hurdles developed by Supreme Court to permit it to postpone or avoid constitutional declarations. One is the requirement that a person challenging the validity of a statute must have "standing" to present the issue. That is to say, he must show that his own legal rights are prejudiced by the statute. Another is the requirement that the issue must arise out of a matured legal controversy, as opposed to an anticipated one.[7] The former requirement ensures the adversarial interest of the parties; the latter, the inescapability of adjudication. Often their effect is to prevent a person from obtaining a legal determination of a law's validity so long as he complies with the law. Hence he must depart from the rule before seeking the protection offered by the Constitution and the institution of judicial review.

These features of judicial review in this country are illustrated by a series of cases brought before the Supreme Court in a 24-year effort to obtain a decision on the constitutionality of a Connecticut statute making it a crime to use contraceptives or to assist others in their use. In 1947 a physician's challenge to the validity of the statute—on the ground that it prevented him from helping several patients whose lives would be threatened by childbearing—reached the Court. The physician sued under the state declaratory judgment statute, which permitted a person, under defined circumstances, to obtain a judicial determination of his legal rights and liabilities under an anticipated but not developed set of conditions.[8] The Court found that he lacked standing to challenge the birth control statute, however. His patients would have had such standing, since the statute directly affected their physical well-being. But the physician could not assert his patients' interests, and he was not asserting that a constitutional right of his own was infringed. Of course,

if he had violated the statute and been prosecuted, there would
have been no problem of standing.

In 1961 another challenge to the statute reached the Court,
again under the state declaratory judgment statute.[9] This time
the suing physician, Dr. Buxton, was careful to assert his standing. He claimed that the birth control statute violated his constitutional right properly to practice his profession. And two
of his patients joined him, claiming that the unavailability of
contraceptive advice presented a danger to their health. Again
the Court declined to pass on the constitutional claim, this time
not because Dr. Buxton and his patients lacked standing but
because there was no ripened controversy requiring a judicial
declaration. The threat of imminent criminal prosecution had
been recognized as an adequate ground for judicial relief, but
here the Court found no such threat in the record. True enough,
the state conceded that the plaintiffs' proposed conduct would
be a violation of the statute and that the attorney general would
prosecute any offenses under Connecticut law pursuant to his
duty. But since the enactment of the statute in 1879 only one
prosecution had been initiated—in 1940—and even then, after
the Connecticut Supreme Court of Errors sustained the legislation, the state dismissed the information. This record, in the
Court's view, combined with the notorious sale of contraceptive
devices in Connecticut drugstores, made the threat of criminal
prosecution academic. Dr. Buxton had sworn that as a law-abiding citizen he was deterred by the statute from giving contraceptive advice. But his "personal sensitiveness" to obeying the
law could not change the fact that in reality he had nothing to
fear.

There was no alternative, then, to breaking the law.[10] Subsequently Dr. Buxton established and advertised a public birth
control clinic in direct violation of the statute and when later
prosecuted invoked the Constitution as a defense. This time
there was unquestioned standing and ripeness. The Court
reached the merits, found the statute unconstitutional, and reversed his conviction.[11]

Surely it would be mistaken, in light of these cases, to say that

Dr. Buxton failed to meet his obligation as a citizen when he acted on his own judgment of the birth control statute's unconstitutionality by violating the statute. That he was free to make that judgment in advance of the Supreme Court's decision is evident from the Court's reversal of his conviction; it is also evident from the Court's twice-repeated declaration that the only way to get the Court to make the decision was to violate the statute and risk punishment.

Of course, in some situations it may not be necessary for a citizen to break the law in order to test it. He may have recourse to declaratory judgment or injunction proceedings, for example. But even when the citizen does have an alternative to breaking the law, the consequence of his doing so remains the same: if his constitutional claim is upheld, he cannot be punished. The fact that he could have obtained a constitutional ruling through a proceeding that did not require him to disobey the law is immaterial.

Moreover, the availability of anticipatory relief through declaratory judgment and injunction proceedings is relatively recent. Traditionally, courts have been reluctant to provide anticipatory relief to test the validity of criminal statutes.[12] And though the trend in recent years has been to extend the remedy, particularly where the threat of prosecution may impinge on such preferred constitutional rights as freedom of speech,[13] the path is still scattered with such obstacles as the requirement of a sufficiently demonstrable threat of prosecution to establish an actual controversy,[14] the ultimate discretionary authority of the courts to entertain such actions,[15] the reluctance of federal courts to intervene in state criminal administration,[16] and particularly in injunction proceedings, the requirement that the plaintiff show irreparable injury in having to defend a possible criminal prosecution.[17] Still, the central consideration for our purposes is that the increasing availability of anticipatory relief constitutes a departure from the traditional procedures,[18] and as such amounts to a supplement to them rather than a substitute for them. Breaking a law and defending against the resulting prosecution by asserting the law's invalidity may be only the traditional recourse of the citizen against unconstitutional legislation, but it remains the most widely accepted.

Indeed, the tradition has been acclaimed as a significant part of the democratic process. Thus one Supreme Court justice observed, "When a legislature undertakes to proscribe the exercise of a citizen's constitutional right to free speech, it acts lawlessly; and the citizen can take matters in his own hands and proceed on the basis that such a law is no law at all."[19] More recently a chief justice wrote, "It shows no disrespect for law to violate a statute on the ground that it is unconstitutional and then to submit one's case to the courts with the willingness to accept the penalty if the statute is held to be valid."[20] The venerability of this tradition is evidenced by the words of Benjamin Curtis, a former Supreme Court justice, who argued to the Senate on behalf of President Andrew Johnson during the latter's impeachment trial a century ago:

I am aware that it is asserted to be the civil and moral duty of all men to obey those laws which have been passed through all the forms of legislation until they shall have been decreed by judicial authority not to be binding; but this is too broad a statement of the civil and moral duty incumbent either upon private citizens or public officers. If this is the measure of duty there never could be a judicial decision that a law is unconstitutional, inasmuch as it is only by disregarding a law that any question can be raised judicially under it. I submit to senators that not only is there no such rule of civil or moral duty, but that it may be and has been a high and patriotic duty of a citizen to raise a question whether a law is within the Constitution of the country.[21]

On this view it is almost as though the Constitution contained the words to be found in the constitution of one contemporary German state: "It is the right and duty of every man to resist unconstitutionally exercised public power."[22]

This argument for legitimated disobedience extends to the person who disobeys a law on the ground that it is unconstitutional. It does not reach one whose grounds for disobeying have nothing to do with the Constitution, even if his lawyer subsequently is able to make a colorable constitutional defense. Such a person also will be immune from punishment if his lawyer prevails, but there is no basis in his case for finding legitimate his initial undertaking to disobey the law. Is the same true for one who conscientiously resists the law on moral grounds and lacks the legal knowledge to see the constitutional implications of his position? If it were, the liberty of legitimated disobedience would extend only to those relatively few with legal sophistication or access to a lawyer before they act. But for the reasons developed by Professor Dworkin in the context of his discussion of draft resistance, it is not.[23] The validity of laws under such constitutional provisions as the due process clause, the equal protection clause, the free speech provision, and many others, depends on judgments of political morality. Hence one who defies a law on a view of political morality that serves, under the Constitution, to make that law unconstitutional as well as wrongful, is entitled to the claim of legitimacy as much as one who knows that those moral views have that legal consequence. One who resists a legal command on grounds of religious conscience, for example, acts no less legitimately than one who knows enough law to invoke the constitutional provision designed to protect the exercise of religious conscience.[24]

Invalid Police Orders, Arrests, and Incarceration

A number of other instances of legitimated disobedience deriving from appeals to the norm of validity are useful to consider, though they are on the whole less significant than the judicial review of statutes and much less consistently recognized.

If a policeman, in the exercise of his office, orders a Black person to leave a park in a Southern town, is the citizen obliged to obey the policeman's order and wait until later to invoke some remedy to challenge its validity? Can the citizen be constitutionally convicted of some crime based on his refusal to obey the policeman's order, even if a court should later determine that the order was unconstitutional? Not long ago the Supreme Court considered just this case.[25] It had little difficulty reaching a decision. The order was found to be an unconstitutional violation of the defendant's rights first because it was designed to enforce racial discrimination in the park, and second because it was based on the possibility of unlawful troublemaking by others rather than on any wrongdoing by the defendant. So much was sufficient to require a reversal of the defendant's conviction: "Obviously, . . . one cannot be punished for failing to obey the command of an officer if that command is itself violative of the Constitution."[26] The policeman's order was treated like a statute: obedience to an unconstitutional order of an official is not required, even though the order has not yet been ruled invalid by a court. The citizen is at liberty to make his own judgment of the order's validity and to act accordingly. If he turns out to be wrong, of course, he is answerable. But if he turns out to be right, he is not answerable in any way—not for disobeying the order, since the order was invalid, and not for undertaking himself to decide in advance that the order was invalid, since he was at liberty to make that decision.

Where the situation escalates into active resistance and perhaps the use of force, typically involved in cases of resistance to unlawful arrest or to the execution of some process, such as serving a search warrant, the interest in the physical welfare of the policeman and the citizen (as well as others) may often produce a contrary answer. Indeed, an increasing number of jurisdictions afford no right to resist an arrest made under color of authority, even if the arrest is later determined to be invalid. The citizen is obliged in this circumstance to yield and submit his case to the courts.[27] As the Model Penal Code concludes, "It should be possible to provide adequate remedies against illegal arrest, without permitting the arrested person to resort to force —a course of action highly likely to result in greater injury even to himself than the detention."[28]

Still, of particular relevance for our purposes is the fact that despite the added consideration of physical danger, the tradition of self-help has been so strong that both under the common law[29] and under much (perhaps most) state law today[30] the prudential view is rejected and the citizen is privileged to use force (short of deadly force) if necessary to resist an invalid arrest.* Where the right to be yielded up is personal liberty, the citizen may make his own judgment of the validity of the order and need not await relief from the processes of the law, even though such a procedure entails the risk of injury as well as the risk of error. A law-and-order model is, of course, incompatible with this view. As Learned Hand observed, "The idea that you may resist peaceful arrest . . . because you are in debate about whether it is lawful or not, instead of going to the authorities which can determine [the question is] not a blow for liberty but, on the contrary, a blow for attempted anarchy."[31] To Judge Hand it was plain enough that the prevailing rule allowed the citizen to take the law into his own hands, and he would have none of it. Whether preserving law and order is more important than protecting "the will to resist arbitrary authority"[32] is an issue we do not argue here. Our concern is to reveal the widely recognized privilege to resist an unlawful arrest (or an unlawful execution of process) as still another instance of legitimated disobedience.

A related self-help issue arises when a person escapes from legal custody or confinement. Is the invalidity of the commitment that led to a person's confinement a basis for defending against the crime of escape as well as a basis for attacking the initial commitment? The case for self-help is much harder to argue here than in the instances previously discussed. The escapee not only disobeys those acting under color of authority and creates a risk of bodily harm but resists officials (his jailors) who are several times removed from the infecting invalid act and cannot be considered responsible for or even knowledgeable of it. Despite these considerations many courts have chosen to legitimate self-help in cases of escape.

In a turn-of-the-century case Ah Teung was convicted for

---

* Similar results are reached in cases of resistance to unlawful process, though here distinctions are made depending on whether the defect in the process is trivial or fundamental. See Annotation, "Criminal Liability for Obstructing Process as Affected by Invalidity or Irregularity of the Process," 10 A.L.R.3d 1146 (1966).

helping his friend Lee Yick escape from jail in Alameda County, California.[33] A federal court commissioner in San Diego had found that Yick was in the country unlawfully, and subsequently a federal marshal had brought him up from San Diego to Alameda County, presumably to await deportation. On Teung's appeal the California Supreme Court determined that since the court commissioner did not enter a formal judgment on his findings and did not order the marshal to remove Yick to Alameda County, the marshal had no authority under federal law to remove him; therefore the Alameda deputy sheriff had no authority to hold him. On this finding the court held that Teung had committed no crime in helping Yick escape:

> An escape is classed as a crime against public justice, and the law, in declaring it to be an offense, proceeds upon the theory that the citizen should yield obedience to the law; that when one has been, by its authority or command, confined in a prison, that it is his duty to submit to such confinement until delivered by due course of law. But when the imprisonment is unlawful, and is itself a crime, the reason which makes flight from prison an offense does not exist. In such a case the right to liberty is absolute, and he who regains it is not guilty of the technical offense of escape.[34]

Though comparable conclusions have been reached in other cases,[35] the defense has also been rejected by many courts, particularly in recent years.[36] One typical case involved a prisoner who escaped from a confinement that a court later set aside as based on an unconstitutional charging procedure.[37] The court concluded that the prisoner's proper remedy was to obtain a judicial declaration of his conviction, not to make and act on that judgment himself: "To say that a prisoner may legally escape from prison on the theory that he was being illegally detained is to strike a blow at the very foundation of law and order."[38]

Significantly, holdings such as these are usually based not only on the availability of other legal remedies and the necessary implications of the law-and-order model, but also on the argument that self-help should be available only where the invalidity is clear and substantial; that is, the order or procedure in question must be "unlawful" or "void on its face" rather than merely "irregular."[39] Of course, automatically placing an invalid order or procedure in the "irregular" rather than in the "void on its face" classification, as most courts now do, is one way to empty the principle of content. But not all courts do so, and even where the defense of self-help is rejected in particular cases, the principle is almost always recognized for extreme cases of unlawful confinement. Accordingly, self-help remains another source of legitimated disobedience that the legal system provides the citizen, even though the legitimating circumstances are more narrowly defined than in ordinary instances of disobedience to statutes. If the citizen is entitled to undertake the act of disobedience only when the invalidity of his confinement is gross and glaring, it only means that a heavier surcharge is put on disobedience. The legitimating principle remains fundamentally the same.

Invalid Judicial and Administrative Orders

In two instances the prevailing approach to the self-help principle turns out to be quite different from that so far discussed. Where the provenance of the peremptory rule is a court order or the action of an administrative agency, American courts on the whole, though certainly not uniformly, take a more restrictive view of the citizen's freedom to depart from the order on his own judgment of its invalidity. These instances are worth examining because they serve to identify areas in which legitimated disobedience is characteristically rejected in our legal system and hence help exhibit legitimated disobedience as a distinct legal strategy to be used or not depending on an assessment of contending considerations.

Judicial Orders. We have grown so accustomed to the citizen's right to disobey invalid statutes (invalid typically on constitutional grounds) that it is easy to miss its significance. We even describe the violation of invalid statutes in the conventional retroactive rhetoric of adjudicative lawmaking, so that it seems inevitable that a person has the right to undertake to disobey them: a law declared invalid was not law; hence a person cannot possibly be held accountable for violating it. But, of course, the existence of such a right constitutes a specific policy decision that need not go the way it has gone; and the very different way the Supreme Court has dealt with punishment for violations of invalid court orders as compared with violations of statutes underscores the point.

On one view, it would appear that the right of a citizen to defy illegitimate judicial authority should be the same as his right to defy illegitimate legislative authority. After all, if a rule that transgresses the Constitution or is otherwise invalid is no law at all, and never was one, it should hardly matter whether a court or a legislature made the rule. Yet the prevailing approach of the courts has been to treat invalid court orders quite differently from invalid statutes.[40] The long-established principle of the old equity courts was that an erroneously issued injunction must be obeyed until the error was judicially determined.[41] Only where the issuing court could be said to have lacked jurisdiction (in the sense of authority to adjudicate the cause and to reach the parties through its mandate) were disobedient contemnors permitted to raise the invalidity of the order as a full defense.[42] By and large, American courts have declined to treat the unconstitutionality of a court order as a jurisdictional defect within this traditional equity principle, and in notable instances they have qualified that principle even where the defect was jurisdictional in the accepted sense.[43]

The United States Supreme Court has run a somewhat broken field through these issues,[44] and it would not be particularly helpful here to trace its entire route. It will be helpful, however, to consider two Supreme Court decisions: the first involved disobedience to a federal court order by John L. Lewis in the 1940's, and the second involved disobedience to a state court order by Martin Luther King in the 1960's.[45]

Lewis was ordered by a federal court to send his mine workers back to work after the mines they had struck had been seized by the United States government. Lewis refused, was cited for contempt, and defended on the ground that the Norris-LaGuardia Act deprived federal courts of jurisdiction to issue injunctions in labor disputes. The trial court rejected his defense and found him guilty of criminal and civil contempt. The Supreme Court affirmed the criminal conviction, agreeing with the lower court that the Norris-LaGuardia Act was inapplicable to labor disputes in which the United States was the employer. As an alternative ground, moreover, it held that even if the injunction were declared invalid, the contempt convictions would be affirmed: even an invalid order must be obeyed until its invalidity is judicially declared by an appellate court. The Court held inapplicable the precedents regarding orders beyond the jurisdiction of a court, on the ground that a court must be regarded as having jurisdiction to determine its own jurisdiction. Only if the claim to jurisdiction was "frivolous and not substantial" would the traditional exception for disobedience to court orders be applied.[46] The exception had no force here, where the defendant's argument that the court lacked jurisdiction turned on a federal statute, "the scope and applicability of which were subject to substantial doubt."[47]

Justice Frankfurter concurred, but only on this alternative ground. The order was invalid, he found, but the judgment for criminal contempt should be affirmed "upon the broad ground of vindicating the processes of law."[48] A "postulate of our democracy," he stated, was that issues of law "must be left to the judgment of courts and not the personal judgment of one of the parties";[49] "no one, no matter how exalted his public office, or how righteous his private motive, can be judge in his own case."[50] Otherwise, society would be ruled not by law but by brute power.[51] "If one man can be allowed to determine for himself what is law, every man can. That means first chaos, then tyranny."[52] Exceptions could be made only where the court was "so obviously traveling outside its orbit as to be merely usurping judicial forms and facilities."[53] It made no difference that interim compliance destroyed the "hard-won liberties of collective action by workers"[54] and that, as Frankfurter in fact concluded, the order was in violation of the Norris-LaGuardia Act. Better that the citizen's rights and interests be sacrificed to compliance with an invalid court order than that the citizen should act on his own judgment of the validity of government power when exercised by courts. Why disobedience to statutes was not subject to the same arguments was not explored.

The King case developed out of a civil rights demonstration in the South. A Birmingham city ordinance made it unlawful to parade or otherwise demonstrate in the city streets without a permit from the city commission. Permits were to be granted by the commission "unless in its judgment the public welfare, peace, safety, health, decency, good order, morals or convenience" required that they be refused. King and his followers tried unsuccessfully to obtain a permit for their demonstration from the police commissioner. When it appeared likely that they would defy the ordinance and march without a permit, city officials obtained a court order prohibiting them from doing so. Stating that the injunction was "raw tyranny under the guise of maintaining law and order," King and his followers defied the court order and held their march. When subsequently cited for contempt, they attacked the constitutionality of the order and the statute with which the order directed compliance on the ground that the order and statute were vague and overbroad, and abridged their freedom of speech. On appeal from their conviction, the Alabama Supreme Court denied their right to raise the unconstitutionality of the statute in the contempt proceedings, following the traditional view that nonjurisdictional error could not serve as a defense to a contempt charge.

The United States Supreme Court found no violation of the Constitution in the Alabama rule, which, after all, paralleled the federal rule announced in the Lewis case,[55] even though the claim of unconstitutionality was based on the "preferred freedoms" protected by the First Amendment, and even though the Court found that the arguments supporting the claim were substantial.* Though the protesters' constitutional arguments were substantial, this was not a case, said the Court, "where the injunction was transparently invalid or had only a frivolous pretense to validity"[56]—and that was the significant criterion. The Court went on to say:

> The rule of law that Alabama followed in this case reflects a belief that in the fair administration of justice no man can be judge in his own case.... This Court cannot hold that the petitioners were constitutionally free to ignore all the procedures of the law and carry their battle to the streets.... Respect for judicial process is a small price to pay for the civilizing hand of law, which alone can give abiding meaning to constitutional freedom.[57]

It is apparent that a citizen undertaking to violate a peremptory rule on his own assessment of its invalidity is perceived differently depending on whether the source of the rule is statutory or judicial. Whether and on what grounds this distinction is defensible we shall not pursue. It suffices for the moment to observe that the law-and-order arguments used in the case of disobedience to court orders are just as appropriate in the case of disobedience to statutes.

One final observation. The Supreme Court's approach to disobedience to court orders does not close the door altogether to legitimated disobedience—almost, but not quite, even here. When a court's claim of authority to act is so weak that it may be called "frivolous"—or in Justice Frankfurter's words, when the court is "obviously traveling outside its orbit"—then the citizen *is* entitled to judge his own case without awaiting the outcome of the judicial process. Thus the principle of legitimated disobedience is not totally rejected. Instead the surcharge exacted on the citizen's reasons for disobeying is increased: not only must the citizen be right; he must be very clearly right to be justified in undertaking to disobey a court order. Inevitably,

---

* Indeed, in a subsequent case involving the conviction of one of the demonstrators for violating the statute rather than the injunction, the Court reversed the conviction on a finding that the statute was unconstitutional. Shuttlesworth v. City of Birmingham, 394 U.S. 147 (1969).

that judgment must remain his to make, notwithstanding the antithetical corollaries of the law-and-order model.

Administrative Orders. The failure to invoke a remedy other than disobedience to challenge the validity of a peremptory rule, which never disqualifies challenges to statutory rules, is a significant issue in challenges to administrative as well as to judicial orders. The problem arises where an administrative agency is empowered to issue rules, whether they be general rules of conduct or specific orders to individuals, that the governing statute makes it a criminal offense to violate. Is a citizen free to challenge the validity of an administrative rule, on constitutional or other grounds, just as he might challenge the validity of a statutory rule—that is, by disobeying the rule and then arguing its invalidity as a defense to a criminal prosecution —regardless of the availability of other means for testing the rule? For example, if it is a crime to hold a meeting in a park without a license from a city department, may a citizen defend against a criminal charge for doing so on the ground that the license was illegally denied him?[58] If it is a crime to sell an article at a price above the ceiling set by a government agency, may a citizen raise the defense of the ceiling's invalidity in a criminal prosecution for overcharging?[59] May a conscript refuse induction and defend against the ensuing criminal charge on the ground that the induction order was invalid?[60]

The answer is generally no. In these kinds of cases the citizen is expected first to exhaust the other remedies available to him for testing the administrative order's validity, whether they be internal administrative appeals or appeals to the courts.[61] If he fails to exhaust those remedies, he may not raise the issue of the order's invalidity as a defense to a criminal prosecution. He may not disobey the order and take his chances in court, as he may in the case of a statutory rule. In effect, his bypassing the available remedies in favor of taking the law into his own hands provides a sufficient basis for punishment even if the rule should be invalid. Thus the possibility of legitimated disobedience is rejected here, much as it is in most cases involving judicial orders.

Two United States Supreme Court cases in this area parallel the Lewis and King cases, previously discussed in connection with judicial orders. The Lewis case is comparable to *Yakus v. United States*.[62] A wholesaler sold meat above the price set by the price administrator during World War II and sought to defend against the ensuing criminal prosecution by raising the invalidity of the price regulation. The Court held that he could not. The Emergency Price Control Act had set up procedures for a review within the agency, to be followed by an appeal to a specially created Emergency Court of Appeal, as means of testing the validity of the administrator's regulations. Therefore the wholesaler, having failed to exhaust these remedies first, was stripped of any defense based on the invalidity of the regulation. For Justice Rutledge, who dissented, this result unconstitutionally infringed the judicial power of the courts:

Once it is held that Congress can require the courts criminally to enforce unconstitutional laws or statutes, including regulations, or to do so without regard for their validity, the way will have been found to circumvent the supreme law, and, what is more, to make the courts parties to doing so.... The idea is entirely novel that regulations may have a greater immunity to judicial scrutiny than statutes have, with respect to the power of Congress to require the courts to enforce them without regard to constitutional requirements.[63]

He advanced the instance of a possible regulation that prescribed different price ceilings for sellers of different races or religions. Would the courts have to enforce this regulation because a seller had not exhausted his other remedies? This thrust evoked a concession from the majority: "We have no occasion to decide whether one charged with criminal violation of a duly promulgated price regulation may defend on the ground that the regulation is unconstitutional on its face."[64] But the conclusion remained that, apart from the "unconstitutional on its face" qualification, the availability of other remedies to test the validity of the regulation disentitled the citizen to make and act on his own judgment of its invalidity.

Yakus was not the last word, however, for there is an incongruity in barring the issue of a rule's validity from a judgment of the defendant's guilt in violating it. In a later case a draftee prosecuted for refusing to submit to induction was precluded from contesting the validity of his classification as a defense, since he could have appealed his classification earlier within the Selective Service System; but the Supreme Court reversed his conviction.[65] A precedent stood in the way—a decision of the same term as *Yakus* that applied its exhaustion principle to Selective Service cases.[66] But the Court elected to introduce a flexibility into that principle by holding it inapplicable unless shown to be necessary in a particular setting to accomplish certain purposes. Those purposes included avoiding the premature interruption of the administrative process, which would interfere with the agency's development of the necessary factual background on which decisions should be based as well as with the application of its discretion and expertise; conserving judicial resources; affording the agency an opportunity to correct its own errors; and preventing the "frequent and deliberate flouting of administrative process," which could "weaken the effectiveness of an agency by encouraging people to ignore its procedures."[67] Absent a showing that these purposes would be seriously implicated, the Court concluded that the "exceedingly harsh" consequences of denying a citizen judicial review of an order when the citizen argued the order's invalidity as a defense against criminal prosecution "should not be tolerated."[68] It chose not to tolerate them in this case, where those purposes, on the facts, would not be served. As for the fear that widespread violation of Selective Service orders would result, the Court concluded that the risk of criminal conviction if the validity of the order were upheld by the courts was an ample protection.

The King case is comparable to *Poulos v. New Hampshire*, in which the Court sustained the constitutionality of a state exhaustion requirement invoked when a criminal defendant tried to challenge the constitutionality of an order denying him a license to hold a religious meeting in a public park.[69] The defendant had had ample opportunity to appeal the denial. His decision to hold the meeting without the license instead of appealing made his punishment constitutional, even though the denial of the license in the circumstances might otherwise have been held to violate his constitutional rights. The public regulatory interest, reasoned the Court, requires compliance with licensing orders until they are invalidated. Delay and the expense and annoyance of litigation "is a price citizens must pay for life in an orderly society when the rights of the First Amendment have a real and abiding meaning."[70] The Court distinguished the present case from precedents in which a statute establishing a licensing scheme was itself found unconstitutional.[71] In those precedents "the statutes were as though they did not exist. Therefore, there were no offenses in violation of a valid law."[72] The dissenting opinion, by Justice Douglas, was similar to that in the King case: since a citizen may "take matters in his own hands" and disregard a statute that abridges his constitutional right of freedom of speech, he should have the same right to "flout the official agency who administers a licensing law" that abridges his freedom, for on the one hand, "defiance of a statute is hardly less harmful to an orderly society than defiance of an administrative order," and on the other, the burden on free speech of awaiting the outcome of litigation is the same in both cases.[73]

Summary

So long as standards for determining the validity of government action exist, citizens subject to peremptory rules and seeking to determine their legal obligations must ask this question: granted that citizens are obliged to obey peremptory rules, are rules that issue from officials necessarily to be taken as valid rules of the legal system?

One answer to this question is simply yes. This is the answer embedded in the law-and-order analysis of a citizen's obligation. So long as the rule issues from an official and purports to be a peremptory rule, the citizen is never at liberty to act on his own judgment of its validity. He must comply with the rule, though while complying he may challenge the rule's validity in the official tribunals established for that purpose.

Our review of the treatment of this question in American law reveals, however, that the law-and-order response is never unqualifiedly given. In dealing with judicial orders judges often speak in these terms and deny defendants' claims on these grounds. But even as they do, they recognize the existence of some extreme point where the invalidity of a judge's action is so gross and patent that the citizen may venture to judge and to act on his judgment to depart from the rule. Thus a contemnor has been held punishable even though the court order he disobeyed was invalid, for "if one man can be allowed to determine for himself what is law, every man can. That means first chaos, then tyranny." Yet he would not be punishable if the court in issuing the order was acting egregiously beyond the law—if it was "obviously traveling outside its orbit." Similarly, a prisoner may not seek to justify his escape on the ground that his commitment was unlawful, since "to say that a prisoner may legally escape from prison on the theory that he was being illegally detained is to strike a blow at the very foundation of law and order." Yet he would be permitted to do so if the commitment was "void on its face."

Moreover, in the single most significant area in American law in which the validity of government action is contestable—statutory law—the courts' response is not the law-and-order response at all. Without any apparent recognition of the import of the choice being made, the system responds in ways that render it legitimate, as we have defined the term, for citizens to make their own judgment of a peremptory rule's constitutionality and to obey or disregard the rule accordingly. Punishment is never imposed if the court accepts the citizen's judgment. Indeed, the processes of legal recourse are often structured in such a way that departing from the rule becomes a necessary condition for obtaining judicial review. Even when this is not so, the availability of means for obtaining relief that do not involve departing from the rule is considered immaterial. And the tradition of vindicating constitutional government by departing from and challenging the disputed rule is regarded as an important historical element in the constitutional ethos.

Legitimated Disobedience and
the Norm of the Lesser Evil

The preceding section tried to show how the appeal to the norm of validity can establish the conditions under which a legal system might legitimate a departure from a peremptory rule. We turn now to another norm that can serve the same function. This norm may be known by various labels, but essentially its standard is whether in the circumstances and on balance it is better in terms of the ultimate ends of criminal law for a person to violate a given rule than to obey it.

In the common law a defense embodying this kind of norm goes under the misleading label of "the defense of necessity"— misleading because it is not physical necessity that is at issue (this is another defense) but moral necessity, which, of course, is not necessity at all but choice. As Prof. Glanville Williams has pointed out, "By necessity is meant the assertion that conduct promotes some value higher than the value of literal compliance with the law."[74] This norm, then, is essentially an open-textured justification based on the judgment that the evil produced by breaching a rule is less than the evil that would follow from complying with it. In the course of the discussion we shall use the term "lesser evil" defense or principle to refer to this norm.

There is substantial though not unanimous agreement that the defense is part of the common law.[75] The cases are few and the scope of the defense indistinct, but common-law commentators from early times to the present have recognized that in the proper circumstances, appeals to the lesser-evil principle may justify disobeying a criminal law. The argument of a sixteenth-century serjeant summed up the tradition:

In every law there are some things which when they happen a man may break the words of the law, and yet not break the law itself; and such things are exempted out of the penalty of the law, and the law privileges them although they are done against the letter of it, for breaking the words of the law is not breaking the law, so as the intent of the law is not broken. It is a common proverb, *Quod necessitas non habet legem.*[76]

And more recently the commentary of the Model Penal Code observes:

Suppose, for example, that the actor has made a breach in the dike, knowing that this will inundate a farm, but taking the only course available to save a whole town. If he is charged with homicide of the inhabitants of the farm house, he can rightly point out that the object of the law of homicide is to save life, and that by his conduct he has effected a net saving of innocent lives.... Property may be destroyed to prevent the spread of a fire. A speed limit may be violated in pursuing a suspected criminal. An ambulance may pass a traffic light. Mountain climbers lost in a storm may take refuge in a house or may appropriate provisions. A cargo may be jettisoned or an embargo violated to preserve the vessel. An alien may dispense a drug without the requisite prescription to alleviate distress in an emergency. A developed legal system must have better ways of dealing with such problems than to refer only to the letter of particular prohibitions, framed without reference to cases of this kind.[77]

The defense has been formulated in statutes in a variety of ways. The criminal code of the largest of the Soviet Union republics makes it a defense to a violation of the code that "the harm caused is less significant than the harm prevented."[78] The German Draft Penal Code accords the defendant a defense where "the interest he protects significantly outweighs the interest which he harms."[79] The New Penal Code of the German Democratic Republic casts the issue explicitly in terms of conflicting duties, stating that a person who commits a "breach of a duty with a view to prevent, by fulfilling other duties, the occurrence of a greater damage, which cannot otherwise be averted" acts justifiably and is not punishable.[80] In the United States the Model Penal Code formulates the defense in terms of whether "the harm or evil sought to be avoided ... is greater than that sought to be prevented by the law defining the offense charged."[81] A recent New York law incorporates a modification of the Model Penal Code proposal to the effect that the injury sought to be avoided must be "of such gravity that, according to ordinary standards of intelligence and morality, the desirability and urgency of avoiding such injury clearly outweigh the desirability of avoiding the injury sought to be prevented" by the law defining the crime; moreover, the evil to be avoided may not rest on considerations "pertaining only to the morality or advisability of the law."[82]

The availability of this norm of the lesser evil as a justification for the citizen's breach of the rule, even more directly than the norm of validity, creates the conditions for legitimated disobedience. As we have seen, the norm of validity does not necessarily have that effect, since a system may choose, in all or in part of its operation, to foreclose a citizen's liberty to exercise his own judgment on the issue of validity by requiring him first to obtain the judgment of a court. But it is, after all, intrinsic to the lesser-evil defense that the court is called upon to approve or disapprove of the choice already made by the defendant to depart from the rule. Thus the decision to recognize the lesser-evil defense is necessarily a decision to legitimate a citizen's undertaking to exercise his own judgment, whereas the decision to recognize the norm of validity may or may not have that effect. As Saint Thomas Aquinas observed, "If . . . the peril be so sudden as not to allow of the delay involved by referring the matter to authority, the mere necessity brings with it a dispensation, since necessity knows no law."[83]

But we must deal at once with a basic objection. It is obvious enough that the lesser-evil defense satisfies the first two conditions for legitimated disobedience earlier suggested: its applicability to the person's conduct falls within the authority of an official (here the court) to determine, and once it is found to apply, it relieves the citizen of his usual liability to punishment for disobedience. However, that the third condition is met, which appears self-evident in the case of the norm of validity, is not self-evident here. This condition is that the norm functions not as a qualification to, and therefore as part of, the rule (so that the upshot of the defense is that the defendant never violated the rule), but as a justification for the citizen's undertaking to depart from it.

That the norm of validity meets this condition is self-evident because the concept of validity applies not to a rule's contents but to its origins; it addresses not the rule's recipient, but its maker. Deriving from a higher level of legal authority, it may deprive a rule of legal effect by determining not that the rule maker in some sense did not forbid the conduct engaged in, but that he had no legal authority to do so. One could say that in such a case the defendant is vindicated because the rule he is accused of departing from never legally existed.

The lesser-evil defense cannot be dealt with in the same way. A plausible argument can be made that where a lesser-evil defense is recognized, the law implicitly includes that defense as a qualification of all its specific rules, with the consequence that to each rule must, in effect, be added the phrase, "provided, however, that appraisal of the balance of evils did not justify the defendant's action." By this reasoning, of course, when the defense is made it serves not to legitimate a rule departure, but to establish that the rule was never departed from. For example, when a defendant is judged not guilty of murder because he acted in self-defense, no one says that the defendant's departure from the rule against murder was legitimated by appeal to the norm of self-defense. One says that the defendant did not depart from the rule, since the crime of murder is not made out when the intentional killing is necessary for the killer's self-defense. Thus the defense of self-defense is included in the rule as a qualification. The same thing could be said of the lesser-evil defense.[84]

The flaw in the argument is its failure to discriminate between the different senses in which the law includes a defense like self-defense, on the one hand, and the lesser-evil defense, on the other. The criminal law includes self-defense in a sense that makes it quite proper to treat it as a qualification to the rules defining criminal conduct. It includes it as a specification of circumstances in which the use of force is not criminal—generally when the actor reasonably apprehends that the force is necessary to protect against imminent unlawful violence threatened by another. The circumstances in which the ends of penal policy will on balance be served by what otherwise would constitute criminal violence have been defined, so that the defense functions as an exception, included in the law, to the definition of the conduct prohibited.

But the law may "include" a defense in still another sense than as an exception. Instead of including the defense by specifying the particular circumstances in which the defense exists, the law may delegate authority to the courts to find a defense made out in terms of some broadly stated policy or principle. The legislature has gone as far as it can (or will) in defining the special circumstances of nonliability appropriate to the ends of its legislation. The task of defining others it remits to the courts on an ad hoc basis as the cases arise. It is in this sense that the lesser-evil defense may be said to be included in the law. The law includes the requirement that the courts assess whether breaching the rule was preferable to complying with it in the circumstances. As Judge Hand put it, the defense "makes the judge ad hoc a legislator."[85]

Therefore, when a defendant appeals to the lesser-evil defense, he cannot be said to be appealing to a qualification of the rule and hence to the proposition that he never departed from the rule. He is appealing to the judge to exercise the authority vested in him by the law to create an ad hoc qualification where none existed before on the basis of the ends of the criminal law. One who breaches a rule and defends on the lesser-evil principle, therefore, is in the position of arguing not that he did not depart from the rule of the criminal law—even taking the rule comprehensively to include its defined exceptions and qualifications —but that his departure should be found consistent with the law's ends. Further, the fact that a court may find the departure justified when it assesses those ultimate ends inevitably legitimates a similar ad hoc assessment of ends by the citizen contemplating the departure—legitimated disobedience, as we have defined it.

Confirming evidence of this distinction between a specifically defined defense that qualifies the rule and an open-textured principle that allows rule departures to be justified in the particular case appears in the different ways courts would perceive the problem of vagueness in the law. It is well established that a rule so vague that a reasonable person seeking to comply could only guess at what it prohibited is unconstitutional. If the lesser-evil defense were regarded as part of each rule of the criminal law, would it not have the effect, in consequence of its open-textured character, of rendering each rule unconstitutionally vague? It is hard to see why not. Yet no court would conceivably hold a penal code unconstitutionally vague because it recognized a lesser-evil defense. The defense simply would not be seen as a qualifying element of each defined crime. A citizen may have to guess at whether a court will use its ad hoc legislative authority to find the defense applicable, but that will not matter so long as he does not have to guess at the meaning of the rule itself. For it is the rule, apart from the possibility of a lesser-evil defense, that tells the citizen what he needs to know to obey the law: the lesser-evil principle is seen not as a further definition of what he must not do, but as a basis for justifying his doing otherwise.

One may find analogous evidence of the distinction in the law between a qualified rule and a rule subject to an open-textured principle in connection with the defense of invalidity. Some constitutional restraints are so vague and undeveloped that they could not be used to define an offense without offending the requirement of specificity. A provision of the Civil Rights Act,[86] for example, makes it an offense for a person, acting under color of law, willfully to deprive another person of his constitutional rights. When a prosecution under this section reached the Supreme Court,[87] the justices divided on whether the statute could be interpreted as requiring actual knowledge

by the defendant that he was depriving another of his constitutional rights. Most agreed, however, that if it could not be so
interpreted the statute would be unconstitutionally vague. For
in that event the citizen would be "referred . . . to a comprehen-
sive law library to ascertain what acts were prohibited."[88] Unconstitutional vagueness, therefore, is created to the extent the
rule defines prohibited conduct in terms of constitutionally protected rights. Now compare the provisions of the Civil Rights
Act with a specifically defined statute whose constitutionality is
put in doubt by provisions of the Constitution and decisions of
the Supreme Court arguably creating a constitutional right that
is violated by the statute. Is it not clear that no degree of unpredictability in what the Court might hold and no amount of uncertainty in the definition of the mooted constitutional right
could themselves serve to invalidate the statute? If the Court
should decide that there is no constitutional right to the prohibited conduct, the rule is valid and enforceable against the
violator, notwithstanding the substantial uncertainty created by
the existence of a vague constitution to which there is recourse.
The defense of unconstitutionality, therefore, like the lesser-evil
defense, is not a qualification of the conduct prohibited—in
which event its vagueness is fatal—but a justification for doing
what the legislature has clearly enough enjoined.*

---

* There is one established exception to the constitutional analogy discussed here. This involves the doctrine of overbreadth, which serves to
invalidate "on its face" a statute that prohibits conduct protected by the
First Amendment as well as conduct that is not protected. It has been
argued that the vice of such statutes is the vice of vagueness, engendered
by the fact that one cannot be certain what conduct the Court would conclude is or is not constitutionally protected. See P. Freund, *The Supreme
Court of the United States* (Gloucester, Mass., 1961), pp. 67–68; Note, "The
First Amendment Overbreadth Doctrine," 83 *Harv. L. Rev.* 844, 871–75
(1970). But the vice is not that of vagueness in general but of the special
danger of vagueness when First Amendment rights are involved in creating
a "chilling effect" on protected expression. For an argument that the law
should go further than it now does and find offensive to due process a conviction under a statute of doubtful constitutionality on any grounds, see
R. Dworkin, "On Not Prosecuting Civil Disobedience," *New York Review
of Books,* June 6, 1968, pp. 14, 20–21.

Let us now recapitulate the argument for legitimated disobedience arising from an appeal to the open-textured norm of the lesser evil. A rule of the criminal law represents the rule maker's judgment that public policies and ends will best be served by prohibiting a defined class of conduct in defined circumstances. How may a citizen lawfully justify undertaking to depart from such a rule? One way is by appealing to a norm of validity; another is by appealing to the open-textured norm of the lesser evil. Such a norm is the rule maker's acknowledgment of the necessary incompleteness of rule making—his acknowledgment that there may be classes of situations in which public ends will not best be served by compliance. In making that norm the basis of a defense, the rule maker empowers the courts to make that judgment after the fact in particular cases and provides a ground on which a citizen may lawfully undertake to justify his departure from the rule.

Legitimated Disobedience and the
Norm of Justifiable Nonenforcement

Thus far we have discussed the legitimation of rule departures that derives from the possibility of appealing to legitimating norms applied by the courts. We shall now turn to another kind of legitimating norm, one that creates the condition for legitimated disobedience not through the courts but through the more informal means of nonenforcement by legal officials.

In the preceding chapter we observed that the police do not always arrest when they know they have probable cause, that prosecutors do not always prosecute when they know they have a provable case, and that juries do not always convict when they know the defendant is guilty under the law. We also observed that the legal system accepts a substantial amount of this nonenforcement either explicitly, by granting officials authority to enforce the law at their own discretion, or implicitly, through the process defined as legitimated interposition. The possibility now arises that these nonenforcement decisions may in some circumstances accord the citizen a liberty to depart from the unenforced rule comparable to that accorded him by the norms applied through the courts. In considering the matter it is helpful to consider nonenforcement decisions in three situations: where there is a settled pattern of nonenforcement, where there is a deliberate policy of nonenforcement, and where there is neither a pattern nor a policy of nonenforcement.

For generations statute books have contained obsolete criminal laws that police and prosecutors have systematically ignored. Prof. Carleton Allen reminds us that such laws have remained on the books in England well into the twentieth century—laws, for example, making it criminal for parishioners not to attend church, providing that Jesuit proselytizers be banished or transported, authorizing ducking as a punishment for common scolds.[89] In the United States we have (or recently have had) laws making it criminal to swear, to eavesdrop on conversations, to extend credit to a minor student, to sell candy cigarettes, to show movies depicting felonies.[90] Does the citizen's usual obligation to comply with criminal laws apply to laws of this sort, whose incompatibility with prevalent community values is manifest both in their quaintness and in their systematic nonenforcement in the face of notorious violations?

Intuitively, many would assume that it does not. But why? If accepted by the legal system, the Roman law principle of *desuetudo*—that persistent and notorious nonenforcement renders a law legally unenforceable—would constitute a norm of validity to which a defendant could appeal to justify not complying. The same would hold if the principle of *desuetudo* were incorporated into the Constitution.[91] But if *desuetudo* is not recognized as a ground for depriving a law of its legal effect—and this is the case in the American legal system—can the notorious nonenforcement of a law be fairly interpreted by the citizen as legitimating his disobedience of it?

Justice Frankfurter's plurality opinion for the Supreme Court in the second birth control case examined above[92] may be taken as answering affirmatively. In this case, it will be recalled, a physician sought an order preventing the enforcement of a birth control law against him on the ground that the law was unconstitutional. "Why do you complain?" the Court in effect asked him. "You know as well as everyone else that that law has virtually never been enforced against anyone despite its notorious violation." "To be sure," we may take the physician as replying. "But it is, after all, a law of the state of Connecticut. It prohibits me from giving birth control advice to my patients. That fact remains, even though the chances of my being punished are quite remote." But even that fact did not satisfy the plurality opinion, for as Justice Frankfurter observed, paraphrasing an earlier dictum of his, "Deeply embedded traditional ways of carrying out state policy—or not carrying it out—are often tougher and truer law than the dead words of the written text."[93] The claim of interference with the physician's asserted rights, therefore, which derived from qualms about violating a law of the state, was found to be remote and speculative, and hence insufficient to make a judicial review of the law's validity of any real concern to the physician. A citizen must take his cue not just from the written law but from the "truer law" deriving from law enforcement patterns. The physician, in short, was being overly fastidious.*

One could take issue with Justice Frankfurter's opinion on various grounds. It could be said, for example, that he should have reached the merits, that his reasoning was a maneuver to avoid a hard issue, or that he should have embraced the conclusion of his logic and invalidated the statute for nonuse. Nonetheless, his insistence that a citizen's obligation with respect to

---

* But compare a recent federal district court decision holding that the absence of prosecutions of married persons for violations of a state sodomy law did not deprive a married couple of standing to enjoin the law's future enforcement: "The failure, however, of the state to prosecute does not answer the allegation of the Gibsons that they fear prosecution. The law is on the books and so long as it remains there it is the duty of the State to carry out the laws. All public officials take an oath to perform the duties of the office to which they were elected or appointed and certainly the major duty of the law enforcing officers is to enforce the criminal statutes." Buchanan v. Batchelor, 308 F. Supp. 729, 733 (N.D.Tex. 1970).

the criminal law cannot be determined from the letter of the law alone reflects a widely shared view. Perhaps this view would not prevail in legal systems like that of the West German Republic where, we are told, there is almost no discretionary power not to enforce the law.[94] But it does in the United States, where pervasive patterns of nonenforcement have impelled the citizen to take criminal prohibitions with a grain of salt. As the American Bar Foundation's study of arrest observed, "Public knowledge of a policy of less than full enforcement in respect to certain criminal statutes results in an attitude by all violators of these statutes that they ought not to be arrested."[95]

No doubt there are several factors contributing to this view of a citizen's obligation before the criminal law. There is first the elemental claim to equal treatment: if some citizens are permitted to violate the law without interference from those charged with enforcing the law, another citizen may not justly be treated any differently, at least if his violation occurs in materially indistinguishable circumstances. This claim of fairness underlies a recently emerging constitutional defense to prosecutions under generally unenforced laws. The issue in these cases, as one court pointed out, is not guilt or innocence, but "whether in a community in which there is general disregard of a particular law with the acquiescence of public authorities, the authorities should be allowed sporadically to select a single defendant or a single class of defendants for prosecution because of personal animosity or for some other illegitimate reason."[96]

A second factor is reliance on previous law enforcement policy. If law enforcement officials have systematically ignored the law's prohibition, a citizen may reasonably expect them to continue to do so. He may not properly be subjected to a sudden reversal of policy. This sentiment also finds frequent expression in the law. A useful illustration is a well-known decision of a federal court of appeals that rejected a finding by the National Labor Relations Board that an employer had committed an unfair labor practice by entering a closed shop agreement with a union that did not represent an appropriate bargaining unit.[97] In entering into that agreement, the employer had indeed violated the National Labor Relations Act, but he was in the construction industry, over which the Board had regularly declined to exercise jurisdiction. When the Board reversed that policy and sought to apply the law to an agreement made at a time when the earlier nonenforcement policy prevailed, the court objected. The Board's action was a violation of due process, the court reasoned, since the retroactive application of its new policy "amounts to adjudging contrary to law actions, which, when taken, were not subject to the applications under the law."[98] Even though the employer knew of the law on the books, his prosecution was unfair, for he was "unable to know, when [he] acted, that [he] was guilty of any conduct of which the Board would take cognizance."[99]

Finally, there is a related factor deriving from the citizen's perception of what he is being told to do. From what source is he to learn what his legal obligations are? He is told by the statutory law that he must not exceed the speed limit, but he is told by law enforcement officials that only if he exceeds the limit by more than ten miles per hour will he be called to account. He is told by the statutory law not to jaywalk, but in Chicago, at least, he is told by the chief of police that the law against jaywalking does more harm than good and will not be enforced.[100] He is told by the statutory law not to gamble at all; but he is told by police and prosecutor that his friendly Saturday night poker game will not be bothered, that only when there is commercial exploitation will the gambling law be enforced.[101] Moreover, these policy decisions by law enforcement officials are not wrongful pretensions to authority but considered judgments the system authorizes the officials to make, either explicitly or by recognizing the officials' right to interpose. In these circumstances would it not be unrealistic for the citizen to construe his obligations from the statutes alone? What is demanded of him is revealed by how law enforcement officials carry out their task.

This is the perception behind Justice Frankfurter's observation that deeply embedded ways of carrying out state policy, or not carrying it out, are truer law than mere words.

Sometimes there is no long-standing pattern of nonenforcement of a statute—indeed, the statute may have been recently enacted—but there is an established policy of nonenforcement in defined circumstances. If the policy is publicly disseminated, this situation is not materially different from the situation of a long-standing nonenforcement pattern, which after all is significant chiefly because it furnishes proof of the existence of a nonenforcement policy of some force. The considerations of fairness, reliance, and the citizen's perception of his obligations remain to support his conclusion that if his proposed conduct is covered by a nonenforcement policy, he may legitimately disobey the criminal statute involved.

The opinion of the federal court of appeals in *United States v. Kartman*[102] deals with the effect of a nonenforcement policy in determining the legal force of a law. In the course of a protest demonstration at an induction center, a deputy federal marshal attempted to arrest a demonstrator for the federal crime of failing to possess a draft card. The defendant intervened to prevent the arrest and in the process kicked the deputy marshal. For this action he was convicted of violating a federal statute that prohibited assaulting and interfering with an officer "while engaged in . . . the performance of his official duties." One of his defenses was that the marshal was not engaged in the performance of his official duty, since the attorney general had instructed federal marshals not to arrest for nonpossession of a draft card unless the Selective Service System had requested such action after an investigation. The trial court disallowed his offer of proof on the ground that the facts would not make out a defense in light of the federal law authorizing the marshal to arrest for an offense against the United States committed in his presence. The appellate court disagreed: the attorney general could deprive marshals of authority to arrest for federal crimes, it said, pursuant to his statutory authority to "supervise and direct United States marshals in the performance of public duties."[103] Hence the defendant in this case could establish a defense by proving that the attorney general had instructed federal marshals not to enforce the draft-card statute. The upshot was that the attorney general's nonenforcement policy altered the statutory duty of federal marshals to enforce the law and deprived those officials of legal sanction—even against a forcible resister—in attempting to arrest for conduct made criminal by Congress.

Another decision that illuminates the argument is that of the Supreme Court in *Redmund v. United States*.[104] Redmund and his wife took nude photographs of each other and mailed the film for processing. They were convicted of causing obscene photographs to be delivered through the mail in violation of the Postal Obscenity Law. Their petition for certiorari from the affirmance of their conviction by the court of appeals was supported by the solicitor general on the ground that the prosecution was inconsistent with the policy previously formulated by the Department of Justice for determining when violations of this act would be prosecuted. That policy stated that "no useful purpose is served by a felony conviction of individuals who have willingly exchanged private letters, although obscene." It therefore confined prosecution to commercial situations, with exceptions not present in this case.[105] On the ground urged by the solicitor general, the Supreme Court granted certiorari, vacated the conviction, and dismissed the information.

The Court's decision, of course, constitutes a recognition of a federal prosecutor's authority to decline to prosecute. Such decisions by now are quite commonplace, however. What makes this decision significant for our purposes is a combination of two factors. First, the Court recognized the prosecutor's authority not only to decline to prosecute in a particular case but to establish a policy of systematic nonenforcement that reduces the scope of the conduct criminalized by the statute. The legislative version of the prohibition was that all obscene pictures are banned from the mail; the prosecutorial version was that they are banned only in commercial situations. Second, the Court recognized the prosecutor's authority not by the ambiguous means of declining to direct remedial action against him, but by the clear, affirmative action of granting his request to reverse an error-free conviction initiated in violation of his nonenforcement policy. In these circumstances it would be pointless to insist that the measure of the citizen's duty is the statutory prohibition rather than the narrower prohibition the prosecutor has decided to enforce.

We now reach the third and most complex nonenforcement situation. Assume there is neither a long-standing pattern nor a publicly established policy of nonenforcement of a particular criminal statute. Might there nevertheless be an argument for legitimated disobedience arising out of the legally accepted power of law enforcement officials not to enforce the rule? Plainly enough, such an argument cannot be construed out of the principle of reliance or the claim to equal treatment, both of which are available only in the presence of a long-standing pattern or a publicly established policy of nonenforcement. For the same reason it obviously cannot be construed out of the perception that the "true" law is reflected in a pattern or policy of law enforcement. If it is to be construed at all, it must be argued on the basis of what law enforcement officials should make the "true" law—that is to say, on the basis that a proper exercise of the nonenforcement authority would entail not enforcing the rule in particular kinds of cases.

Let us start with a famous example of a carefully considered policy of nonenforcement to show how the case might be made. When Robert H. Jackson was attorney general of the United States, he wrote a letter to Sen. Millard E. Tydings explaining why he declined to prosecute Drew Pearson for a criminal libel against Tydings uttered in the course of one of Pearson's broadcasts. Jackson's reasons were that a policy of enforcement would make journalism a dangerous profession, would invite a flood of demands for prosecution, would discredit law enforcement when prosecutions failed, and would inhibit the freedom of the press when prosecutions succeeded. Therefore, he concluded, so long as the aggrieved individual had a civil remedy and there was no breach of the peace or other public injury, he would follow a policy of nonenforcement.[106]

Now after that policy was articulated and established, a case for legitimated disobedience could clearly be made. But what of the situation before Jackson spoke, assuming past policy failed to reveal a clue? A citizen might argue in favor of legitimated disobedience at this point as follows. "The statute prohibits me from defaming senators and others with untruths. Yet the 'true' law depends on how the attorney general will use his legal power of nonenforcement and not simply on what the statute proscribes. If the attorney general exercises responsible and proper judgment, he will not enforce the prohibition: enforcement would make journalism a dangerous profession, discredit law enforcement, and hamper freedom of the press; moreover, the defamed person has an adequate civil remedy. I don't know whether or not the attorney general will make these judgments. Hence one of the important elements that constitute the 'true' law is indeterminate. There is no way of finding out what the attorney general will do but to exercise my best judgment of what he ought properly to do and act on it. If I'm right I won't be prosecuted. If I'm wrong I will be. But my undertaking the decision to disobey on these grounds is legitimate."*

This is an argument that cannot be brushed aside if some of the propositions we advanced earlier are accepted. We argued that the norm of validity and the lesser-evil norm furnish a basis for legitimated disobedience because a citizen may appeal

---

* Or consider the reasons advanced by Professor Dworkin for not prosecuting those who disobey the draft laws out of conscience: "One is the obvious reason that they act out of better motives than those who break the law out of greed or a desire to subvert government. Another is the practical reason that our society suffers a loss if it punishes a group that includes—as the group of draft dissenters does—some of its most thoughtful and loyal citizens. Jailing such men solidifies their alienation from society, and alienates many like them who are deterred by the threat." "On Not Prosecuting Civil Disobedience," *New York Review of Books*, June 6, 1968, p. 14.

to them as a ground for relieving him of his usual liability to punishment for disobeying the rule. And we just argued that a norm of nonenforcement, when it has become established through a long-standing pattern or policy, furnishes an equivalent basis for legitimation. But why should it matter that the norm of nonenforcement has not been given a clear content in the particular case? In constitutional matters, for example, it is not only the clear cases of unconstitutionality that provide a basis for legitimation: a novel claim of invalidity based on the amorphous character of the due process clause functions just as well as an established claim based on a more specific clause of the Constitution. And the lesser-evil defense deals by definition with situations that were not specifically provided for in a law. Therefore, it could be argued, just as a citizen in deciding whether or not to obey a rule is at liberty to make a judgment on its validity and on the bearing of a lesser-evil evaluation, so he is equally at liberty to make a judgment on the propriety of its enforcement.

A very important qualification is needed at this point in the argument. After all, it is not simply a calculation that the citizen will "get away with" disobeying a rule that produces legitimated disobedience. We would make no claim to legitimated disobedience for a person who calculates that he will not be caught, or that the evidence available will not convict him, or that the prosecutor can be induced by political pressures not to prosecute. What distinguishes instances such as these from legitimated disobedience is the ground on which a citizen makes the judgment that the law will not be enforced against him. Dr. Buxton, the physician who violated the Connecticut birth control statute, disobeyed the law on the ground that it was unconstitutional. If another physician had violated the law at about the same time simply in the hope that he would not be caught, he would have been in a very different position. For then, unlike Dr. Buxton, who appealed to a legitimating norm recognized by the legal system, he would be appealing to no norm at all.* The

* Of course, a person might violate a law simply in the hope he would not be caught and still raise the constitutional defense as an afterthought

reporter who defames a senator in our hypothetical case would be rather in the position of Dr. Buxton. He too would be appealing to a legitimating norm—a proper and rational policy of nonenforcement by the Attorney General that, if adopted, would modify the law on the books. As Chief Judge Bazelon recently had occasion to observe, the "standards which guide prosecutors in the exercise of their discretion are as much a part of the law as the rules applied in court."[107]

Of course, not every reason a prosecutor might have for not prosecuting serves as a legitimating norm. The distinction between reasons that do so serve and those that do not is similar to the distinction drawn by Prof. Norman Abrams between reasons for not prosecuting that do and those that do not yield to meaningful systematization. The reasons that do not yield to meaningful systematization and do not serve as a basis for legitimated disobedience are those consisting of practical factors, such as "the prosecutor's belief in the guilt of a suspect, the likelihood of a conviction, the possibility of obtaining the suspect's cooperation in other matters, the prosecutor's concern about his record for obtaining convictions, the influence of the law enforcement agents involved, and the general character of the offender." The reasons that do are those that are "linked to particular offense categories" and respond to a generalization, whether consciously formulated or not, to the effect that certain kinds of conduct should not be prosecuted, even though they fall within the scope of the statutory prohibition.[108]

There are at least two differences between an appeal to the Constitution and an appeal to the proper exercise of prosecutorial discretion that argue against the conclusion that the latter appeal furnishes a basis for legitimated disobedience.

First, a citizen who appeals to the Constitution has an opportunity to argue his case in court, whereas a citizen who appeals to the proper exercise of prosecutorial discretion usually does

---

when later prosecuted. But then, although he too would be nonpunishable if the law were held unconstitutional, his initial decision to breach the law would not have been legitimate. What we are concerned with are the grounds for a citizen undertaking to depart from a rule.

not. But the fact that the second citizen may be deprived of an opportunity to argue his case does not disentitle him from relying on what he has reasons for concluding would be a proper exercise of discretion by the prosecutor. Moreover, he might well have an opportunity to argue his case in the prosecutor's office, and it cannot make a difference that he argues his case before the official exercising authority rather than before an agency reviewing its exercise. Suppose a statute established an administrative board within a prosecutor's office with jurisdiction to review the prosecutor's decision to prosecute or not to prosecute at the behest of a defendant or complainant.[109] If an appeal to a norm of the proper exercise of prosecutorial discretion before such a reviewing agency may establish a basis for legitimated disobedience, an appeal before the prosecutor himself should do so just as well.

Second, the grounds of a constitutional appeal are a body of law rooted in the text of the Constitution; thus there are standards of explicit law to appeal to. A person appealing to the proper exercise of prosecutorial discretion has more difficulty finding a basis for his argument, since there is no explicit law he can cite. But as we argued earlier, the discretion enforcement officials have, whether by delegation or through interposition, is not the discretion to act willfully but the discretion to exercise sound judgment consistent with the ends of the legal system. It is to the criterion of sound and proper judgment that the citizen may make his appeal, undeveloped and unformulated though this criterion may be at any particular time. Formally, the objection of an absence of a legal standard could be met by a statute providing, for example, that in establishing a nonenforcement policy a prosecutor should be guided by the public interest. In fact, this is precisely the condition that prevails without an explicit law so stating.

In developing the argument for legitimation through appeal to norms of justifiable nonenforcement, we have focused on the role of the prosecutor. Manifestly the argument would be precisely the same for the role of the police, where the issue is the decision to arrest rather than the decision to prosecute. It is perhaps less obvious that the argument is equally applicable to the nullifying powers of juries. A jury, after all, has the authority to acquit "in the teeth of the law" even more clearly than a prosecutor has the power to reduce the scope of a statute by exercising his nonenforcement authority. Hence a case for legitimated disobedience may be made whenever a citizen is able to adduce a set of reasons why he should be acquitted comparable to the kinds of reasons he might give in arguing that he should not be prosecuted.

Let us consider some of the arguments that may be made against this position. First, one might argue that in the case of the jury there is no background of principles and policies out of which a norm leading to acquittal can be established. But this is surely not so. Juries can and sometimes do respond to their sense of the system's governing ends in concluding that conviction is inappropriate despite the defendant's guilt. Indeed, the very existence of background ends and policies a jury may appeal to is an important part of the argument for jury nullification as legitimated interposition. Thus the very same arguments that Attorney General Jackson found persuasive in deciding not to prosecute Drew Pearson would have been no less relevant and forceful for a jury deciding whether to acquit Pearson, had a prosecution been instituted.

Second, one may object that juries are not continuing institutions capable of formulating and adhering to a policy. They are ad hoc bodies sitting exclusively to judge the case at hand and no other. As such, they have no institutional concern with past or future jury determinations, and hence no concern with policy beyond the case before them. Still, why should that matter? For the case at hand juries are at liberty (so we have argued in Chapter Two) to return an acquittal contrary to the law and the evidence by appeal to social ends; and these ends must include the kind of considerations a prosecutor might be expected to rely on, even though they may include others as well. To be sure, a jury's decision to acquit applies only to the case at hand, whereas a prosecutor may formulate a nonenforcement policy to govern an entire class of cases. But for the defendant's purposes a basis for legitimated disobedience in the case at hand is enough.

A third possible objection is that a defendant is not free to argue to the jury reasons why it should acquit contrary to law. But it is not clear that he may not make such an argument in some form. And even if he may not, the fact that the jury is at liberty to consider precisely the reasons he would have argued is sufficient to create the conditions for legitimated disobedience.

Summary

We have tried to show in this chapter that in our legal system the obligations of the citizen with respect to mandatory rules are less unremitting than the law-and-order model would have them. In a number of instances of potentially broad scope, the citizen may justifiably undertake to depart from a peremptory rule by appealing to a set of norms afforded by the legal system itself. In a number of significant contexts, then, the citizen's role has the characteristics of a recourse role. Just as the official is at liberty to undertake to depart from rules of competence, as we have seen in the preceding chapter, so the citizen is at liberty to undertake to depart from the peremptory rules constraining him. And the legitimation of rule departures turns out to be neither incomprehensible nor alien, as the rule-of-law and law-and-order models would have it, but a distinctive and pervasive feature of the functioning of the American legal system.

CHAPTER FOUR

Legitimation as a Social Strategy

IN ORDER to assess the force of the legitimation of rule departures as a social strategy we must undertake four tasks: to contrast legitimated interposition and legitimated disobedience; to review the problem to which legitimated disobedience and legitimated interposition respond; to examine the variations in legal systems' structures and functions that cause them to be more or less open to legitimated rule departures of both sorts; and to sketch at least the policy considerations that, given the problem legitimation meets, dictate the degree to which legitimation may be provided for in a legal system.

Interposition and Disobedience Contrasted

While both forms of legitimation enable a role agent justifiably to undertake departures from the mandatory rules constraining him in his role, the justifying argument in the two forms are differently derived. To use our earlier terminology, the contexts of evaluation of different roles—in this case the roles of citizen and official—yield different propositions of appropriateness for decisions to undertake rule departures.

The differences in these propositions of appropriateness stem from differences in the nature and source of the obligations imposed by rules constraining citizens, on the one hand, and officials, on the other. Mandatory rules constraining citizens acquire their obligatory force from the fact that they are authoritative commands backed by the threat of punishment in the event of violation. As observed earlier, the import of the possibility of punishment for the citizen's obligation, in contrast to its effect as threat, is that it signals that an authoritative demand is being made on persons in their role as citizens. Of course, such rules may be addressed to officials as well—criminal laws against accepting bribes, for example. But even so, the basis for the obligation is the same. By contrast, rules addressed solely to officials may be mandatory even though they do not take the form of authoritative commands backed by the threat of punishment. These rules derive their obligatory force on another ground: namely, that they stipulate the terms under which the official is vested with authority. Hence the official incurs the obligation to comply in his very act of assuming the official role.

The preceding two chapters have developed the consequent differences in those propositions of appropriateness that support legitimated interposition and legitimated disobedience. A citizen's disobedience is legitimated when the legal system incorporates some norm to which the citizen may appeal as the basis for justifying his departure from a rule, and when the citizen is not liable for punishment at least in the event the legal official determines the norm to be applicable. The legal system may incorporate the norm explicitly, as in the case of the norm of validity and the norm of the lesser evil, or by tacitly accepting it, as in the case of the norm of justifiable nonenforcement. In either event, for legitimation to take place there must be legal recourse against the citizen for his rule departure (in the form of criminal prosecution, contempt proceedings, or the like) and he must invoke a legitimating norm as a ground for justifying his action. So he is at liberty to judge for himself whether a legitimating norm applies to a rule departure he is about to undertake, and even to undertake the rule departure if his judgment so prompts him; but the final judgment whether his appeal to the legitimating norm will be sustained and punishment precluded is made by a legal official or institution, usually a court of law.

The legitimation of an official's interposition differs in a number of ways. First, there is no legal recourse either against the official who undertakes a rule departure or against the legal effectiveness of his action. Indeed, the absence of legal recourse is an important element in the argument that such departures are legitimated by the legal system. Professor Hart has referred to a system of rules as being "inefficient" when "no agency [is] specifically empowered to ascertain, finally and authoritatively, the fact of the violation."[1] This aptly describes the system of rules constraining the official when legitimated interposition occurs.

Second, there is no explicit legal standard by which to judge when an official's rule departure is justifiable, as there is in most cases of a citizen's legitimated rule departures. Insofar as we may say that the official has discretion to depart from a rule, the discretion is, in the language used earlier, deviational. Since the legal system does not formally acknowledge the official's power of deviation, it cannot consistently establish criteria for deviating. This, however, is not to say that the official has a liberty to follow his purely personal inclinations. For interposition to achieve legitimacy, identifiable public policies or ends must exist to justify the official in departing from the rule. Those ends, as argued earlier, may be the ends of the official's role, the ends of other roles affecting or affected by the official's actions in his role, institutional ends, or background ends. But the law never openly articulates these ends as ends that may be employed to justify a rule departure.

Third, the legal system never subjects the official's judgment to depart from a rule to review, though the official may be called to account within the bureaucracy by higher officials. Legal vindication, an essential step in legitimated disobedience, is absent in legitimated interposition. A jury's decision to acquit, for example, is untestable, even though the jury may have acquitted "in the teeth of the law." To this extent, of course, legitimated interposition offers the official a wider freedom to depart from a rule than legitimated disobedience offers the citizen. The disobedient citizen labors under the contingency that he may be formally punished if his defense is rejected. The interposing official is bound only by his self-restraint and informal pressures of criticism.

It was out of regard to these differences that we chose to speak

of legitimated disobedience by the citizen and legitimated interposition by the official. The citizen disobeys a rule and defends
his act by appealing to a legitimating norm before a court or
other official with final authority to determine whether he is
right. The official interposes his own judgment that to depart
from a rule constraining him in his role will serve, rather than
disserve, the social purposes his role exists to accomplish.

Legitimation as a Response to a Dilemma

The central significance of the legitimation of rule departures
by a legal system is that it constitutes a response to a perennial
dilemma of legal ordering, a response that tends to go unnoticed
as a legal response at all. The dilemma is this. On the one hand,
a fundamental function of a legal system is to set restraints on
the judgments of individuals through a regularized ordering in
the larger interest of protecting other individuals. Those who
hold the state's coercive power are confined within collectively
determined limits of what is appropriate and desirable. As Wil-
lard Hurst observed in discussing the question of legitimacy,
"Any kind of organized power ought to be measured against
criteria of ends and means which are not defined or enforced by
the immediate power holders themselves. It is as simple as that:
We don't want to trust any group of power holders to be their
own judges upon the ends for which they use the power or the
ways in which they use it."[2] By the same token, citizens subject
to the restraints imposed by officials must not be their own
judges of how the use of government power bears on them and
their own interests. It is as critical for the overall success of social ordering through law that citizens observe the constraints
set by officials as it is that officials observe the constraints collectively set on their exercise of government power. In both cases
self-determined judgments of ends and means subvert the enterprise of collective ordering in the social interest.

On the other hand, for reasons we have explored, these goals
of rule ordering can never be totally achieved, for no rule of law
can prescribe adequately for every set of circumstances in human

life it potentially governs. Given the unpredictability of events and the ever-shifting pressures of interests and demands, it is inevitable, particularly in a dynamic society, that at some point the collectively determined means and ends embodied in the rules of law will badly disserve the social interest.

How can a sensitive legal system respond to this dilemma? Certainly there are many ways. It can establish responsive and dynamic lawmaking processes, legislative, judicial, and administrative; it can explicitly delegate powers of discretion to officials; it can enact laws that attempt to anticipate the kinds of circumstances that might compel exceptions and qualifications. But even such efforts will probably not suffice. For as fast as a legal system may change its rules, it is unlikely to match the speedy and eccentric pace of circumstances and the subtle shifts in a society's priorities. What further response can a legal system make, then, without turning the law into an inflexible bureaucracy or yielding finally to the ultimate wisdom of personal over public judgments?

Some would say that no further response can be made: the legal system has gone as far as a legal system can in providing for unforeseeable circumstances and changing social demands. At times when the means prescribed by law are inharmonious with the law's ends, sensible people will act sensibly outside the law. Officials and citizens simply will substitute their own judgment for the law's judgment and act accordingly. So long as those instances are reasonably few and confined, all is well. The gap between the law in action and the law in books may be reduced, but it can never be closed.

In our view this answer misrepresents the phenomena it purports to describe and underestimates the potential of legal systems to provide rule ordering adaptive to change. The conceptions of legitimated interposition and disobedience identify ways in which such adaptations can be made within the legal system. Actions that are conventionally viewed as extralegal adjustments through rule violation may be seen as actions that at times are legitimated by the legal system. So jury nullification, police and prosecutorial rule departures in law enforcement, and even a citizen's disobedience to a rule may be actions within the law though outside its rules. By legitimating rule departures under certain circumstances legal systems can provide for the disparity between the rule's demand and the demand of the moment. Rule departures become not simply extralegal actions of individuals that compensate for the inadequacy of law, but sometimes, when legitimated, a part of the legal framework itself by which rule ordering is made adaptive to unforeseen circumstances, change, and conflict.

But is it merely a quibble to insist, as we do, that legitimated rule departures occur within the legal system rather than outside it? We think not. More is involved than how one may choose to stipulate the extent of a legal system. For all would acknowledge to be parts of the legal system those actions and responses that, in the preceding chapters, we relied on as establishing legitimated rule departures. How individuals respond to rules may or may not be regarded as part of the workings of a legal system. But how courts, legislatures, administrative agencies, and other official bodies respond to individuals who depart from rules must be considered part of the workings of a legal system in any meaningful understanding of the phrase; and it is those responses that raise the question of legitimation.

Openness to Legitimation in Legal Systems

The preceding two chapters have examined the legal system of the United States in order to assess the nature and extent of legitimated rule departures by officials and citizens. To gain a further perspective on the significance of legitimation as a social strategy we shall now turn to a more theoretical question. What kinds of legal arrangements make a legal system more or less open to legitimated rule departures?

The kind of system that would be totally closed to legitimated rule departures has already been discussed. It is the system that adheres totally to the rule-of-law and law-and-order models, in which individual judgments contrary to a mandatory rule are totally excluded and any attempt at principled rule departure is necessarily considered an act of usurpation in the official or an act of rebellion in the citizen. The plan in the following pages is to examine what would be required to take a legal system increasing distances beyond these classic models. Since the legal arrangements that give rise to legitimated disobedience and legitimated interposition are different, it is necessary to consider the possibilities of increasing openness separately with respect to each.

Legitimated Disobedience

Among the conditions for legitimated disobedience discussed in Chapter Three, two are readily amenable to alterations that expand or contract a legal system's openness to legitimated disobedience. One is that the system must recognize some legitimating norm to which the citizen may appeal as a justification for undertaking to depart from a mandatory rule. The other is that in some circumstances the system must accept the appeal to this norm as some basis for relieving the citizen of his usual liability to punishment for his rule departure. Let us consider now how each of these conditions might be dealt with to create systems increasingly open to legitimated disobedience.

The Scope of the Legitimating Norm. The presence of a written constitution enforced by a supreme court with powers of judicial review exercised in the course of adjudicating cases plainly serves to open a system to legitimated disobedience. A system like that of the United Kingdom, which works on the concept of parliamentary supremacy, on its face is substantially less open to legitimation than that of the United States, for there are no judicially enforceable norms superior to the parliamentary authority to which a citizen may appeal to justify his departure. Even given a written constitution enforceable through judicial review, however, a system may be more or less open to legitimated disobedience depending on two circumstances: the nature of the constitutional restraints on government authority and the way the system's judiciary perceives its role in interpreting and applying constitutional norms.

The constitution makers determine the first circumstance. A

constitution may contain only narrowly conceived restrictions on government authority—that taxation must be direct, that only one branch of the legislature may initiate fiscal measures, that certain procedures must be followed in the enactment of legislation, and the like. The possibilities of appealing to such norms to justify a rule departure have limited effect. But a constitution that incorporated broad principles and ethical norms as constitutional standards would be quite different. For example, a constitution providing that all laws must be just in their formulation and their application and must comport with the highest human ideals would open every law to challenge on virtually any ground a citizen might conscientiously claim.*

But as important as the norms incorporated in the constitution is the approach the supreme court takes to its responsibility of interpreting and applying those norms. Consider two extremes. Supreme Court A applies no principle of deference to the legislative judgment. It reads constitutional provisions broadly with a minimum regard for their actual wording or for the specific apprehensions that prompted them. Their "emanations" and "penumbras" are as influential as their language and history. They are regarded as infinitely flexible instruments through which the court translates the ethos of the times, as it interprets that ethos, into legal restraints on government power. Moreover, the court readily undertakes to interpret and apply any provision of the constitution, irrespective of the extent to which interpreting a particular provision might require the exercise of social, economic, or political preferences. Not only does Supreme Court A decline to develop principles designed to defer or avoid adjudicating constitutional issues, but it seeks out and exploits every available op-

---

* Consider Professor Dworkin's observations on the American Constitution: "In the United States, at least, almost any law which a significant number of people would be tempted to disobey on moral grounds would be doubtful—if not clearly invalid—on constitutional grounds as well. The constitution makes our conventional political morality relevant to the question of validity; any statute that appears to compromise that morality raises constitutional questions, and if the compromise is serious, the constitutional doubts are serious also." "On Not Prosecuting Civil Disobedience," *New York Review of Books*, June 6, 1968, p. 14.

portunity to do so. Indeed, the court may regard itself as having the power of total discretion to determine the law with no obligation whatsoever, except perhaps that of doing justice as it sees it. Accordingly, not even the rule of *stare decisis* will have force, since the constitution is seen as a living document that changes and grows with changing events and changing courts. Supreme Court A is in fact the "super-legislature" and the wholly "judicially activist" body that our own Supreme Court is from time to time hyperbolically accused of being.[3]

Supreme Court Z is at the opposite extreme. It attempts a policy of slavish deference to the legislative judgment, placing an almost unbearably heavy burden of proof on challengers to constitutionality. It declines to pass on constitutional issues unless the necessity of doing so is utterly inescapable. It reads constitutional provisions as narrowly as possible in order to minimize its authority to restrain the exercise of government power. It sees the constitution as static; denies its own authority to expand meanings once given; sees itself bound by the most rigorous self-imposed restraints; eschews all but the most traditionally accepted modes of legal reasoning.

Obviously the system in which Supreme Court A sits is far more open to legitimated disobedience than the one in which Supreme Court Z sits. Court Z has restricted the provisions of the constitution that may invalidate mandatory rules and it has narrowed and crystallized the grounds under which other provisions may invalidate rules. Court A, on the other hand, has eliminated these restraints and, in assuming the role of a free moral agent, has opened wide the possibilities of invalidation, and hence of legitimated disobedience. To label Supreme Court A a super-legislature is close to the mark. By virtue of the way it has perceived and structured its role, it approaches the status of an overt lawmaking agency. And given that it exercises its authority through the process of adjudication, it must rely on rule departures by citizens to provide the occasions for its lawmaking. In such a system rule departures ultimately become an extension of the franchise.

Now the United States Supreme Court is neither Court A

nor Court Z, but falls somewhere in between. Moreover, its location between those extremes is not static. Over its history the Court has moved sometimes in the direction of one extreme, and sometimes in the direction of the other. At any period one is able to find elements of both traditions of adjudication at work in the Court's decisions. The important point for our purposes is that these shifts in the Court's view of its role increase or decrease the extent to which citizens are permitted and encouraged to act according to their own judgment rather than according to the rules, since the possible grounds for legitimated disobedience are expanded by one tradition of adjudication and contracted by the other.

Similar considerations apply to the second norm we have discussed—the lesser-evil norm. The more explicitly it is recognized as a legal defense and the more broadly it is defined, the more a defense based on this norm opens the system to legitimated disobedience. As we saw in Chapter Three, the lesser-evil defense was only ambiguously recognized at the common law under the principle of necessity. Jurists like James Fitzjames Stephens recognized the need for such an ultimate defense but opposed its clear articulation on the ground that explicit recognition would invite a wider use of the defense than is desirable, thus weakening the force of the criminal law. The codification approach to the criminal law substantially defeats this strategy. Where the defense exists in the Continental countries, it is embodied in the code. Recent revisions of American substantive criminal law, influenced by the Model Penal Code, have followed the Continental tradition in articulating an explicit lesser-evil defense. Making the defense more visible and treating it like other justifications tends to remove its mystery as an intangible last resort and makes its invocation more likely in a broader range of circumstances.

How a legal system defines and applies the lesser-evil defense has the same effect on the system's openness to legitimation as how the system defines and applies constitutional defenses. The defense may be confined to cases in which the greater evil consists of certain specified kinds of injuries, such as death or great bodily harm;[4] or it may be broadly applicable to cases in which the greater evil consists of any kind of evil greater than that sought to be prevented by the criminal law in question.[5] The defense may be unavailable for certain kinds of criminal offenses, like homicide;[6] or it may be applicable to all offenses. It may be confined to situations of dire physical emergency;[7] or it may reach all circumstances, regardless of the source of the greater evil or the suddenness of its appearance. Finally, it may be made inapplicable to certain kinds of individual judgments. For example, the lesser-evil defense enacted by the New York legislature does not reach where the citizen's judgment rests only on the morality or advisability of the statute as such or of the statute as applied to a particular case. Thus it is unavailable to "the crusader who considers a penal statute unsalutary because it tends to obstruct his cause, and the like."[8] These possible formulations of the defense show that the greater the range of citizen judgment authorized under the defense the more open the system is to legitimated disobedience.

In the remaining kind of legitimated disobedience discussed, law enforcement officials rather than courts apply the legitimating norm. Our argument was that where law enforcement officials may exericse discretion, whether delegated or deviational, to decline to enforce a rule for reasons founded on their own judgment of the rule's appropriateness in certain circumstances, the citizen has a correlative ground for departing from the rule.

The factor that most directly controls the extent of this kind of legitimation in any legal system is the degree of discretion enforcement officials are permitted to exericse. When the official cannot exercise any discretion, of course legitimation by appeal to the norm of justifiable nonenforcement cannot occur. When the official can exercise discretion, much depends on the criteria he may appropriately invoke and the range of crimes to which he may apply his discretion. If, for example, the criteria for nonenforcement are confined to norms already incor-

porated in acceptable legal defenses, the possibilities of legitimated disobedience are not enlarged as they would be if the
criteria extended beyond the norms otherwise incorporated in
the system. A lesser-evil criterion bearing on the exercise of
prosecutorial discretion, for example, would not further open
a system to legitimated disobedience if the system already incorporated this norm as a defense. It would have this effect,
of course, in a system that did not otherwise incorporate the
norm. A criterion for justifiable nonenforcement such as that
invoked by Attorney General Jackson in the Senator Tydings
libel case, which amounted to a judgment of the social utility
of the law itself, plainly would extend the possibilities for legitimated disobedience. So would the criteria advanced by Professor Dworkin when he suggests that draft resisters not be prosecuted when the law is arguably unconstitutional, the defendants are conscientiously motivated, and their actions do not
invade the moral rights of others.[9]

The nature of the official's discretionary authority, as well as
the criteria governing nonenforcement, may affect the system's
openness to legitimated disobedience. Discretion not to enforce
the rules opens the system to legitimation. But deviational discretion opens it up less than delegated discretion. This tends
to happen for two related reasons.

First, when nonenforcement discretion is delegated rather
than deviational, it is likely to be more widely exercised by
officials and to be more clearly perceived by citizens as a sanc-
tioned legal response that may serve to legitimate their rule
departures. We have already seen, for example, that the deviational status of jury discretion itself tends in part to explain
the limited impact of this power of nullification on the system.[10] Indeed, a major argument against converting the jury's
deviational discretion into an avowed delegated discretion by
instructing the jury that they are at liberty to depart from the
judge's legal instructions is that the conversion would lead
juries to exercise their discretion more widely.[11] To the extent this conversion occurred, the enhanced prospect of jury

nullification and its legally authorized nature would widen the possibilities of legitimated disobedience through the citizen appealing to the prospect of jury nullification to justify his rule departure.

Second, the explicit delegation of nonenforcement authority tends to produce pressures to regularize and publicize the criteria of nonenforcement. We have already seen this occurring as prosecutorial discretion emerged from its twilight deviational status into an explicitly delegated discretion. Indeed, some have urged that public regulations be adopted specifying the circumstances in which rules would not be enforced. To the extent this kind of development occurs, citizen judgment to depart from a rule by appeal to these articulated grounds of nonenforcement is facilitated.*

In sum, a system will be increasingly open to legitimated disobedience to the extent it recognizes norms that furnish a basis for justifying a rule departure, whether these norms be superior substantive norms or norms of nonenforcement, and to the extent that it grants discretionary authority to its officials to interpret and apply these norms. If the discretionary authority granted to the system's officials is delegated, the system is more open to legitimated disobedience than if the authority is deviational. Even so, deviational discretion has an effect similar in kind, if not in extent, to that of delegated discretion. Thus we may say, with respect to our larger concern with legitimation generally, that the more open a system is to legitimated interposition, the more open it will be to legitimated disobedience.

Liability to Punishment. As seen earlier, the argument for legitimated disobedience requires not just that the legitimating

---

* Of course, it is consistent with these arguments to recognize that in some situations grounds of action acceptable for deviational discretion may not be acceptable for delegated discretion. This will typically be the case where the policy favors the official's dispensing with the rules in particular circumstances but does not favor explicitly articulating this preference. Compare Louis Jaffe's observation on the use of informers, quoted in the note on page 78 *supra*.

norm exist, but that it have a legal effect on the citizen's liability to punishment for disobeying a rule. The task now, therefore, is to consider the variety of responses a legal system might make to the actor's punishability in light of his appeal to one of these legitimating norms and to assess the extent to which various responses tend to open or close the system to legitimated disobedience.

Assume a citizen has acted in contravention of a peremptory rule and seeks to establish his nonpunishability nonetheless by appealing to a legitimating norm. Two principal questions arise. First, if he turns out to be right, how much does it count *against* him that he took it upon himself to make the judgment that he was at liberty to depart from the rule? Second, if he turns out to be wrong, how much does it count *for* him that he acted in conscientious reliance on the legitimating norm? Different answers provide different levels of openness to legitimated rule departures.

One clarifying point should be made before considering the variety of possible responses to these two questions. While a number of different responses may be given to the first question when the norm appealed to is that of validity (indeed, we saw a number of these responses in the last chapter), only one answer is possible in the case of the other norms. The very recognition of the norms of the lesser-evil and justifiable nonenforcement implies the shielding of the actor from punishment if he is right. The lesser-evil norm functions solely to create a defense where the actor has disobeyed a rule. And in the case of the norm of justifiable nonenforcement, what it means to say that the citizen is right in his assessment of the norm is that the law enforcement official accepts it as a ground for not enforcing the law against him, in which event the citizen necessarily will not be punished. The second question, however, of what happens when the citizen is mistaken, permits a variety of responses for all the relevant norms.

We shall begin with those answers to the two questions that most sharply restrict legitimated disobedience and then consider those that increasingly open the system to it. This requires dealing first with the question of how much it counts against the citizen that he undertakes to depart from a rule, even when he is right.

The most extreme answer asserts that it counts against the citizen altogether that he took the judgment upon himself, so that his punishability for disobeying the rule is undiminished by the content or applicability of the norm invoked. This response would represent the unqualified law-and-order position. The citizen's duty is to obey the rules; he may not take it upon himself to judge that in light of some norm he may depart from them. Only the courts can make that judgment, and until they have done so the citizen's duty is to comply with the rules. That a citizen who chooses to depart may have been right in his understanding of an applicable norm does not relieve him of his liability to punishment. Thus the first judicial response to the issue of punishability completely closes a legal system to legitimated disobedience. If the analysis in Chapter Three was correct, however, that response is never actually given in the American legal system, though much judicial rhetoric and theory asserts or implies it.

The second response also accepts the general principle that citizens are obligated to obey peremptory rules in advance of a judicial determination of the applicability of a legal norm, but it recognizes exceptions under certain circumstances, either singly or in combination. This is the actual response of the American legal system, rather than the first, when law-and-order values purportedly have controlling weight. These circumstances, to the extent the American experience may be relied on as a guide, will include the following: that the citizen is not only right but clearly right in his assessment of the norm; that other adequate remedies are unavailable, so that it is necessary for the actor to depart from the rule in order to test it; and most generally, that the nature and extent of the interest imperiled by obedience to the rule outweigh the interest imperiled by departure from it.

Some of the examples discussed in the last chapter show how these circumstances may affect a citizen's obligation to obey the rules. In the case of judicial orders, the old equity principle required compliance whether the order was valid or not, so long as the issuing court had jurisdiction. Under this principle constitutional defects are generally treated as nonjurisdictional. Yet where the issuing court's claim to legal authority was "frivolous and not substantial," or where the court was "so obviously traveling outside its orbit as to be merely usurping judicial forms," or where the order "was transparently invalid or had only a frivolous pretense to validity," a citizen who violated it would be relieved of his liability to punishment. In the case of administrative orders, a citizen is not permitted to raise the issue of validity, constitutional or otherwise, unless he has already exhausted whatever internal agency or judicial review remedies he had available. But exceptions may be made if the order is "unconstitutional on its face" or under certain other circumstances, such as those in which a citizen's interest in personal liberty is at stake (e.g., draft cases) and the public interest in requiring him to exhaust his other alternatives is not shown to be strong.

In the third possible response the standard situation is the other way; that is, the citizen, being right in his assessment of the relevant norm, is no worse off for venturing to act on his own judgment, except in special circumstances. Those circumstances might include the inverse of those just discussed, serving now as grounds for depriving the citizen of his normal nonpunishability rather than for entitling him to an exceptional nonpunishability. Thus a citizen invoking a particular legal norm as a defense would be relieved of his liability to punishment except, for example, when he was not clearly right in his assessment of the norm, or when adequate remedies other than disobedience were available, or when the interest imperiled by departure from the rule outweighed the interest imperiled by obedience to it. Aside from possibly shifting the burden of proof from the defense to the prosecution, however, the third response as qualified by these exceptions probably differs from the second less in functioning than in formulation.

On the other hand, the third response would differ functionally from the second if the exceptional circumstances were more narrowly defined. Thus a legal system would be further opened to legitimated disobedience if the third response were always given except, for example, when the defendant's motives for departing from the rule disqualified his defense in some respect. The Supreme Court's decision in *Dennis v. United States* suggests an exception of this sort.[12]

A federal statute denied the services of the National Labor Relations Board to any union whose officers failed to file affidavits stating that they were not Communists. Instead of challenging that law directly—for example, by suing to require those services without the affidavits—the union officers filed false ones. When subsequently prosecuted for conspiracy to defraud the United States government, they defended on the ground that the law requiring the affidavits was unconstitutional. But the Court declined to reach the constitutional issues, on the ground that the officers were in no position to raise them:

They were indicted for an alleged conspiracy, cynical and fraudulent, to circumvent the statute. Whatever might be the result where the constitutionality of a statute is challenged by those who of necessity violate its provisions and seek relief in the courts is not relevant here. The indictment here alleged an effort to circumvent the law and not to challenge it—a purported compliance with the statute designed to avoid the courts, not to invoke their jurisdiction.[13]

Breaking the law and invoking its unconstitutionality as a defense is one thing. Evading the law surreptitiously and attempting to defend on the ground of its unconstitutionality when caught is another. The former is recognized as a legitimate avenue of redress for a law-abiding citizen; the latter is not. As a consequence the union officer's convictions were affirmed, even though the Court very likely would have found the statute unconstitutional had it considered the issue.*

This use of bad motive to disqualify the defendant's claim to nonpunishability based on a legitimating norm recalls the commonly adduced moral requirement for civil disobedience that the citizen act openly and stand ready to accept any legal punishment appropriate. The use of motive as a ground for moral approbation, however, is quite different from the use of motive as a ground for depriving a defendant of a legal defense otherwise available. This second use of motive is unusual, but it is plainly one possible ground for denying a defense based on an otherwise applicable legitimating norm.

Another instance of an exception to a standard rule of nonpunishability is the increasingly accepted position with regard to unlawful arrest. As the Supreme Court has held, a citizen cannot be punished for a criminal offense based on his refusal to follow a policeman's unconstitutional order. Still, in many jurisdictions, if the order takes the form of an arrest by one known to be a policeman—an order, that is, to submit to the policeman's custody backed by the threat of physical force—resistance may constitute a criminal offense even if the order proves unconstitutional. The reason, it will be recalled, is the enhanced potential for physical harm in following the usual rule and the availability of substantial, if not complete, legal redress after arrest.

The fourth response to the issue of punishability holds that in no circumstances does it count against the citizen that he ventured to act on his own judgment. If the citizen turns out to have been correct in his assessment of the invoked norm, he cannot be punished. This approach has prevailed in the American system with respect to statutory rules, particularly where the norm is based on the Constitution. Apart from an eccentric

---

* Shortly before, the Court had declared unconstitutional an amended version of the non-Communist affidavit provision that differed in minor and immaterial ways from the original. United States v. Brown, 381 U.S. 437 (1965).

case like *Dennis*, the defendant's motives in violating the rule are immaterial. Equally immaterial are such considerations as how clearly right his assessment was, so long as the court agrees with it; whether adequate alternative remedies were available; or whether the interest imperiled by obedience to the rule outweighed the interest imperiled by departure from it. As we have seen in Chapter Three, a defense of unconstitutionality, if upheld, precludes punishment regardless of any of these considerations.

This last response to the first question provides the maximal openness to legitimation. If the citizen turns out to be right, it counts against him not at all that he undertook to make the judgment in advance of its declaration. If we are to consider a fifth response to punishability that would open the system still further, we must turn to the second question: how far may it count *for* the citizen that, even though he turns out to be wrong, he conscientiously relied on the legitimating norm to justify his action?

For example, a draft protester prosecuted for criminal trespass for occupying a draft office might argue that his act of protest was an exercise of free speech protected by the First Amendment. The courts might well reject the argument on the ground that the physical occupation of the draft office was no more an exercise of free speech than a blow to the face of a political adversary, which also expresses one's opinion. Still the courts might find the defendant nonpunishable if they accepted two principles: first, they would have to recognize a defendant's mistake in interpreting the law governing his behavior as a legal defense, at least in some circumstances; and second, they would have to recognize his mistake in assessing the meaning and applicability of the legitimating norm as a mistake in interpreting the law.

English and American law generally hold that a person's mistake as to the criminality of his conduct constitutes no defense, even if the mistake is bona fide and reasonable. It follows *a fortiori* that it cannot be a defense either to misapprehend the meaning of any legitimating norm. There have been exceptions to these principles, but they provide little basis for extending legitimated disobedience by making the nature of the citizen's mistake of the legitimating norm relevant to his liability to punishment.

One exception is where the defendant's mistake results from his reliance on a judicial holding that is rejected in his case for the first time.[14] In *James v. United States*, for example, an embezzler was convicted of failing to report embezzled income on his tax return. The Supreme Court rejected his defense that embezzled income was not reportable under the law, but it nonetheless reversed his conviction on the ground that one of its earlier decisions supported the defendant's view.[15] Although no one rationale for this conclusion obtained majority support, most of the justices would probably have agreed that the principle that all are presumed to know the law is inappropriate in the unusual case where a court changes the law in midstream. The same conclusion is reached on comparable grounds where a court has changed its interpretation of the Constitution after the defendant acted in reliance on the court's earlier position. In a well-known state case the defendant was convicted of violating a state prohibition law that the state supreme court had previously held unconstitutional. On appeal, the court took occasion to overrule its earlier decision, this time upholding the constitutionality of the statute. But it also reversed the defendant's conviction.[16] Ignorance of the law is no defense, but a citizen is entitled to govern his conduct in accordance with the law as previously interpreted by the state or federal supreme court.* At least in one instance, then—where the defendant's erroneous belief in the unconstitutionality of a statute rests on a judicial declaration to that effect by the highest court within the jurisdiction—his mistake in assessing the legitimating norm renders him nonpunishable.

Another occasion when the defendant's mistake concerning the constitutionality of a statute may constitute an acceptable

---

* Though not by an inferior court, according to State v. Striggles, 202 Iowa 1318, 210 N.W. 137 (1926).

defense occurs when he erroneously concludes that the statute he obeys is constitutional. For example, several public officers were criminally prosecuted for failing to levy a tax they were obliged to levy under one statute but not entitled to levy under a subsequent statute, declared unconstitutional after the defendants' conduct. The state supreme court reversed the conviction: "Until the subsequent statute was declared to be unconstitutional by competent authority, the defendants, under every idea of justice, and under our theory of government, had a right to presume that the lawmaking power had acted within the bounds of the Constitution, and their highest duty was to obey."[17] This exception is of a piece with the one previously discussed: since it is the duty of a citizen to obey the law as it is authoritatively expressed, he may not consistently be punished for relying on a judicial decision (at least of the highest court of the jurisdiction) or a statute to guide his conduct.

A third exception may arise when statutes are interpreted to require that the offender be aware of the unlawfulness of his conduct. The Supreme Court's decision in *United States v. Murdock* is illustrative.[18] Murdock was convicted of the crime of willfully refusing to furnish requested information to the Bureau of Internal Revenue. In making his refusal he had relied on his constitutional privilege not to incriminate himself, fearing state prosecution on the basis of the requested disclosures. At this time the Supreme Court had not decided whether a person in a federal tribunal could constitutionally refuse to answer on account of probable incrimination under state law. Subsequently, however, it held that he could not.[19] In this situation the Court reversed Murdock's conviction, even though he relied on a constitutional privilege he did not have, on the ground that he was entitled to have his good-faith mistake of constitutional law taken into account on the issue of whether he willfully refused to furnish the information.*

---

* *James v. United States*, the embezzled-income case discussed above, is subject to a comparable explanation. Since in that case the defendant had relied on an explicit interpretation of the law later rejected, however, it is strongly arguable that the same result would have followed there even without the requirement of a willful violation. 366 U.S. 213 (1961).

Apart from these exceptions, it is well established that a defendant's mistaken belief in the unconstitutionality of a statute no more constitutes a defense than any other mistake of law. If he turns out to be right, he will not be punished. But if he turns out to be wrong, his reliance on the Constitution is irrelevant. This position is so widely accepted that there have rarely been occasions for courts to assert it explicitly—though, of course, the countless cases in which convictions have been affirmed upon rejection of the defense of unconstitutionality leave no doubt of its authority. Still, the principle has been clearly articulated in a few cases, and it may be helpful to consider some of them.

In *Keegan v. United States* German Bund members were convicted during World War II of counseling draft evasion.[20] The Supreme Court reversed on the ground that the statutory requirement of evasion connoted a fraudulent intent ("stealthily and by guile") to circumvent the law. It held this requirement inconsistent with the actions of the defendants, who, in order to test the constitutionality of the draft law's discrimination against Bund members in employment rights, urged their supporters to register for the draft but not to accept service. Chief Justice Stone dissented on the basis of a different reading of "evasion," which he took to mean resisting or avoiding the law, and hence was in a position to make the standard riposte to a defendant seeking a test of a statute's constitutionality:

Plainly one who would assail the validity of a statute in a test case can do so only by violating its provisions, here by knowingly counseling another to evade registration or service in the armed forces. One who thus evaded or counseled evasion of military service could not defend on the ground that he violated the act in order to test its constitutionality. He nevertheless does the act which the statute prohibits and nonetheless intended to do it even though his purpose was to establish that the statutory prohibition is unconstitutional. There is no freedom to conspire to violate a statute with impunity merely because its constitutionality is doubted. The prohibition of the statute is infringed by the intended act in any case, and the law imposes its sanctions unless the doubt proves to be well founded.[21]

The same reply was made to Susan B. Anthony when she defended against an illegal voting charge on the ground that she believed the state law denying the vote to women to be in violation of the Fourteenth Amendment.[22] Once the constitutional issue was decided against her, no defense remained:

Miss Anthony knew that she was a woman, and that the constitution of this state prohibits her from voting. The necessary effect of her act was to violate it.... She undertook to settle a principle in her own person. She takes the risk, and she can not escape the consequences. ... No system of criminal jurisprudence can be sustained upon any other principle.[23]

When a defendant invokes a constitutional defense, then, the American legal system offers no greater compromise with the law-and-order model of a citizen's obligation than to hold him immune to punishment if he turns out to be right. If he turns out to be wrong, he is punishable. So much is to be expected in a system working on the general premise that mistake of law is no defense. The exceptions—where the defendant acted in reliance on a holding of the highest court, which later changed the law, or on the validity of a statute not yet invalidated by the highest court—are essentially consistent with the fundamental premise that a citizen's duty is to obey the law as it is expressed by the legal institutions of the state.

The American legal system's response to a defendant's mistake concerning the lesser-evil defense is the same. Whether the evils of disobeying a criminal prohibition are less than the evils of complying with it in a given case is a matter of law—unformed law, but law nonetheless.[24] To the extent that the lesser-evil defense is offered to a defendant, it is offered on the same terms as a constitutional defense. If the defendant turns out to be right on the law—in this case, that is, if the court agrees with his assessment of the balance of evils—he is immune from punishment, but not otherwise. Our own legal system, therefore, committed to the premise that mistake of law cannot constitute a defense, in general rejects the further opening of the system to legitimated disobedience that would be obtained by precluding punishment when a citizen mistakes the meaning of a legitimating norm. But what are the possibilities for legitimated disobedience in a system less committed to rejecting the mistake-of-law defense?

In 1952 the supreme court of West Germany, in response to long-standing academic criticism, overturned its past rulings and held that a mistake by the defendant about the criminality of his conduct, whether based on ignorance, on a mistaken interpretation of the statutory prohibition, or on a mistaken interpretation of justificatory privileges, could constitute a legal defense.[25] The court reasoned that blameworthiness is a necessary condition for guilt; hence where mistake of law is inconsistent with moral blameworthiness, guilt should not be attached. Moral blameworthiness does not exist, the court found, if the defendant was not aware that his conduct was unlawful or wrongful, and if a proper application of his moral sensitivities would not have led him to such an awareness:

> As a free and moral agent and as a participant in the legal community, the individual is bound at all times to conform his behavior to law and to avoid doing the wrong thing. He does not fulfill this duty merely by avoiding that which seems to him clearly to be the wrong thing; rather he must attempt to determine whether that which he plans to do is compatible with the legal imperatives of the system. He must resolve his doubts by reflection or investigation. This requires that he apply his moral sensibility. . . . If despite the moral sensitivity that can fairly be demanded of him, the individual does not perceive the wrongfulness of his contemplated action, then his mistake is to be viewed as ineluctable; the act would be, for him, unavoidable. In a case of this sort, the individual cannot be blamed for his conduct.[26]

The conscientious objector—one who is aware of the criminality of his conduct but rejects the moral judgment of the legislature—was excluded from the reach of this defense: "The culpability of the morally committed violator consists in his knowing that he substitutes his own system of values for that of the legal community."[27] But what of the objector who bases his claim on a legitimating norm, such as the lesser-evil principle or the constitution? The West German court has addressed both situations.

A defense based on a mistaken lesser-evil principle was dealt with in a case that shortly followed the court's mistake-of-law decision.[28] A physician charged with murder for participating in selecting sickly, unproductive persons for execution under the Nazi regime argued that his participation had enabled him to reduce the number of lives taken by striking names from the execution list. The court concluded that the physician might have a defense, not because he chose the lesser evil in accordance with the law—the court found that the necessity principle did not extend to taking innocent lives—but because the existence of a defense in this circumstance was controversial. Thus, in accordance with the recently reformulated mistake-of-law doctrine, the defendant could be found to have acted without blame, since he believed his conduct was right. This application of the mistake-of-law defense to the lesser-evil defense, though contrary to American law, is consistent with the apparent import of several Continental codes. The Swiss code, for example, authorizes the court to absolve from punishment a defendant who "commits the act believing he has legal justification for it";[29] and the Hungarian code precludes the punishment of a person who erroneously assumes that his criminal act is not dangerous to society and has "well-founded reasons" for making this assumption.[30]

A defense based on a conscientious but mistaken constitutional interpretation was presented in a 1968 case.[31] Owing to his religious beliefs, the defendant, a Jehovah's Witness, refused to permit a blood transfusion to be given his infant child, even though he was advised by the hospital physician that the child would soon die without it. The physician then notified the local judge of the guardianship court, who came to the hospital and instructed the defendant that his refusal to grant permission constituted a violation of a section of the Penal Code making it a crime to fail to provide aid to an endangered person. When the defendant persisted in his refusal, the judge appointed the physician temporary guardian of the child and the transfusion was successfully carried out. Subsequently the father was prosecuted under the section of the Penal Code the judge had informed him of.

Throughout the criminal proceedings the defendant based his defense on a clause of the West German constitution protecting religious freedom. The lower court rejected his constitutional claim and convicted him on the ground that he was merely a conscientious objector and hence not entitled to the mistake-of-law defense. The appellate court also rejected his constitutional claim on the merits, but it reversed his conviction on the ground that he was entitled to the mistake-of-law defense. Even though the defendant had been instructed by the local judge on his duty under the law, the court found that his defense relied on a mistaken interpretation of relevant legal norm—the constitution—and not simply on a moral or political norm. It apparently did not matter that he justified his refusal to allow the transfusion in terms of his religious convictions rather than in terms of the constitution, because the moral claim he asserted was itself arguably embodied in the religious-freedom clause of the constitution. Since there had been no previous cases clearly resolving the constitutional issue against him, the court concluded that the defendant had made a personally unavoidable mistake of law inconsistent with blameworthiness and hence inconsistent with guilt.

These developments in West German law clearly move in the direction of enlarging the autonomy of the citizen under the law. By withdrawing the threat of punishment even if the citizen misjudges the law, so long as he acts without blame, and by doing so even when he misjudges the import of legal defenses based on the lesser-evil principle and the constitution, the system has moved significantly away from the traditional law-and-order view of a citizen's obligations, farther indeed than our own. Why should this have happened in West Germany in the 1950's? The Nazi experience may have had much to do with it. A major legal and social issue of the post-Nazi period was how to deal with the many officials and private persons who committed acts that were lawful, even justifiable under Nazi law, but were serious crimes under the law of postwar Germany.[32] If the defendants in these cases were to be denied their defenses under the Nazi positive law prevailing when they acted, it was necessary not only to adduce a superior legal norm that deprived the relevant Nazi law of its authority, but also to conclude that the defendants, at least in these extreme circumstances, were obliged as citizens—not merely permitted—to undertake to act on their own judgment of the force of these norms. In taking this course the German courts moved a good distance from the law-and-order model of a citizen's obligations. Doing what one is told was not only rejected as the model of right citizen behavior; it could serve as the foundation of criminal liability.

But if this view stood it could not be restricted to the Nazi cases. These cases forced the courts to focus on the predicament of the citizen before the law, the whole law, not just its positive enactments; and in so doing to enlarge the responsibility of the individual to embrace, at least to some degree, the task of making his own judgments on the whole force of the law. This had to have consequences beyond the Nazi cases. The change in the law with respect to errors of law and its application to mistaken lesser-evil and constitutional judgments may be seen as part of those consequences.

In considering the possibilities of a comparable development in American law, we must note an important difference between German and American law in the standard governing when mistake of any kind is a defense. We have, of course, so far in this discussion been assuming a defense arising from a mistake as to a governing norm that requires the mistake to meet a certain standard; that is, not every such mistake is a defense, but only those of a certain kind. A general way to express that standard is in terms of the distinction between reasonable and negligent mistake. The German standard of negligence as a basis for criminal liability generally includes the capacities of the defendant to have known better if he had tried. However, the typical American standard of negligence excludes this subjective element and asks only whether the mistake would be reasonable in the person of normal capacities. Therefore, any expansion of legitimated disobedience in this country through the recognition of the defense of mistake of law* would no doubt rest on the generally prevailing standard of negligence, so that the relevant question would become whether the defendant's judgment on the law, even though incorrect, was consistent with the judgment "a law-abiding and prudent person" would make.[33]

The sixth judicial response to punishability, and the final one we shall consider, would abandon any qualification concerning the character of the defendant's argument to the norm apart from an elemental colorability, which we have posited as a necessary condition for any instance of legitimated disobedience. Instead it would rest on the defendant's motives in departing from the rule, either entirely or in conjunction with other conditions not bearing on the legal weight of his argument.

In a lesser-evil defense, for example, the defendant's violation of a criminal statute would be justified by his conscientious belief that he was choosing the lesser of two evils. That the law, as interpreted by the court, strikes the balance differently, or that the balance struck by the defendant was unreasonable, would not work against him. He would not be punished so long as he acted conscientiously.

In a constitutional defense, likewise, the defendant's actual belief that the constitution justified his conduct would suffice to make it so. In *Murdock*, the self-incrimination case discussed

* For example, Professor Dworkin has argued that even if the Supreme Court eventually rejects the position of the draft-law resisters, it should "acquit" those convicted prior to its decision on the ground that until it spoke the validity of the law was doubtful and it is unfair to punish men for disobeying a doubtful law. "On Not Prosecuting Civil Disobedience," *New York Review of Books*, June 6, 1968, pp. 14, 20.

above, the statute Murdock was accused of violating required that the offender be aware of the unlawfulness of his conduct. This approach, extended to cover all crimes, no matter how they were otherwise defined, would make a defendant's belief in the rightness of his constitutional claim determinative of his nonpunishability. Plainly it would open a system to legitimated disobedience considerably further than the five judicial responses previously considered.

A variation of this approach has been advanced by some in the recently revived debates over civil disobedience in the 1960's. Harvey Wheeler, for example, has attempted to develop a case for making constitutionally protected civil disobedience available to anyone who violates a criminal statute, no matter how clearly and recently the courts had rejected the constitutional defense claimed by the defendant, so long as certain conditions exist: that the defendant have committed no violence; that he have evidenced an intent to make a constitutional challenge to a specific law or government action; and that there be a direct relationship between the defendant's conduct and the law or action objected to. Wheeler argues that a defendant in these circumstances would be acting no less consistently with the constitutional ethic than one whose constitutional claim was validated by the courts; and even if his claim had no foundation under the courts' holdings, he could still appeal to the nation's "true" or "emergent" Constitution of the future rather than to the "transitory, fallible Constitution of the present." The justification for his proposal is the desirability of "reactivating the people—the political order as a whole—as participants in elucidating the most fundamental principles of the emergent Constitution."[34]

Our purpose in the foregoing account was principally to illustrate some of the possibilities of engineering a greater or lesser degree of openness to legitimated disobedience into the structure of a legal system. We will shortly return to some of these possibilities in discussing the values and risks of the legitimation of rule departures. But first we must consider briefly the problem of deliberately engineering different degrees of openness to legitimated interposition within a legal system.

Legitimated Interposition

It is not hard to see how the incidence of legitimated interposition might be reduced. It might be done in precisely the ways Professor Davis and other critics of unchecked and assumed discretion have been urging—essentially by engineering visibility and accountability into the exercise of discretion through the means we discussed earlier. On the other hand, it is difficult to see what deliberate modifications one could make in the structure of a legal system to create a greater openness to legitimated interposition. This follows for obvious reasons. A system's openness to legitimated disobedience is determined largely, though not entirely, by explicitly recognized legal norms and by explicit legal decisions defining the conditions of punishability. These are readily amenable to manipulation. But interposition, as an evolved institutional accommodation to unpredictable stresses within the system, turns so much on unformulated norms and informal relationships that it is much less amenable to manipulation. Who could possibly have planned, for example, the institution of the jury as we know it today or the institution of plea-bargaining?

To be sure, one might increase the occasions where an official is accorded final authority to act on his own judgment without recourse against the official himself or against the legal effectiveness of his acts. Achieving this result would entail casting rules of competence in nonconstitutive forms, so that their breach would not affect the legal effectiveness of an official's actions, and at the same time declining to vest authority in the official in the form of delegated discretion. But, it must be noted, this would not necessarily ensure the expansion of legitimated interposition. It might just as readily increase the unrestrained abuse of power, for interpositional justification depends on accommodating role support from officials in other roles in what we called an ecology of roles, and this response is essentially unplannable.

The Values and Risks of Legitimation

We turn now to another question that is equally essential in considering legitimation as a social strategy. Why would one want to build a greater openness to legitimated rule departures into a legal system? What is to be lost and what is to be gained by doing so? These questions require a rather more direct treatment than the incidental discussions so far presented. Let us start with the risks, for in our effort to identify legitimation as a coherent legal conception and as part of the reality of legal arrangements, we may seem to have been partisan proponents of its extended use.

Though "rule of law" and "law and order" have indeed become shibboleths in much current political discourse, they also encapsulate a fair estimation of the risks of rule departures by citizens and officials, an estimation that a society ignores at its peril, as the very history of law and politics has shown. After all, subjugation of royal rule to the rule of law was the signal achievement of English constitutional law, while the further development of the principle of the rule of law offered the citizen protection against the many lesser rulers exercising state power. A commitment to government by rules enforceable through courts open to all citizens sheltered the citizen from the arbitrary power of ministers and lesser bureaucrats as well as from the tyranny of kings. The official's obligation to serve the legal order was matched by a corollary obligation of the citizen. So that he might be protected against the self-determined and therefore the often self-interested judgments of others, officials and citizens alike, the citizen yielded the freedom to act on his own when the law through its neutral processes had made a preemptive judgment. All this represented no mere mindless worship of the virtues of law and order for their own sake but a commitment to those "wise restraints which set men free." Freedom from the willful impositions of fellow citizens and officials might constitute a relatively restricted sense of freedom as a political ideal. Nevertheless, it was that sense of freedom that lay at the heart of the classic liberal tradition; and any denial of the obligations of citizens and officials that made that freedom possible had the most powerful presumption against it.

The force of that presumption, it must be emphasized, is not just a matter of history; it has acute contemporary relevance. Experience with even the delegated discretion of administrative officials seems to have blunted much of the enthusiasm of the 1930's and 1940's for discretionary government. Perceived then as a sensitive and flexible instrument for administering the extended legal regulation demanded by social and technological change, discretionary government now seems to many an "Alice-in-Wonderland of unchanneled, unreviewable, untrammeled discretion" wherein "the police, prosecutors, and petty bureaucrats in our local and national governments are free to run loose."[35] Dicey, as observed earlier, rejected all but the most narrow discretion because of the evils of arbitrariness, unfairness, and abuse of authority inherent in the exercise of government authority unrestrained by rules of law. Today few are inclined to dismiss the fear of these evils as the paranoia of conservatives; instead it is seen in large measure as justified by the unhappy condition of modern government. Moreover, the fear of arbitrariness and unfairness is seen as warranted no less when the exercise of discretion is ameliorative rather than detrimental.[36] And even though the elimination of delegated discretion has appealed to few as a likely answer to its attendant problems, a serious movement for reform has developed aimed at curbing the excesses of discretion by confining it, structuring controls on its exercise, and developing a system of checks against its abuses;[37] or by instituting an invigorated judicial review, establishing more specific legislative standards, or invoking a rejuvenated doctrine of illegally delegated authority.[38]

If the problem of the use and misuse of delegated discretion is so vexing, what shall we say of deviational discretion as a means of administering government? The exercise of delegated discretion, after all, is at least acknowledged and visible. Action is taken within a context of legal restraints even when those restraints, lacking the rigor of rules in the narrow sense, consist of statements of purposes and policies, specifications of what may or may not count as a relevant consideration, procedural constraints controlling how judgments must be reached, or the judicial review of clearly erroneous judgments ("abuse of discretion"). None of these confining and disciplining influences touch actions that by definition entail decisions to exceed precisely those kinds of restraints and that, when legitimated as instances of interposition, are insulated from effective review. In consequence, the dangers of excessive delegated discretion, so well documented in recent literature, are magnified many times in the case of deviational discretion.

The root problem is that deviational discretion gives no occasion for reform. Where the traditional controls of delegated discretion prove inadequate, as in many areas of modern government, it is possible to consider better controls, such as those just summarized. But deviational discretion is impervious to control; indeed, it is essentially an escape from controls. It can only be disciplined by converting it into a species of delegated discretion. Indeed, when Professor Davis and others argue for imposing controls on the exercise of discretionary power by police and prosecutors, they are in our terms urging the conversion of powers of deviational discretion into powers of delegated discretion.[39]

As the danger of increasing increments of legitimated interposition in a legal system is the increase in the unrestrained power of rulers and lesser bureaucrats, so the danger of increasing increments of legitimated disobedience is the weakening of the legal order from the citizen's side. No legal system other than one built solely on force can function without general acceptance among its citizens of the obligation to comply with the rules. But as the circumstances widen in which the citizen may deem his obligation to comply overcome on his own estimate of the force of some potentially legitimating norm, the functioning of that sense of obligation is put in jeopardy.

The dangers of legitimated disobedience were pointedly expressed by Justice Frankfurter when, in rejecting the right of an enjoined person to judge the validity of a court order, he wrote: "No one, no matter how exalted his public office, or how righteous his private motive, can be judge in his own case. That is what courts are for.... If one man can be allowed to determine for himself what is law, every man can. That means first chaos, then tyranny."[40] There is unmistakable hyperbole in these invocations of chaos and tyranny, but the Justice did not miss in identifying the kind of peril that may follow when citizens are permitted to take the law into their own hands. Indeed, some have speculated, plausibly enough, that the Supreme Court contributed to the wave of disobedience in the 1960's through its vindication of statutory law violations by members of the civil rights movement in the 1950's. Prof. Martin Shapiro has observed that the social consequence of the Segregation Cases was

an extended period in which a whole generation of liberal youths were taught (by headlines in the papers, and demonstrations in the streets) that some laws were legal, that some were not, and that it was moral, good and constitutional to break some of the laws of some of the states.... We cannot turn the canons of moral outrage against one set of laws and expect the untutored to make the crucial but sophisticated distinction between disobeying "bad," in the sense of unconstitutional, laws, and "bad" period laws.... Thus it might well be argued that the principal impact of the Warren court has been to reduce the quantum of fidelity to law present in our society.[41]

This is to speak only of the hazards to "fidelity to law" of so much legitimated disobedience as our system now embraces. Those hazards augment substantially in systems with even greater latitude for legitimation than our own. For a central issue in ruling through obligations is the degree to which a citizen owes it to the law to comply with a peremptory rule. In a law-and-order model he owes it to the law to comply without qualification. In our own system, at least with respect to statutory rules, he owes it to the law to comply subject to a liberty to gamble on his being right about the invalidity of a rule. In a system where he owes it to the law only not to make unreasonable misjudgments of the invalidity of the rule or the justification of his action, the surcharge exacted by his obligation to comply is substantially reduced. In a system where he owes it to the law only to make conscientious claims with respect to these issues, the surcharge soon approaches zero. In sum, the more extensive the grounds for legitimated autonomous judgment, the greater the threat to the effectiveness of ruling through obligation. Moreover, the most extensive modes of enlarging the grounds for legitimated disobedience create difficulties of another kind for governing through peremptory rules: since they entail the enlargement of defenses against punishment, they also weaken the effectiveness of ruling through threat.

Consider, for example, the expansion of grounds for legitimated disobedience that would result if it were a defense that the lawbreaker reasonably misjudged the applicability of either a constitutional norm or the lesser-evil norm. From one point of view the argument for rejecting the conventional principle that mistake of law is no defense, as such an expansion in effect requires, seems more persuasive when the mistake is one of constitutional law. In conventional mistake-of-law cases the injustice of absolute liability is counteracted, at least in the more serious crimes, by the patent wrongfulness of the conduct, which should serve to dissuade a potential wrongdoer even if he is unaware of the criminal prohibition in question. But where the defendant defends his departure from the rule by appeal to the Constitution (and we are assuming a reasonably based appeal), he is acting consistently with the proper role of the citizen in resisting unconstitutional encroachment. In the event that the Supreme Court rejects his claim (perhaps by a divided vote), to punish him is to impose punishment in the total absence of any fault in his conduct as a citizen.

From another point of view the argument for accepting reasonable mistake as a defense is less persuasive where the mistake pertains to a constitutional issue. Given the indeterminacy of many provisions of the Constitution and the rate at which the Supreme Court has discovered new meanings in them, such a defense would open a large, if uncertain, ground for escape from liability. Moreover, applying the requirement of reasonableness would be even less manageable for constitutional defenses than for conventional defenses. Was it reasonable for Susan B. Anthony to invoke the equal protection clause in 1873 against a New York statute forbidding women to vote?[42] For a Connecticut doctor to assert a constitutional right to give birth control advice?[43] Would it be reasonable for students participating in a sit-in at a local draft board to claim that their conduct was protected by the First Amendment? Judgments of what constituted a reasonable constitutional defense would be hardly less perplexing and uncertain than judgments of what constitutes a valid constitutional defense. One might think that at least where the Supreme Court has recently denied a claim, there would be no reasonable basis for making it again, as in the case of the Southern resistance to the Segregation Cases.[44] But the Court's reversal in the 1940's of its position on the compulsory flag salute within a period of three years suggests that even this test would be unworkable.[45] It cannot be said that the Supreme Court's pattern of adjudication over the years, especially recent years, has denied litigants a fair hope of reversal.

Still more potentially damaging to the effectiveness of ruling through obligation, and through threat as well, is an expansion of grounds for legitimated disobedience that would look to the lawbreaker's motive as a basis for a defense. Such a defense would tend to reduce the citizen's legal obligation to the moral obligation felt by one who maintains the Athanasian attitude.[46] To be sure, even this defense would require that the defendant's legal argument be at least colorable. But if the force of the obligation to comply were confined to the citizen's subjective perceptions, very little would remain of the surcharge exacted by legal obligation. A principle requiring only that the citizen act in good faith would exert scarcely any pressure at all to comply with a peremptory rule.

The risks, then, of extending the possibilities for legitimating rule departures are serious indeed. They threaten both our freedom from the tyranny of office and our orderly and consistent mode of conducting social affairs. They are the very risks that argue against any policy that imposes an anarchic principle for the behavior of officials and citizens. We shall pursue that trail no further. Because legitimation as a social strategy, like any social strategy, possesses values as well as risks, we turn now to assessing some of the principal values of the legitimation of rule departures—values that, despite the risks, may possibly prove compelling.

Consider legitimated interposition first. Its most obvious advantage is that it can increase a legal system's flexibility and responsiveness. We have already observed in some detail how strict adherence to the rules precludes sensitive adaptation to the infinite ingenuity of events. Government by rule is government in gross—justice wholesale, as it were. Sometimes rule makers have an insufficient grasp of the intricacies of the activity to be regulated, or of precisely how to compromise among conflicting policies, or even of what the relevant policies are, to dispense with the ad hoc judgment of officials. Often the wisest rule making takes the form of ongoing interactions between the lawmakers making rules and the officials making judgments. It is wisdom as old as Aristotle that we can rarely, if ever, dispense with the need for mediation between the generality of the rule and the palpable human values of the particular case. And beyond these considerations, the accommodation among groups and forces in contention in a dynamic, open society that generates any particular set of rules is inevitably temporary. Even when one knows what one wants to achieve, and how to achieve it, it may not be possible politically to obtain consensus on rules. Ends and means are in a constant state of flux and reexamination, so that the formal processes of rule changing, even when they work, may work too slowly to make transitions with a minimum of pain and disruption.

Legitimated interposition responds to the inadequacies of strict rule-ordering in two ways. First, it provides a mechanism for preserving justice in special cases, thus ameliorating the effects of the bureaucratic mentality that follows the rules come what may. Second, it creates a certain looseness in the joints of the legal system that allows for a salutary adaptation to social conflict and change by legal officials in the process of enforcing the law. Legitimated interposition thus acts to buffer the shock of social conflict and change on the formal legal structures.

As we acknowledged earlier, there are other strategies for achieving these ends—responsive mechanisms for legal change, imaginative formulations of exceptions to legal rules, and most important, the deliberate use of delegated discretion. But the advantages of legitimated interposition remain, and it is instructive to consider them briefly against the background of the other strategies.

To begin with, these other strategies are restricted in ways that legitimated interposition is not. Formal legal change is inevitably sluggish, particularly in a democratic society; it has to lag behind need, since it must await the marshaling of a consensus and the stirring of bureaucratic mechanisms. Built-in exceptions to rules have the obvious limitation Professor Wigmore pointed out long ago: "Not even the general exceptions that the law itself may concede will enable the judge to get down to the justice of the particular case, in extreme instances."[47] Delegated discretion inevitably comes wrapped in constraints of some kind, loose though they may be, and breaking even these constraints may at times be necessary to serve larger ends. Generally, delegated discretion may fail to ease the tension between constraints and ends where that tension is generated by the more radical challenges of social and political forces.

Further, it is not always obvious at what points in the system delegated discretion should be granted, or within what constraints and in what terms it should be articulated. In the normal course of events it is primarily after experience with the administration of rules in certain areas that the desirable scope of discretion comes to be perceived clearly enough to justify explicit incorporation. Legitimated interposition has at least the virtue of serving as an interim measure. No legislative body has to decide to grant a dispensing power to an official. The liberty to depart from the rules tends to evolve along with the need; it does not have to be deliberately engineered. Then, with the passage of time, and the accumulation of experience, legitimated interposition may be converted into delegated discretion, as we have seen in the growing acceptance of police and prosecutorial nonenforcement powers. The very recent emergence of prosecutorial plea-bargaining from a rather clear instance of legitimated interposition to one of delegated discretion is a dramatic example. In sum, the history of legitimated interposition reveals that it performs a genuine adaptive function during the twilight period before formal legal rules are changed.

Next, as suggested before, interposition can in some instances actually confine the scope and extent of departures from mandatory rules within narrower bounds than delegated discretion. Interposition, because it is less visible and not officially approved, tends to work interstitially and narrowly; there is a higher surcharge on acting outside the rules than on acting at one's own discretion with the rules as a guide. This is the point made by Kalven and Zeisel in a passage quoted earlier: "Perhaps one reason why the jury exercises its very real power so sparingly is because it is officially told that it has none."[48] It is also the point made by Stephens nearly a century ago when he argued that an explicitly recognized defense of necessity (which he conceded a judge would allow in any event) would run the risk of multiplying the occasions on which people would venture to depart from a rule: "There is no fear that people will be ready to obey the ordinary law. There is great fear that they would be too ready to avail themselves of exceptions which they might suppose to apply to their circumstances."⁴⁹

Finally, there are times in the administration of the law when preserving appearances performs a socially useful function. The strategy of legitimated interposition allows the appearance of absolute adherence to the law to be maintained, while at the same time providing in reality for some degree of accommodation. Consider the example of lawmaking by the courts. For a judicial system to be effective, it must be accepted by the parties who submit their disputes to it. To state boldly that cases are determined by what the judge deems desirable rather than by the strict application of the law could hinder the public's acceptance of the judicial resolution of controversy. As K. G. Wurzel observed:

> A European judge is no Oriental sage who is to point out the right course to the parties by virtue of his own higher wisdom. The only authority on which everybody relies, when they assemble together, the injured party and the wrongdoer as well as the judge, is exclusively and solely the will of the State, embodied in the laws that have been broken. This being so, the judge would hardly supply the wants of the parties if he allowed any doubt to arise but what these commands of the State are really sufficient to settle every contention.⁵⁰

The criticism that this state of affairs amounts to calculated hypocrisy in the legal system has some truth in it, of course, but not the whole truth.⁵¹ Some tension between what is said and what is done in the legal system as elsewhere may be benign and useful. There is an element of theater in the law, but this is not to say that it is all farce.*

Turning now to legitimated disobedience by citizens, we may identify several distinct but related values of its incorporation into legal systems. First, a judicious allowance for legitimated

---

* Similarly, the objective of securing obedience to the rules of the criminal law would tend to be disserved by proclaiming explicitly that law enforcement officials may choose not to enforce the rules at their discretion. The strategy of legitimated interposition makes it possible to adapt the criminal law to individual needs while maintaining a solid front against disobedience.

disobedience, ironically enough, tends to reinforce a citizen's acceptance of legal obligations by reducing tensions between the law's formal demands and the broader moral sensibility that leads a citizen to respect the law in the first place. This is particularly true where the legitimating norms derive sustenance from the moral preconceptions of the community, as is the case with many constitutional defenses and with the lesser-evil defense generally.

Second, legitimated disobedience tends to expand individual freedom, a virtue in itself. The fundamental utility of government by law consists in ensuring one's freedom from being subjected to the arbitrary action of others, citizens and officials alike. The fundamental utility of legitimated disobedience in a legal system consists in extending another kind of freedom: namely, the freedom to act according to one's judgment when the reasons for doing so seem so great that they outweigh an acknowledged legal obligation to act otherwise.

Third, legitimated disobedience furthers the democratic commitment to citizen participation in government. There is no *a priori* reason why that participation must end with the political processes that precede the promulgation of laws. Certainly there is potential for the citizen to make a substantial contribution to the adaptability, the justness, and the acceptability of legal institutions, as well as of the laws themselves, to the extent that he may legitimately challenge their entitlement to control as new situations arise, participate actively in shaping their contours, invoke anterior commitments of the community from which they may have strayed, and venture to act on his own judgment of ultimate ends so that new conceptions of justice may have their day in court—in short, to the extent that society's conception of citizen participation in the political process is enlarged to embrace the administration of the laws as well as their formulation.

Plainly, then, a legal system that makes allowances for legitimated disobedience captures some of the moral force of civil disobedience. But there are significant differences between the two. Whereas civil disobedience converts the citizen into a free moral agent and makes his conscience king, legitimated disobedience requires him to justify departing from the peremptory rules of the law within the law itself, taken to include the variety of legitimating norms the legal system makes available.[52] Of course, to the extent that the legitimating norms depend on judgments of personal and political morality, and to the extent that officials in interpreting these norms assume a wide-ranging authority to make judgments of personal and political morality, legitimated disobedience tends to overlap with civil disobedience. To the extent that the legitimating norms and their interpretation reflect legal constraints on the applicability of personal and political moral judgments, however, it does not.

The difference between legitimated disobedience and civil disobedience has deep moral significance. Legitimated disobedience implies the acceptance of the grip of the law, since it requires an appeal to a standard of justification the law itself has made available; the constraining force of the peremptory rule being disobeyed is recognized precisely through an appeal to the system that gave the rule its force in the first place. Thus whereas civil disobedience gives conscience free rein, legitimated disobedience restricts its exercise, both by demanding that the citizen present not only reasons for his actions but reasons of the strongest sort, and by imposing constraints on those reasons themselves. Legitimated disobedience implies autonomy, then, but autonomy within limits. One might say that it requires a different sort of conscience than civil disobedience—a conscience in which the legal order constitutes not only part of the subject matter of a judgment but part of the context of evaluation in which the judgment is made.

We may conclude by observing that legitimated rule departures, whether by a citizen or by an official, are not in irreconcilable conflict with the principle of legal ordering but present the classic challenge of establishing appropriate restraints to preserve the integrity of a legal system while at the same time maintaining a fitting sensitivity to the individual judgment of those the system is designed to serve. In establishing such restraints there is good reason to be wary of granting, through the formation of recourse roles, the authority to depart from mandatory rules, lest that authority be abused. At the same time there is a twofold argument favoring the careful consideration of those features of legal systems that tend to preserve or extend recourse roles.

The first part of the argument is that no human system can ever fully insure itself against the subversion of its ends by those working within it. All systems depend on a minimum of good will and good sense, no matter how complex, how checked, how guaranteed. Lacking these, any system, whether or not it incorporates recourse roles, may end in disaster.

The second part of the argument is that all grants of freedom, including grants of freedom of speech and freedom of assembly, incur risks. It is no less reasonable for society to take the risks involved in a hedged and restricted freedom to depart from mandatory rules than to take the risks involved in any other freedom. In any event, the choice we face in engineering legal systems is not solely between a system that denies any possibility of legally justifiable rule departures and one that incorporates such possibilities without limit. It is rather whether to accept or to ignore the challenge to create legal systems that under given historical circumstances may attain the most salutary mix of individual autonomy and supervening law. For this last achievement, it goes without saying, no manual exists.

CHAPTER FIVE

Legitimation and the Idea
of a Legal System

THAT A LEGAL system may sometimes justify departures from its own mandatory rules, that persons in the roles of citizens and officials may sometimes fairly claim that they were legally justified, given their assessment of the merits in the case, to undertake departing from a mandatory rule, has been our constant theme. To support it we tried to show how certain legal events and processes, such as case testing, jury acquittals, and prosecutorial discretion, along with judicial behavior like the employment of legal fictions, constitute legal means for legitimating genuine departures from mandatory rules. Yet, because the concept of a legitimated rule departure requires for its intelligibility a suitable concept of a legal system, we must now at the end shift focus from the citizen's or official's in-system justifications of his rule departures to those general features of legal systems that make possible, and lead to, such justifications. Once the implications of legitimation for the concept of a legal system and for the meaning of legal obligation have been considered, the notion of a legitimated rule departure may seem less like a foreign body to be removed as quickly as possible from the eye of jurisprudence.

Principles of Acceptance in Legal Systems

If some legal systems have mechanisms for legitimating rule departures, an adequate concept of a legal system must not only acknowledge the existence of mandatory rules but also recognize the existence of principles to guide the individual in obeying those rules. That is, a legal system must be understood to determine not only what the individual's obligations are but how those obligations are to be taken. The latter function is served in a legal system by what we shall call for convenience principles of acceptance.

That a citizen may be entitled to disobey a statutory rule or the order of an officer in the light of a constitutional provision is one principle of acceptance in the American legal system. That a jury is entitled to acquit despite the court's instructions on the law is another, inferred in part from the finality of such acquittals and the nonaccountability of juries that render them. But in some legal system other than our own a principle forbidding a citizen to disobey a statutory rule or the order of an officer despite the justification afforded that citizen by the constitution would also be a principle of acceptance. So also would be a principle depriving a jury of the liberty to acquit counter to a court's instructions.

Principles of acceptance may be seen both as elements of a legal system and as factors in the deliberations of individuals in their roles as citizens and officials. As elements of a legal system, principles of acceptance establish the conditions under which individuals in their roles must obey or may depart from the mandatory rules of the system; and they are incorporated in all the complex ways we have discussed in considering legitimated interposition and legitimated disobedience in chapters Two and Three. As factors in the deliberations of individuals, principles of acceptance are the relevant propositions of appropriateness that enable a citizen or official to determine whether he is at liberty, given his assessment of the merits of his case, to depart from a mandatory rule. Because principles of acceptance are the ultimate criteria determining how peremptory rules and rules of competence are to be applied, and because they are typically inferred from the working of the system rather than explicitly formulated, we call them principles rather than rules. Because they provide how obligations are to be accepted by receivers of the law, we call them principles of "acceptance."

Although mandatory rules do purport to tell a receiver of the law what he must and must not do, they cannot, owing to certain pervasive features of legal systems, tell him all he needs to know in order to undertake appropriate action as a citizen or official. All legal systems raise at least a potential question of the legal validity of mandatory rules. Most legal systems engender recurrent and major tensions between the prescribed ends of legally defined roles and the rules laid down in advance for the achievement of those ends.* Also, mandatory rules will not suffice to answer questions raised in consequence of the delegated or deviational enforcement discretion incorporated into the law as a response to means-ends tensions. To the degree that legal systems raise issues of legal validity requiring rules and procedures of some complexity to settle, to the degree that they generate tensions between prescribed means and prescribed ends, and to the degree that they institute discretion as a response to those tensions, we call them developed legal systems. Clearly, the more developed the systems, the more acute will be the need to articulate principles of acceptance to guide the conduct of citizens and officials under the rules.

Legal Validity

For the receiver of the law, legal validity raises at least two issues. Before he can be in any position to conclude that he has an obligation to obey a rule, he must first have ascertained that the rule maker is indeed authorized to make the rule. Is the receiver of the law to accept as valid the rules made by anyone claiming to be the true prince, so long as he looks like the true prince? Such a question can always be raised in a legal system. An answer, either way, would be a principle of acceptance. A

---

* Where the ends of the role are varied and no adequate principle for priorities is established, there too, of course, legal systems may create tensions that role agents must resolve. A similar situation holds also for roles that prescribe a plurality of means. We have restricted discussion here to means-ends tensions for purposes of simplicity and because the tension that underlies most of the instances of rule departures we have professed to discover in our legal system is between means and ends.

principle of acceptance must exist to tell people how to proceed.

Second, the receiver of the law must have ascertained that the rule itself satisfies whatever criteria the system has established for validity. Principles of acceptance must tell him what to do when he is uncertain of the rule's validity. To insist that the citizen or official need only know that he is obliged to obey all mandatory rules emanating from rule makers can mean only that the citizen or official must accept as valid all rules presented under color of authority. The law-and-order model has been read into the legal system and, in effect, an appropriate principle of acceptance postulated. Further, to defend the sufficiency of mandatory rules to guide conduct on the ground that they are not mandatory unless they are valid leaves the citizen or official uninformed about the validity of the rule and about whether it is up to him to make that judgment. The simple existence in legal systems of criteria for validity does not, and cannot, help him. Be those criteria few or many, simple or complex, a distinction exists between validity-conferring rules and the principles by which a citizen or official must judge that validity has indeed been conferred, or is likely to be conferred.

Principles of acceptance, therefore, are inevitable to the extent that validity is a necessary condition for legal rules. However, the importance of such principles in any particular system will vary. In legal systems with relatively few articulated restraints bearing on the validity of government action and with limited means of recourse for raising them, such principles may be relatively insignificant. On the other hand, in a system like the American legal system, where constraints on government action are many and complex and are embedded in a written constitution subject to interpretation and application by courts in the normal processes of adjudication, their significance is substantial. In such a system the articulation of a system of principles to guide receivers of the law in the presence of mandatory rules—a system complementary to the system of procedures and criteria for determining legal validity—becomes a practical necessity.

Means Versus Ends

A vital problem remains even when the validity of a rule is not in doubt. Mandatory rules, like all legal rules, are, after all, tools for the achievement of ends. But even the most incontrovertibly valid legal rule may not always prove adequate to the purposes for which it was instituted. In changing societies with complex problems and few clear solutions, there are, and must be, recurrent disparities and consequent tensions between legal means and the social ends they are meant to serve; and the more complex the society, the greater these tensions are likely to be. To some extent it is possible to compensate for the limitations of a rule by delegating discretionary authority to officials or even by qualifying the rule to establish specific conditions under which a citizen need not follow it. But, as we stated earlier, these techniques cannot resolve the means-ends tensions in a system entirely. Indefinitely extended discretion would diminish the force of a mandatory rule into a mere consideration to be taken into account by the official when he makes his judgment. And specific conditions under which a citizen may disobey a rule, laid down in advance, would almost inevitably be inadequate to some unforeseeable circumstance, just as the rule itself was.

Principles of acceptance are necessary to respond to the tensions that may remain between the legal means and the social ends of a system that have been structured into the context of evaluation of the role, when other techniques have been exhausted. When such tensions are felt by a citizen or official, is he to follow the rule, or is he to depart from it and serve the end? Since there is always a question whether the advantages of allowing an official or citizen to depart from a rule outweigh the disadvantages, legal systems must make choices, explicitly or implicitly, among the responses to mandatory rules they will tolerate or encourage and those they will not. Principles of acceptance represent such choices. They may entitle or disentitle an official to depart from a rule of competence when in his judgment compliance would constitute a disservice to the end of the rule itself or to the entire system of rules of which it is a part. Such a rule of competence may be a general rule for the conduct of the office, like the rule requiring judges to adhere to *stare decisis* or the rule requiring juries to follow the instructions of the judge; or it may fix the extent to which officials charged with enforcing other rules against citizens are required to do so, like the arguable rule that the police must arrest and the prosecutor prosecute all known offenders. On the other hand, principles of acceptance may entitle or disentitle a citizen to judge for himself that to depart from a peremptory rule under certain circumstances would better serve the ends of the system. They might, for example, leave it to the citizen to determine in the first instance that departing from a rule would result in a lesser evil than obeying it, while leaving it to the courts to judge after the fact whether he has decided correctly.

The Discretion of Officials

When legal officials have either delegated or deviational discretion to determine the classes of cases covered by peremptory rules they may or may not enforce, the citizen is left with a puzzle. The law forbids a form of conduct under circumstances A, B, and C. But officials charged with enforcement of the law enforce it only, or for the most part, under circumstances A and B. Moreover, they do so, when they act in their official roles and not as usurpers, in accordance with a variety of principles and policies and in view of a network of ends that the legal system itself provides. What, then, are citizens to make of their obligations toward the peremptory rule under circumstance C? The approved policies and principles of the enforcing agency's role may function like so many constitutions in their effect on the force of the rule as it applies to the citizen. Principles of acceptance must tell the individual how far he enjoys a liberty, comparable to the liberty of one who appeals to a constitutional norm, to undertake to depart from the terms of the rule, given his judgment that the agency's approved policies and principles justify not enforcing the rule against him. Whether those principles and policies are more or less explicitly announced in the organization of the agency's role or whether they are implicitly developed in the course of the exercise of discretion, principles of acceptance are needed to resolve the citizen's puzzle and thereby to realize the purpose of the law to rule through obligations.

So it is that in consequence of questions of validity, questions of means-ends tension, and questions involved in the existence of enforcement discretion, a developed legal system cannot dispense with principles of acceptance to tell the receiver of the law how to proceed under what are for him conditions of uncertainty about his legal obligation.

Principles of Acceptance and Legal Theory

Essential as principles of acceptance are, they have, surprisingly enough, been overlooked by many legal theorists. Of course, it is not surprising that principles of acceptance play no part in Hobbesian or Austinian attempts to derive the law from the will of a sovereign power. But one would think that natural-law theory, for example, with its limits beyond which positive law might not go and remain valid, would provide for legitimated rule departures and at least implicitly take principles of acceptance into account. Yet such a conclusion would be overhasty for the following reasons. First, and most obvious, while natural-law theory justifies rule departures, it justifies them morally through an appeal to norms outside the legal system. That is the justification of civil disobedience, to be distinguished from the justification that legitimates disobedience in our account. Second, even if one establishes the principles of natural law as implicit parts of a legal system's norm of validity, still that will not have established those principles as principles of acceptance. A norm of validity does not tell a receiver of the law how to proceed if he is uncertain of the legal validity of a mandatory rule, nor does it provide for the possibility of legitimated rule departures when the mandatory rule is admittedly valid. Third, it must be remembered that the question of who makes the judgment that a violation of natural law has indeed occurred and what he may properly do about it has always been a sticky point for natural-law theory. That sticky point is precisely the point of principles of acceptance. Last, natural-law theory characteristically deprives the positive law of any obligatory status when it conflicts with the rules of natural law. A traditional way of saying this is that when this conflict arises we are back in the state of nature. In the state of nature the citizen faces no problem of surcharge, no possibility of a genuine conflict between legal means and legal ends that he might properly take it upon himself, through appropriate principles of acceptance, to resolve.

Perhaps one might think that legal realism, insofar as it embraces a predictive theory of law and a pragmatic emphasis on the "bad man's" point of view, would reach to legitimated rule departures and principles of acceptance. But though the realist characteristically takes the point of view of the receiver of the law, it is no accident that he does not encounter principles of acceptance. His primary interest is to determine what the law demands, not to identify the bases on which a law's demands may be accepted or rejected. The acceptance or rejection of the law is left strictly up to a receiver who makes his decision by weighing the consequences of disobeying, as though there were no further issue, no question of a surcharge. The individual's acceptance or rejection of a law's demands, therefore, becomes a prudential matter that bears no particular relation to the liberties granted him or the rules constraining him in his role. It has nothing to do with his acceptance of his obligations as a citizen or official. Hence, at least the traditional realist would see no need for principles of acceptance.

Prof. H. L. A. Hart's views, as they bear on principles of acceptance, are of particular interest. One might think that Hart, who has cogently argued against the adequacy of the "external point of view" that underlies a predictive theory of law and in favor of an "internal point of view" that emphasizes the binding force of obligation, would have been sensitive to the problems to which principles of acceptance respond. Certainly, when

Hart formulated his rule of recognition he seems to have concerned himself with the problems faced by receivers of the law under conditions of uncertainty:

> The simplest form of remedy for the uncertainty of the regime of primary rules is the introduction of what we shall call a "rule of recognition." This will specify some feature or features possession of which by a suggested rule is taken as a conclusive affirmative indication that it is a rule of the group to be supported by the social pressure it exerts.

The rule of recognition, he continues, is "the *proper* way of disposing of doubts as to the existence of the rule." Further, whenever a rule of recognition is accepted, both citizens and officials are provided with "a conclusive identification of the primary rules of obligation."[1]

Yet in truth Hart's rule of recognition serves to obscure the need for principles of acceptance, not to satisfy it. In "disposing of doubts as to the existence" of a rule, the rule of recognition establishes legal standards for determining a rule's validity; but it does not resolve the doubt of the receiver of the rule about whether he is free to act on his own judgment of how those standards apply to a rule confronting him. If the receiver of the rule must act before an authorized official or body has pronounced on the issue, how will he know whether to act on his own judgment or not? Rules of recognition do not provide the answer, but principles of acceptance do.

Nor, it seems to us, does Hart's concept of the "open texture" of the law constitute a recognition of the need for principles of acceptance, though its bearing on the serious problem of the adequacy of judicial roles might seem to argue otherwise. Hart has written, in a passage that has provoked much controversy:

> The open texture of law means that there are, indeed, areas of conduct where much must be left to be developed by courts or officials striking a balance, in the light of circumstances, between competing interests which vary in weight from case to case. Nonetheless, the life of the law consists to a very large extent in the guidance both of officials and private individuals by determinate rules which, unlike the applications of variable standards, do *not* require from them a fresh judgment from

case to case. The salient fact of social life remains true, even though uncertainties may break out as to the applicability of any rule . . . to the concrete case. Here, at the margins of rules and in the fields left open by the theory of precedents, the courts perform a rule-producing function which administrative bodies perform centrally in the elaboration of variable standards. In a system where *stare decisis* is firmly acknowledged, this function of courts is very like the exercise of delegated rule-making powers by an administrative body.[2]

We may note, first, that Hart considers a rule at its core—as opposed to its margins—sufficient to guide both officials seeking to apply the rule and citizens seeking to obey it. Of itself, the core of a rule gives no occasion, therefore, for principles of acceptance. Yet we have argued in this book that even when what a rule demands is clear enough, departures from the rule may under certain circumstances be legitimated by the legal system; hence the recognition of "open texture" does not point to principles of acceptance, at least at the core.

How decisions may be made at the margins of a rule, however, rather than at its core, is the main issue raised by Hart's concept of the open texture of the law. Certainly the indeterminacy of rules does raise questions for citizens that might have led Hart to principles of acceptance had he considered the consequences of the law's open texture for citizens as he does for officials, particularly judges. But even Hart's consideration of the judge's problem in making decisions at the margins of a rule does not lead him to principles of acceptance: "at the margins of rules and in the fields left open by the theory of precedents," the indeterminacy of rules is seen to imply not that the court may sometimes need to exceed its delegated authority but that the court may exercise a function "very like the exercise of delegated rule-making powers." To Hart the necessity of reaching decisions when rules and precedent are not compelling implies a delegated discretion, not a deviational one. Thus no question of legitimated rule departure arises, and no need for principles of acceptance is created.

The central question that Hart's discussion does raise is whether the judge's role may properly be interpreted to include a delegated rule-making authority. If the possibility of legitimated rule departures is not acknowledged, those who think that the judge's role does not include any rule-making powers will differ from Hart only on whether a legal system, properly conceived, compels a uniquely correct solution to every legal problem and hence precludes a rule-making discretion. However this question were decided, of course, one could still raise the issue of rule departures—and hence of principles of acceptance—for the roles of other officials, or for that matter for the role of the citizen.

It does seem, then, that legal theories as diverse as natural-law theory, legal realism, and Hart's version of legal positivism—not to mention sovereignty theories like those of Hobbes and Austin—have overlooked principles of acceptance. The prevalence of this oversight, even in theories that at first glance would seem most likely to recognize principles of acceptance, requires an explanation. This explanation is partly to be found, we propose, in a set of underlying assumptions these theories have all made about the nature of legal obligation.

The Producer's View of Legal Obligation

Most writers on law and politics, and particularly those who share the diverse theories of law that have just been considered, seem to accept a concept of legal obligation that makes it essential that such an obligation serve as the exclusive determinant of proper action by those whom it obliges. We shall refer to this as the producer's concept of legal obligation. This concept rests on a theory of obligation (the producer's theory) that accepts the following premises:

1. Legal obligations exist to rule the actions of men.

2. All mandatory rules impose legal obligations.

3. The legal obligation imposed by a mandatory rule can be fulfilled only by doing the thing demanded or abstaining from the thing prohibited. To think that the mandatory rules of the law merely present considerations for a citizen or official to take into account in planning his actions is to mistake the nature of

the law's demands and hence the meaning of legal obligation. If the lawmakers in a system want to present an official or citizen with a consideration to be taken into account, the legal means exist to make it clear that they are doing so. A mandatory rule, which expressly forbids or demands certain conduct, aims to do more: it "lays down the law," and in doing so, imposes an obligation to comply.

4. Hence either a mandatory rule cannot legitimately be departed from, or it is not a mandatory rule and the obligation it imposes is not a legal obligation. A departure from a mandatory rule may be justifiable on moral or social grounds, but not on legal grounds.

Accordingly, legal obligations are by nature unremitting and any legal obligation makes a claim to serve as the exclusive determinant of proper action by those it obliges.

Clearly, the producer's concept of legal obligation makes legitimated rule departures anomalous and principles of acceptance unnecessary. If a legal obligation exclusively determines the proper action of those it obliges, no logical ground remains for legitimated rule departures and no problem remains for principles of acceptance to resolve. In effect, therefore, that concept embodies the viewpoint of the lawmaker—of the producer of the law—in contradistinction to the viewpoint of the receiver, since it makes it logically necessary that in any legal system legal officials are entitled to make and enforce the law without interference from the judgment of the receivers of the law. Assuming the producer's concept, most legal and political philosophy thereupon proceeds to examine the forms of government that would best exercise the authority government necessarily has.

Although the legal theories sketched in the preceding section are diverse in many respects, all of them implicitly or explicitly accept the premises of the producer's theory. Certainly these premises are more or less explicitly accepted by Hobbesian and Austinian theorists. Hart, the legal realists, and the natural-law theorists would not deny that legal obligations exist to rule the actions of men, though the realists view legal obligations solely from an external point of view and define them that way. They would all also agree that mandatory rules impose legal obligations, though natural-law theory limits the validity of mandatory rules in a way that Hart and many others do not. There is no disagreement that to satisfy his obligation to a mandatory rule the citizen or official does the specific thing it requires. As a result, though none deny that developed legal systems raise issues of legal validity, exhibit means-ends tensions, and incorporate enforcement discretion—features of a legal system that raise questions for the receiver of the law beyond that of determining what the mandatory rules of the system require—all the theories considered nevertheless hold that mandatory rules suffice to tell the receiver of the law what he must or must not do. Thus all of them overlook the need for principles of acceptance.

The Rational-Bureaucratic Model of a Legal System

Now we submit that the producer's theory of legal obligation is based on only one of many possible models for a developed legal system. That model exhibits the following characteristics, among others.

First, there is a sharp functional division between the ruler and the ruled, even if the legal system provides for a rotation of authority among the citizenry. This assumption is reflected in the first three propositions of the producer's theory—namely, that legal obligations exist to rule the actions of men, that they are imposed by mandatory rules, and that they can be fulfilled only by doing the thing demanded or abstaining from the thing prohibited. In other words, it is in the nature of a legal system that some members of a society have exclusive authority to determine the legal obligations of all members of the society, and by the same token, that the other members have no authority to determine legal obligations at all. In that way a state comes to be conceived of as a distribution of coercive powers among individuals who, in virtue of their roles, have a monopoly on those powers.

All the varieties of legal theory touched on above assume such a sharp division between the rulers and the ruled. The very insistence of the legal realist that judges act as lawmakers suggests how deep the assumption goes. Even natural-law theory does not really reject the notion that legal authority in a system is a monopoly; it simply restates the concept of authority to include criteria for the monopoly's legitimacy. Legal positivists may find the source of legal authority in secondary rules, in a basic norm, or, in an older tradition, in a sovereign; but all take for granted that legal authority is to be vested exclusively in certain individuals and not in others.

Second, the model for legal systems presumed by the producer's theory typically constructs legal systems on the ideal of the rule of law, which requires those in authority to rule solely according to law. This ideal, of course, excludes kadi justice as a characteristic of developed legal systems, just as the notion that legal authority in a system is a monopoly excludes from the category of legal systems those that, like a purely moral system, have rules but no special authorities. In a genuine legal system justice requires both a designated authoritative voice and a justified judgment that the authoritative voice is duty-bound to render.

But the requirement of a justified judgment creates an obvious difficulty. If receivers of the law are obliged to obey the justified judgments of those in authority, it follows that they must be assured somehow that the judgments rendered to them are indeed justified. Yet, if legal authority is a monopoly, only the authorities themselves have the power to render judgments on the propriety of their judgments. Hence a means must be found to bridge the possible gap between what the authorities say and what the law would have them say.

A resolution of the difficulty is sought through a hierarchical system of appeals that provides legal recourse. Since only the authorities have the power to make and administer the law, an appeal to a higher authority by a defendant who believes his action justified can have only one of two consequences: either the authorities find that the defendant did in fact depart from a rule, in which case his appeal is rejected, or they find that he did not, in which case his appeal is sustained. Under no circumstances do they find that he had a liberty to depart from a rule, for such a finding would require an acknowledgment of the citizen's legal authority to undertake to depart from a rule under certain circumstances — to take the law into his own hands, as it were. To sustain the appeal of a defendant who thinks his action legitimate, the authorities find instead that the rule the defendant departed from was never a rule at all. Thus the practical gap between the voice of authority and the rule of law is papered over by the retroactive way of speaking remarked on earlier in this book—a way of speaking that denies the possibility of justified rule departures and thereby preserves the ideal of the monopolization of legal authority by those who fill certain legal roles.

We now come to a third characteristic. The producer's theory requires that a legal system be both consistent and complete. It must be consistent, since if one can derive from the legal system incompatible obligations, to that extent an obligation cannot be presented as the exclusive determinant of proper action by individuals. And the system must be complete for all actions it purports to rule, since it will not succeed in ruling those actions for which an insufficient ground exists to reach a conclusion. It seems, then, that the rule of law we saw presumed by the producer's theory cannot be achieved unless every legal issue that a legal case can raise can be decided by some rule or rules of law and unless incompatible decisions are not equally grounded in the law. For unless these conditions hold, the resolution of cases must rest upon the discretion, deviational or delegated, of the judge.

It is interesting to observe that the use of the device of retroactive explanation itself testifies to the strength of the requirement of consistency and completeness. For the whole point of such explanations consists of allowing one to say of a case that seemed not to be decidable before a given legal decision was reached that it only seemed to be undecidable—actually, the uniquely correct decision was implicit in the law all along, waiting only to be stated, and the opinion that decided the case expressed the true law. Consistency and completeness are guaranteed, even if by a purely formal move. Of course, all of this implies only that the diverse legal theories touched on above as embodying the producer's theory of the law have in fact required consistency and completeness for legal systems, not that they have necessarily recognized that requirement in their exposition.*

The fourth and final characteristic of that model of legal systems the producer's theory of obligation demands is as follows. If obligations are imposed on receivers of the law, and those obligations are the exclusive determinants of proper action, then receivers of the law are entitled to legally correct decisions. In place of principles of acceptance and the possibility of a legitimated rule departure, the receiver of the law receives

---

* As we have already observed, Hart does not make the requirement of consistency and completeness absolute for legal systems, although he does seem to say that one may expect that requirement to function for officials for the most part. Cases in which, as a consequence of the open texture of the law, that requirement does not hold then become more or less inevitable lesions in the law as it stands in relation to circumstance, to be handled by a delegated rule-making power. The question, then, has been raised whether Hart, given his positivistic theory of legal obligation, can consistently acknowledge such lesions and extend to judges "strong discretion." For the positivistic theory of obligation, it is argued, "holds that a legal obligation exists when (and only when) an established rule of law imposes such an obligation. It follows from this that in a hard case—where no such established rule can be found—there is no legal obligation until the judge creates a new rule for the future. The judge may apply that new rule to the parties in the case, but this is ex post facto legislation, not the enforcement of an existing obligation." Dworkin, "Is Law a System of Rules?" in R. S. Summers, ed., *Essays in Legal Philosophy* (Berkeley, Calif., 1968), p. 59. In effect, Hart *ought* to accept the view that uniquely correct decisions are always determinable even if he does not; such an acceptance, Dworkin argues, would be possible on the proviso that "a legal obligation might be imposed by a constellation of principles as well as by an established rule."

We need not attempt to mediate the difference between Hart and Dworkin. Our argument is not inconsistent with principles, as well as established rules, functioning in the law. We are concerned with authoritative formulations that impose obligations, whether those formulations be in the form of rules or principles. In our sense, the term mandatory rule includes principles taken as mandatory. Our argument concerning the remittability of legal obligations remains whatever the source of the obligation.

an entitlement to justice according to the rules. He can demand that his obligations be clearly stated and that the rules be correctly applied, but he is not at liberty ever to function as the judge of his own case.

In sum, then, underlying the producer's theory of legal obligation is the view that a legal system must exhibit the monopolization of authority, the requirement that judgments be rendered according to law, consistency and completeness, and, for receivers of the law, an entitlement to legal justice. We may now give its proper name to this model of a legal system that makes the producer's theory of obligation self-evident and legally legitimated rule departures incoherent. We have in effect been articulating, in only slightly different terms, the third of Max Weber's pure types of legitimate authority, the rational-bureaucratic, in which the validity of a mandatory rule's claim to be obeyed rests on "a belief in the legality of patterns of normative rules and the right of those elevated to authority under such rules to issue commands (legal authority)." Authority is monopolized by certain members of society and accompanied by principles for justifying legal action. "Patterns of normative rules" enable those in authority to impose legal obligations on "rational grounds." So it is where authority derives from a rational-bureaucratic system, which Weber describes as a central feature of the modern state, rather than from tradition or charisma.

Not only are offices created and rules established to be administered, but the other premises of the producer's theory are explicitly advanced. We find Weber asserting that "every body of law consists essentially in a consistent system of abstract rules." Furthermore, the administration of law is held to consist of the application of these rules to particular cases: "The administrative process is the rational pursuit of the interests which are specified in the order governing the corporate group within the limits laid down by legal precepts and following principles which are capable of generalized formulation and are approved in the order governing the group, or at least not disapproved by it." "Technical training" provides the means of ensuring that the actual decisions of authority have legal justification, that the legal system is in fact administered according to its rules, and that the system's rules are rational in the sense of being consistent and complete. The major purpose of bureaucratic activity then becomes the determination of violations and compliances, with the citizen's entitlement to a right decision shored, in Weber's words, "by a right of appeal and of statement of grievances from the lower to the higher"—in effect, by provision for recourse through a hierarchical appeal process essential to the producer's theory.[3]

Of course, identifying the main features of the producer's theory of legal obligation in Weber's portrait of the law as a rational-bureaucratic system neither proves nor disproves the theory's validity.* But it does tend to make manifest that the theory depends upon a specific ideal that is subject to evaluation, not upon logical necessity. Assuming this is the case, there must be other possible modes of organizing social relations than the rational-bureaucratic and other concepts of legal obligation than the producer's.

An Alternative Model of a Legal System— Checks and Balances

We have suggested that principles of acceptance have been omitted by many legal theories owing to certain common assumptions about the nature of legal obligations and legal sys-

---

* For a discussion of Weber's evaluation of the rational-bureaucratic order, see P. Selznick, *Law, Society, and Industrial Justice* (Russell Sage, 1969), especially pp. 76–77. The following remarks by Selznick (p. 78) suggest that when we identified Weber's account of that order as the presupposition of a theory of obligation that precludes the possibility of a legitimated rule departure, we were doing no injustice to Weber's overall view of bureaucracy: "In his most direct analysis, Weber hardly mentioned the place of purpose in bureaucracy. He simply takes it for granted that bureaucratic organization is a rational instrument subordinate to given ends.... For him bureaucracy was not a dynamic institution committed to solving problems and attaining objectives. He saw it rather as a relatively passive and conservative force preoccupied with the detailed implementation of previously established policies. In such a setting purpose lacks creative significance. It is not in the foreground of bureaucratic awareness." We should say that in such a setting not only does purpose lack creative significance, it fails to function internally to the role, to provide the possibility of recourse roles.

tems. Our task now is to consider the nature of a legal system in which legitimated rule departures might be seen as a means of achieving some of the system's objectives rather than as evidence of the system's imperfection. Then it will be possible to consider a theory of legal obligation that would embrace principles of acceptance capable of legitimating departures from rules. Since the rational-bureaucratic model of a legal system precluded legitimated rule departures in consequence of the four characteristics discussed above, an alternative model that would accommodate legitimated rule departures must have different characteristics.

First, it must be capable of mitigating the monopolization of authority by members of society in certain legal roles. That is, at least some receivers of the law as well as lawmakers must be acknowledged to have some authority to determine legal obligations if legitimated rule departures are to be seen as a functional element in a legal system. Receivers of the law, it must be remembered, include both officials and citizens.

Second, an alternative to the rational-bureaucratic model that would accommodate rule departures must qualify the central commitment of the rational-bureaucratic order to the rule of law. Yet it must not do so in a way that implies the collapse of system and the rule of lawlessness. In the alternative model we seek, recurring doubts concerning the legal justification of the judgments reached by authoritative voices will appear less as imperfections in a rational-bureaucratic structure than as necessary consequences of change and complexity for which the legal order makes systematic provision. There will be no need to resort to retroactive explanations to assure oneself that the legal system has been working effectively as a legal system.

Third, incompleteness and inconsistency must be accepted as necessary concomitants of the system's response to social change and to the complexity and indeterminacy of social objectives. Sometimes in a particular case either no strictly legal judgment can be made to stand or incompatible judgments can equally well be derived. In such an event, since by hypothesis there can be no legal justification prior to the judgment, justification may have to wait for subsequent legal developments—developments for which the judgment itself may end up providing at least a practical ground. Until the future vindicates it, however, that judgment rests upon a gamble that it is, and will be recognized as, the sort of decision the law ought to be rendering in that kind of case. As Hart observed in a not dissimilar context, "Here all that succeeds is success."* So it was with *Marbury v. Madison*, which has become an integral part of constitutional law even though its original grounds have been questioned.

Last, while a rational-bureaucratic system entitles receivers of the law to the one uniquely correct decision, in a system that legitimates departures from rules the receiver of the law may sometimes claim an entitlement to the "justice" he would have received if the maker of the law had departed from the legal rule. He is, as it were, entitled to an "incorrect" judgment under certain sorts of circumstances. Moreover, if the rules of the system are indeed either inconsistent or incomplete in the circumstances of their application, he may find himself at most with a claim to some one decision of a class of different possible decisions. Then his entitlement may reduce to a claim to influence or to participate in the processes by which judgments are made, rather than to be given a legally correct judgment. But we do not wish to press questions of possible entitlements further than to suggest that there are other ways of dealing with entitlements than the rational-bureaucratic way. Those other ways are hardly neat or simple, but some of them may be workable—and, from a practical point of view, at least, more descriptive of the true state of an individual's entitlement before our law than the view

---

* H. L. A. Hart, *The Concept of Law* (Oxford, Eng., 1961), p. 149. In fact, Hart here comes close to formulating a theory of deviational discretion for courts. It is a formalist error, he tells us, to think that "every step taken by a court is covered by some general rule conferring in advance the authority to take it, so that its creative powers are always a form of delegated legislative power. The truth may be that, when courts settle previously unenvisaged questions concerning the most fundamental constitutional rules they get their authority to decide them accepted after the questions have arisen and the decision has been given. Here all that succeeds is success."

derived from considering the legal system according to the rational-bureaucratic model.

What sort of legal system will it be that has the above four characteristics? What structural characteristics of a legal system will cause it to exhibit these functional characteristics and make rule departures expected parts of the system?

An alternative to the rational-bureaucratic legal system is, in fact, described in a widely known tradition of political theory, and one particularly relevant to the American political experience. That political theory is the theory of checks and balances, which describes a system so organized that its various discrete parts in the performance of their functions check and balance rather than interlock and reinforce one another. Instead of defining the offices that comprise a system's parts in terms of entirely separate and distinct responsibilities, powers, and privileges, the theory of checks and balances distributes responsibilities, powers, and privileges to overlap from office to office, and hence promotes conflict. Moreover, the system of checks and balances makes such a distribution not accidently, but in order to prevent the abuse of government power. For example, the power of the presidency specifically includes the conduct of foreign affairs and the disposition of the armed forces, while Congress alone has the power to make war. In theory, at least, a check on the President's conduct of foreign affairs and employment of the armed forces would be secured by his need to calculate the willingness of Congress to support the possible consequences of his policies, which could limit the abuses of an adventuristic foreign policy. Such at least is the traditional way in which American political theory and practice have adopted Montesquieu's famous principle* that to avoid the abuse of

---

* See Madison, writing in *The Federalist*, Modern Library College ed. (New York, n.d.): "From these facts by which Montesquieu was guided, it may clearly be inferred that, in saying 'There can be no liberty where the legislative and executive powers are united in the same person, or body of magistrates,' ... he did not mean that these departments ought to have no *partial agency* in, or no *control* over, the acts of each other. His meaning ... can amount to no more than this, that where the *whole* power of one department is exercised by the same hands which possess the *whole* power of

government power, matters must be so disposed (in constitutions) that one power of government will check another.[4]

Now, of course, Montesquieu's principle and the classic theory of checks and balances that instantiated it were designed to constitute a strategy for limiting and impeding the government's freedom of action in matters concerning the liberty of its citizens through the organization of a political constitution. But can it be that Montesquieu's principle is susceptible to an even wider application than it has historically received? Are the concepts of power, of abuse of power, of power checking power, applicable not only to the distribution of ultimate government authority among the legislative, executive, and judicial branches, but also to the actions of individual officials, and of citizens as well, in the very processes of administering government through rules and obligations?[5] If so, we would have an alternative to legal systems built on the rational-bureaucratic model—a system of checks and balances in which rule departures, in virtue of the structural characteristics of the system, become intelligible as possibly lawful events. The problem is to show how and why Montesquieu's principle might be extended to explain and justify legitimated rule departures. Let us first consider the extension of the principle to individual government officials.

It is possible to contemplate such an extension because while Montesquieu himself formulated his principle in the language of mechanics and conceived of both law in civil society and law in physical nature as species of the same genus, he nevertheless gave his powers the same signification as that we are familiar with in actual legal systems. Indeed, if Montesquieu's principle was to fulfill its express function and serve as a principle for organizing a political constitution, his special way of formulating it could constitute only an interpretation of the sociological fact

---

another department, the fundamental principles of a free constitution are subverted." (No. 47, p. 314.) "Unless these departments [legislative, executive, and judiciary] be so far connected and blended as to give to each a constitutional control over the others, the degree of separation which the maxim [of separation of powers] requires, as essential to a free government, can never in practice be duly maintained." (No. 48, p. 321.)

that made the principle operative, namely, that powers are definable in terms of a system of legal rules, that to speak of the legislative, judicial, and executive powers is to generalize how a system of rules empowers individuals in certain sets of offices to perform certain acts. So it happens that the powers of policemen or jurors, as of chief executive or legislator, are all alike constituted of duties, prescribed instrumentalities, procedures, rights, and privileges of the sort discussed throughout this book. And a fact of central importance for the extension of the principle emerges: the powers referred to in Montesquieu's principle in order to achieve their effect require the exercise of the powers of other roles. Such is the nature of legal roles. But since powers are given effect through the powers of other legal roles, a consequence crucial to the theory of checks and balances follows: the powers of Montesquieu's principle are intrinsically of the sort that officials other than the individual exercising such a power may frustrate in the exercise of their own defined powers.

In short, the notion of power checking power is an entirely natural one not merely for the relations among executive, judiciary, and legislature, but for the legal system at large, if indeed one wishes to organize a legal system in which all the parts do not automatically interlock and sustain one another, and to accept the consequences. Montesquieu's principle, so far as the notion of power checking power goes, becomes peculiarly applicable to social conditions for which it is impractical to organize an ecology of legal roles invariably sustaining one another, or in which there is no way of doing so without incurring outweighing disadvantages. It is an old story that such circumstances will prevail when the materials to be organized by the legal system are of major complexity and when unanticipated transformations in social circumstances occur with fairly high frequency.

The concept of the abuse of power in Montesquieu's principle would seem to present no intrinsic obstacles to the extension of the principle. To be sure, the abuses Montesquieu had in mind were chiefly infringements of what he considered to be the liberty of subjects. But there are many ways through which officials may abuse their powers not directly tied to that liberty. Power is subject to abuse in our proposed extension of the concept of the abuse of power for the same reason that it is subject to abuse in the reading of Montesquieu's principle that has become general in American political theory: the grant of power can rarely, if ever, be made exactly coextensive with and proportionate to the ends it is established to achieve. The President, for example, might indeed be empowered in his role of commander-in-chief to take only those measures necessary to the defense of the nation. But what constitutes defense, and what an appropriate measure? For officials generally, as their duties exceed those of the most routine jobs, and not only for the President, no feasible way exists to settle all such issues in advance, with the consequence that the abuse of power remains always imminent, even for some of the more humble officials of the legal system. It is with such an imminence in view that it becomes reasonable to oppose one power to another in ways Montesquieu, or even the classic theory of checks and balances, did not contemplate.

Certainly, the actual criteria of abuse present no difficulties to the envisaged extension of Montesquieu's principle. Rather, the extension appears particularly apt. Criteria for determining abuses of power—criteria like Montesquieu's own liberty and principles of natural law—are built into the functioning of political systems often very informally and only in the most general way. But criteria for determining abuse by an individual official of the legal system may be lodged not merely in the provisions of the criminal law, to which he, like anyone else, is subject, but in the specific structure of his particular legal role.

Montesquieu's principle, therefore, states a possible strategy for the construction of a legal system of checks and balances extending well into the processes of administering government through rules, provided only one is willing to accept consequences that neither Montesquieu nor classic political theory have found acceptable and that are crucial to the present argument. Those are consequences for the domestication of rule departures within the legal system. To apply Montesquieu's principle throughout the reaches of the legal system, one must be willing to complicate the structures of the system in ways that will justify agents in their official roles sometimes taking the judgment of their roles upon themselves—as, all through this book, we have seen happening in the American legal system. This will be necessary, on the extended theory of checks and balances, because official roles often impose an obligation to comply with the rule addressed to agents in those roles by officials in other roles, at the same time that such compliance may complete or expedite the abuse of power. It may follow then that the only way to prevent the abuse of power will be through checking that power by means of a departure from a mandatory rule. So it is that to the very degree an official finds justification for his rule departures in terms of the ends of his role, and that justification is supported by the workings of the legal system, the legal system will have applied Montesquieu's principle of controlling the abuse of power through the institutionalization of a system of checks and balances.

Consider, for example, our paradigm case of interposition, the jury acquittal in the face of court instructions that demand conviction. The judge instructs the jury; the jury applies the instructions. Yet conceive of the jury as checking or balancing the power of the judge—and, therefore, sometimes the legislature for which he may speak—and it is apparent that the only way the jury can function to check the legal power of the judge is by interposing its own judgment. The price of checks and balances introduced into the court system for the sake of ultimate ends is the legitimation of rule departures, departures sustained within the legal system in ways already discussed. Conversely, legitimated rule departures impose on the legal system a system of checks and balances.

Let us turn now for a final extension of Montesquieu's principle to the place of citizens within the legal system. Any account of an alternative to the rational-bureaucratic system must include an account of the role of the citizen in the system. Despite the fact that Montesquieu's principle was hardly formulated for subjects of the law, but aimed to protect them by the constraints it placed on rulers, the argument for the accommodation of citizen rule departures under Montesquieu's principle quite parallels the argument for the accommodation of official rule departures under that principle. Of course, we do not mean that Montesquieu's principle must be extended to citizens if it is extended to officials. The point is merely that it is perfectly feasible to give citizens as well as officials a checking power over the actions of officials for the sake of the application of a framework of norms that define the abuses of power by officials—provided that the legal system set up the role of citizen to permit legitimated disobedience. For since the citizen's role is defined in terms of his obligation to comply with mandatory rules, he cannot have a lawful power to check or arrest the abuse of authority without having the liberty of departing from those rules. In our own system, as we have seen, the legal justification of citizen action through the appeal to the Constitution, through the lesser-evil principle, or through discretionary nonenforcement by officials has the inevitable consequence of justifying citizens' taking it upon themselves to disobey some mandatory rule and of extending the system of checks and balances. That it is so extended escapes notice because people, in virtue of their implicit commitment to a rational-bureaucratic system, find the acceptance of rule departures within a legal system incomprehensible.

It may be objected that to speak of extending Montesquieu's principle to citizens misrepresents the concept of power. We do not, of course, mean to assert that a difference does not exist between the specific powers of officials and the peculiar, reactive power of citizens with respect to rules that they may consider legally unjustifiable in themselves or as leading to consequences that the legal system never intended. But it is not clear that to admit this much is to give very much. It is the legal system, after all, not their own political morality, that accords citizens liberties that enable them, under special conditions, to depart from legal rules. It is the legal system that provides them with the ultimate ends in virtue of which they may justify their behavior. It is the legal system, finally, that provides them with procedures and arguments in virtue of which they may defend their disobedience as a legitimated act. The "spirit of the laws" justifies the extension. Both officials and citizens, through the extension of Montesquieu's principle to the sphere of their action in which they are bound by mandatory rules, receive an effective power to modify the roles they enact.

That the system of checks and balances possesses the characteristics we found necessary for an alternative to the rational-bureaucratic system is now manifest. Extended to official legal roles, it patently involves the modification of the rule of law that we found to characterize such a system, and without lapsing into lawlessness. For the system of checks and balances is a possible system of law constrained by the variety of legitimating norms we discussed in earlier chapters. Extended to citizens, the system of checks and balances necessarily blurs the sharp division between ruler and ruled that we found to characterize an alternative to the rational-bureaucratic system. Given the checking and balancing of official by official, the system leads us to expect inconsistency and incompleteness. And, of course, instead of invariably entitling receivers of the law to legally correct decisions, the system of checks and balances offers the possibility of decisions that are more just in terms of the ultimate purposes of the legal system, even though, given the state of the legal system at the time, they are legally incorrect.

The place for principles of acceptance in the extended system of checks and balances is also apparent. Whereas in the rational-bureaucratic system, one principle of acceptance alone is needed —namely, to follow all mandatory rules that come to one under color of authority—in the extended system of checks and balances, the legal system must provide principles for determining when to comply with such rules and when not to, unless the system is to collapse into chaos. For strictly speaking, of course, there can be no working legal system that consists exclusively of powers checking and balancing one another. Just as systems of law may be more or less open to legitimated rule departures, so they may more or less extensively incorporate Montesquieu's principle. When they do so to an appreciable extent, one speaks of a system of checks and balances. It also follows that, insofar as the extended theory of checks and balances applies to a legal system, mandatory rules cannot suffice to tell the receiver of the law what he must or must not do.

An Alternative View of Legal Obligation

Since, on the extended theory of checks and balances, mandatory rules cannot suffice to tell the receiver of the law what he must or must not do, the producer's concept of legal obligation cannot account for legal obligation as such. A more catholic view of legal obligation than the producer's must find the nerve of the obligation of the receiver of the law not in the unremitting character of the obligation—which, indeed, a rational-bureaucratic system postulates—but elsewhere.

Such a view of legal obligation does not deny that legal obligations exist in order to rule the actions of men, that mandatory rules impose legal obligations, or that the mandatory rules of the law present more than considerations for a citizen or official to take into account in planning his actions. Since the principle of checks and balances constitutes a possible basis for a legal system, this view of legal obligation allows that a mandatory rule can sometimes legitimately be departed from while the obligation it imposes remains a legal obligation. Hence the "exclusive determinant of proper action" will be found in the combination of mandatory rules and principles of acceptance. Finding it there will accommodate both the producer's perspective in viewing the law and the receiver's. The unremitting character of legal obligations in rational-bureaucratic systems stems from the special principles of acceptance that it incorporates.

The view that the obligations finally binding on citizens and officials are the product of mandatory rules and principles of acceptance, and hence that the obligations imposed by mandatory rules are not necessarily unremitting, calls for at least two assurances, which we shall now attempt to provide: that it makes sense to speak of an obligation imposed by a mandatory rule as at once remittable by principles of acceptance and still a genuine obligation; and that the purpose of legal obligations, which is to rule the actions of men, is not defeated by taking mandatory rules as something else than the sole determinants of proper action.

A central feature, then, of the view of legal obligation alternative to the producer's is that it presents the legal obligations mandatory rules impose as a species of garden-variety obligation. For when it holds that receivers of the law have an obligation to comply with a rule of law and also that they sometimes may be justified in not complying with it, the alternative view holds no more than is in fact normally held of obligations—and this despite the superficial difficulty of explaining how an act one "has to" perform in virtue of some obligation may also be an act one does not "have to" perform.

Consideration of an ordinary, nonlegal instance of dealing with obligations may help smooth the apparent paradox of legal obligation. Daily experience, after all, seems to confirm that obligations may at once genuinely obligate one to a specific performance and, under certain circumstances, be remittable. If I borrow a sum and promise to return it on a certain day, I have not merely obligated myself to take into serious consideration paying the sum back, for that would be compatible with not paying the sum back. I have obligated myself to paying the sum back. On the other hand, even granting that the obligation of my promise was to repay the sum at a certain time, it seems strange to deny that circumstances might arise in which it would be wrong to pay the sum back. Never to default on an obligation though the heavens fall is a possible strategy for dealing with obligations, of course—but perhaps most people would find that strategy not merely imprudent but positively immoral, and a definition of obligation that made it logically necessary peculiar indeed. So it is that ordinarily one speaks not merely of prima facie obligations that one satisfies by according them a certain weight, but of obligations that under certain circumstances one rightly fails to discharge. This way of speaking is possible because those circumstances are determined by a body of moral principles—partly specified, partly not—built into the structure of moral experience and serving as background rules governing noncompliance with obligations. For example, not everything and anything serves to release a person from a promise, provided only that he values those things strongly enough. He may place an extraordinary emphasis on his own comfort and sincerely judge that the importance of that comfort far outweighs the importance of keeping his promise, but we would not ordinarily say that he was therefore justified in not keeping his promise. For while he possesses many good reasons for not keeping it, he does not possess what earlier we called "damned good reasons"—reasons, that is, the appropriateness of which has been supported by the general practice of morality. On the other hand, that the promisor's child would die if he did not buy medicine with the money he had promised to return would constitute more evidence than the promisor needed to justify, morally, his not returning the money. Everything depends on what, in the moral climate, may be expected of a person. At the same time, those expectations can never be completely formulated in advance and the process of not abiding by the moral rules has, when occurring within certain limits, the consequence of gradually changing the content of our moral obligations.

Observe, now, that the law of contracts itself formulates principles comparable to the moral background principles in virtue of which we are judged justified in not having discharged our promissory obligations. Generally, the grounds for excusing a breach of contract are put in terms of impossibility of performance and frustration of purpose.[6] An opera singer who does not perfom as promised because of illness is not held for breaking a promise,[7] nor is a renter who rents an apartment at a high rate to watch a coronation and refuses to pay when the coronation is cancelled,[8] nor is a contractor who promised to rebuild the second floor of a building and fails to do so when the building burns down.[9] The temptation here, as in the case of other justifiable rule departures, is to evade the paradox of a remittable obligation by offering a retroactive explanation. Courts may explain these holdings on the ground that no breach actually occurred, since the circumstances that served to excuse the nonperformance were an "implied condition" of the original promise. But even then, as Corbin observes, "They are aware they are holding the promise to be conditional because they think that justice so requires, justice based upon custom, business practices, the mores of the community."[10] In other words, the courts introduce background ends into the law.*

Accordingly, while it is precisely the force of having a legal obligation that one must comply despite all sorts of strong reasons for not doing so, it does not follow that therefore there are *no* reasons whatsoever that could justify noncompliance. And it does not follow any more than it follows that because some reasons are not good reasons for breaking a promise, no reasons are. Remittable obligations exist as paradoxes only if one confuses the two sorts of reasons: those that derive from the essential structure and ends of the practice in which the obligation occurs and those, however weighty, that do not so derive. In the legal context the principles that make some reasons for departing from rules appropriate reasons and some, however strong on the

---

* Cf. Lord Wright, in Denny, Mott & D. v. Fraser & Co. [1944] A. C. 265, 275: "The court has formulated the doctrine [of frustration] by virtue of its inherent jurisdiction, just as it has developed the rules of liability for negligence, or for the restitution or repayment of money where otherwise there would be unjust enrichment. I find the theory of the basis of the rule in Lord Sumner's . . . pregnant statement that the doctrine of frustration is really a device by which the rules as to absolute contracts are reconciled with the special exceptions which justice demands. Though it has constantly been said by high authority, including Lord Sumner, that the explanation of the rule is to be found in the theory that it depends on an implied condition of the contract, that is really no explanation. It only pushes back the problem a single stage. It leaves the question what is the reason for implying a term."

merits, unavailing are, if anything, still more developed, in the form of principles of acceptance, than are the moral presuppositions that may sometimes justify breaking a promise.

The quarrel, then, between the producer's theory of legal obligation and the more inclusive account we have advanced of it cannot be resolved in favor of the former by appealing to the incoherence of remittable obligations. For the legal obligations that mandatory rules impose share with other obligations the same general structure that dissipates any paradox of remittable obligations. The question that remains is whether in assimilating legal obligations to other sorts of obligations that remit we have not denied legal obligations their special function to rule the actions of men. How can legal obligations rule if they can be overcome? At least this last assurance is necessary: that we do not give away the presupposition of the inquiry announced at the beginning, namely, that legal systems be considered to rule men not merely through threat or advantage, but through obligation.

The assurance is hard to give, however, only if one assumes that the alternative to having the law rule the actions of men through unremitting obligations is to have the law rule the actions of men through threat or reward. Yet, after all, what evidence is there that if obligations are made remittable, the possibility of ruling through obligations will be eliminated and the only way to rule will be by threats and rewards? The proposition might perhaps rest on psychological grounds: men are such that, as soon as they see that their obligations may under some circumstances be justifiably resisted, they will resist them on all occasions when it suits their convenience. But while it is undoubtedly true for some people that they give no person or thing obedience at all unless they give unquestioning and unqualified obedience, that is surely not true of everyone and must be resisted as holding for most people by anyone who thinks a democratic society viable. Far more likely, the reason why anyone would believe that either obligations are not remittable or the law must rule otherwise than through obligation is the assumed truth or desirability of a certain sort of theory: law is a question of authority; the flow of authority is one way; break the flow of authority and the gravest consequences ensue for society. It is, politically, better that obligations be unremittable —we *ought* to opt for the rational-bureaucratic legal order. Yet even if the system of law under which obligations are unremittable is a better system, it hardly follows that the rules must rule our consciences absolutely in order to rule them at all; and whether it would be better to live in a rational-bureaucratic order than in a legal system characterized by the judicious application of checks and balances must surely depend on the nature of society and what we hope for from ourselves and others.

How, then, might legal obligations rule the actions of men on the assumption that they might be remittable? Through the way most "ruling" of autonomous men occurs—through the presentation of reasons to obey so strong that the individual will consider carefully, and in a structured and ordered way, his refusal to comply. Rules of the law may still function, then, to produce order, though the order be less than total and not invariable; and, in any case, that is the way most ruling works. In sum, we may conceive of mandatory rules imposing obligations as elements in an interaction through which legal communities of producers and receivers of rules control their affairs. In such a community the conduct of men is neither subject to obligations as the exclusive determinants of proper action nor controlled simply by threat or reward.

If the possible varieties of legal systems are recognized in a way that the producer's theory precludes and its alternative makes feasible, students of legal systems may perhaps examine on their merits the issues involved in ruling the conduct of citizens and officials through obligations. They may also reach a more realistic appraisal of what happens in our own legal system to the actual constraints on officials and citizens as they face the law.

On Conceiving of the Law

How ought we to conceive of the law if the conception must be broad enough to include the possibility of legitimated rule departures? Let us try a final synopsis.

Most legal theorists have followed the rational-bureaucratic model of a legal system, in which the law comprises a complete and consistent set of rules aimed at exclusively determining the actions of those subject to them, plus, perhaps, a set of rules, principles, or procedures to be followed in generating the first set of rules. We have tried to alter that conception in two ways. First, we called attention to principles of acceptance, necessary features of developed legal systems that guide the deliberations of receivers of the law under complex and unsettled conditions. Second, we tried to show that the notion of an obligation derived from a mandatory rule as the exclusive determinant of proper action is gratuitous; there is no *a priori* reason why a mandatory rule, in order to rule, must impose an unremitting obligation and rule absolutely. An alternative system of checks and balances is possible in which the obligations imposed by mandatory rules are tempered by principles of acceptance that permit rule departures and in this way serve the ultimate ends of the system. Such an alternative is not only conceivable but in use.

In conceiving of the law we have in effect applied a simple precept of what Charles Sanders Peirce called the logical conscience. In order to avoid blocking the way of inquiry, this precept warns us not to employ restrictive definitions that exclude real possibilities from consideration. Theories about the nature of legal systems, from which are derived all sorts of propositions about the entitlements of defendants, the obligations of officials, and the nature of proper judicial reasoning, run the same risk as theories about the nature of art—namely, that substantive choices of particular programs in the domain will be defended on the basis of a prescribed concept of the domain. In such a case the need for a defense has been obviated.

The commitments justifying one's substantive choices have been implanted in the theory and then read out from the theory as discoveries.

We have proposed, then, a way of conceiving of the law that can include both rational-bureaucratic systems and systems organized on the principle of checks and balances, along with a broad spectrum of systems in between. So to conceive it exhibits the law as a far more remarkable and serviceable tool than might otherwise be supposed. In such a conception legal systems can be seen as vehicles for turning indeterminacy and conflict into socially creative forces, as well as for giving form and certainty to agreement and established patterns. The law imposes order, and in an orderly way. But it may also admit the impulses of disorder in the shaping of its acts.* In a partially disorderly way, in an only partially explicit fashion, the law may channel into its processes the beliefs, aspirations, and guesses both of those who make and apply its rules and of those obliged to obey them. The law itself accepts the challenge to legitimate departures from its own rules. Hence a system providing for the legitimation of rule departures reminds us again of an analogy between law and art: the development of one as of the other draws vitality from embracing within itself a random element. In sum, to the extent it is proper to speak of the law as a system, it now seems the sort of system that in the very process of its internal operations surrenders self-enclosure and completeness in order to accept, and capitalize on, influences from that outside milieu in which it is immersed. In still another sense, therefore, one may repeat after Holmes that the life of the law is not logic, but experience.

* In a recent work Professor Ehrenzweig has examined the psychological roots of the impulses behind the formulation of the law as well as those behind the divergent attempts to account for it. See A. E. Ehrenzweig, *Psycho-analytical Jurisprudence* (Dobbs Ferry, N.Y., 1971).

Notes

Notes

Chapter One

1. H. L. A. Hart, *The Concept of Law* (Oxford, Eng., 1961), p. 39.
2. T. Parsons and E. A. Shils, eds., *Toward a General Theory of Action* (New York, 1962), p. 24.

Chapter Two

1. H. L. A. Hart, *The Concept of Law* (Oxford, Eng., 1961), pp. 30, 33.
2. W. Holdsworth, *A History of English Law*, 10 (London, 1938): 647.
3. A. Dicey, *Introduction to the Study of the Law of the Constitution*, 10th ed. (New York, 1961), pp. 202–3.
4. F. Hayek, *The Road to Serfdom* (Chicago, 1944), pp. 72–73. A modern study of administrative agencies concludes: "The rule of law stands for the view that decisions should be made by the application of known principles or laws. In general such decisions will be predictable, and the citizen will know where he is. On the other hand there is what is arbitrary. A decision may be made without principle, without any rules. It is therefore unpredictable, the antithesis of a decision taken in accordance with the rule of law." Gr. Brit. Committee on Administrative Tribunals (Franks Committee), Report, Cmnd. No. 218, at 6 (1957).
5. L. Duguit, *Traité de droit constitutionnel*, 3d ed. (Paris, 1927), p. 681.
6. Dicey, *supra* note 3, at 202.
7. K. C. Davis, *Discretionary Justice* (Baton Rouge, La., 1969), p. 44.
8. Examples of legislation embodying the three standards respectively are Interstate Commerce Act §207(a), 49 *U.S.C.* §307(a) (1964); Federal Power Act §206, 16 *U.S.C.* §824(e) (1964); and Federal Trade Commission Act §5(a)(1), 15 *U.S.C.* §45(a)(1) (1964).
9. Davis, *supra* note 7, at 216–17 (footnotes omitted).
10. *Id.* at 4.
11. Dworkin, "Is Law a System of Rules?" in R. S. Summers, ed.,

Essays in Legal Philosophy (Berkeley, Calif., 1968), pp. 45–56. See also Dworkin's "Social Rules and Legal Theory," 81 *Yale L.J.* 855 (1972).

12. See generally W. Forsyth, *History of Trial by Jury* (1852), pp. 192–214, 259–98; P. Devlin, *Trial by Jury* (London, 1956).

13. 26 Hen. 8, c. 4, §2 (1534).

14. See J. Thayer, *A Preliminary Treatise on Evidence at the Common Law* (1898), pp. 162–78.

15. 124 Eng. Rep. 1006 (C.P. 1670).

16. Devlin, *supra* note 12, at 89.

17. *Id.* at 90–91.

18. See, e.g., Case of the Seven Bishops, 87 Eng. Rep. 136 (K.B. 1688); The King v. Shipley, 99 Eng. Rep. 774 (K.B. 1784); The King v. Withers, 100 Eng. Rep. 657 (K.B. 1789).

19. The Libel Act of 1792, 32 Geo. 3, c. 60, §1.

20. Howe, "Juries as Judges of Criminal Law," 52 *Harv. L. Rev.* 582, 583–84 (1939).

21. Trial of Peter Zenger, 17 State Trials 675 (1735); People v. Croswell, 3 Johns. Cas. 337 (N.Y. 1804).

22. Commonwealth v. Porter, 51 Mass. (10 Met.) 263 (1845) (yes).

23. Sparf v. United States, 156 U.S. 51 (1895) (no).

24. United States v. Battiste, 24 F. Cas. 1042 (No. 14,545) (C.C.D. Mass. 1835).

25. For the exchange in New York see People v. Croswell, 3 Johns. Cas. 337 (N.Y. 1804); in Vermont, State v. Croteau, 23 Vt. 14 (1849); in Massachusetts, Commonwealth v. Anthes, 71 Mass. (5 Gray) 185 (1855); and in the Supreme Court, Sparf v. United States, 156 U.S. 51 (1895).

26. The history of the controversy in the United States is related in Howe, *supra* note 20, and by the exhaustive majority and dissenting opinions in Sparf v. United States, 156 U.S. 51 (1895). Justice Gray, dissenting, observed: "Until nearly forty years after the adoption of the Constitution of the United States, not a single decision of the highest court of any State, or of any judge of a court of the United States, has been found denying the right of the jury upon the general issue in a criminal case to decide, according to their own judgment and consciences, the law involved in that issue—except the two or three cases . . . concerning the constitutionality of a statute." *Id.* at 168. See also United States v. Moylan, 417 F.2d 1002, 1005–7 (4th Cir.), *cert. denied*, 397 U.S. 1064 (1969).

27. Letter from Jefferson to L'Abbé Armond, July 19, 1789, in *Writings of Thomas Jefferson*, ed. P. Ford, 35 (New York, 1895): 104.

28. U.S. National Comm'n on Law Observance and Enforcement, *Report on Criminal Procedure No. 8*, at 27 (1931).

29. Howe, *supra* note 20; Sparf v. United States, 156 U.S. 51, 168 (1895) (Gray, J., dissenting).

30. *Ga. Const.* art. 1, §2–201; *Ind. Const.* art. 1 §19; *Md. Const.* art. XV, §5.

31. Rouse v. State, 136 Ga. 356, 71 S.E. 667 (1911); Beavers v. State, 236 Ind. 549, 141 N.E.2d 118 (1957); Bridgewater v. State, 153 Ind. 560, 566, 55 N.E. 737, 739 (1899); Giles v. State, 229 Md. 370, 183 A.2d 359 (1962).

32. Wyley v. Warden, 372 F.2d 742, 745 (4th Cir. 1967).

33. See, e.g., United States v. Battiste, 24 F. Cas. 1042, 1043 (No. 14,545) (C.C.D. Mass. 1835) (Story, J.); Commonwealth v. Porter, 51 Mass. (10 Met.) 263,280 (1845) (Shaw, C.J.); Forsyth, *supra* note 12, at 261.

34. See United States v. Dougherty, 473 F.2d 1113 (D.C. Cir. 1972); United States v. Moylan, 417 F.2d 1002, 1005, (4th Cir.), *cert. denied*, 397 U.S. 1064 (1969); United States v. Sisson, 294 F. Supp. 520, 523 (D. Mass. 1968); Sax, "Conscience and Anarchy: The Prosecution of War Resisters," 57 *Yale Review* 481 (1968); Van Dyke, "The Jury as a Political Institution," 16 *Cath. Lawyer* 224 (1970); Scheflin, "Jury Nullification: The Right to Say No," 45 *So. Cal. L. Rev.* 168 (1972).

35. United States v. Moylan, 417 F.2d 1002, 1007 (4th Cir.), *cert. denied*, 397 U.S. 1064 (1969), quoting Sparf v. United States, 156 U.S. 51, 101–2 (1895).

36. Cal. Jury Instructions—Criminal, CALJIC 1.00, at 2 (1970).

37. People v. Croswell, 3 Johns. Cas. 337, 345 (N.Y. 1804).

38. "Can the Jury do it with power, and without right? When we say of any forum that it can do, and may hazard the doing a thing, we admit the legal power to do it. What is meant by the word hazard? If they choose to do it, they have then the legal right. For legal power includes the legal right. This is really only a question of words. But in the exercise of this right, moral ideas are no doubt to restrain, for the conscience ought to decide between the charge, and the evidence which ought to prevail; one side or the other." *The Law Practice of Alexander Hamilton*, ed. J. Goebel, 1 (New York, 1964): 828–29.

39. People v. Croswell, 3 Johns. Cas. 337, 368 (N.Y. 1804). See also Sparf v. United States, 156 U.S. 51, 173 (1895) (Gray, J., dissenting).

40. United States v. Maybury, 274 F.2d 899 (2d Cir. 1959).

41. Dunn v. United States, 284 U.S. 390 (1932).

42. Horning v. District of Columbia, 254 U.S. 135, 138 (1920).

43. Steckler v. United States, 7 F.2d 59, 60 (2d Cir. 1925).

44. United States *ex rel.* McCann v. Adams, 126 F.2d 774, 775–76 (2d Cir. 1942).

45. E.g., *Fed. R. Civ. P.* 49.

46. United States v. Ogull, 149 F. Supp. 272 (S.D.N.Y. 1957).

47. United States v. Spock, 416 F.2d 165 (3d Cir. 1969).

48. *Id.* at 181, quoting United States v. Ogull, 149 F. Supp. 272, 276 (S.D.N.Y. 1957).

49. 416 F.2d at 182, quoting Skidmore v. Baltimore & O. Ry., 167 F.2d 54, 70 (2d Cir. 1948) (L. Hand, J.).

50. 416 F.2d at 182.

51. Duncan v. Louisiana, 391 U.S. 145, 153 (1968).

52. *Id.* at 156, 157.
53. *Id.* at 187.
54. Pound, "Law in Books and Law in Action," 44 *Am. L. Rev.* 12, 18 (1910).
55. Devlin, *supra* note 12, at 154.
56. *Id.* at 160.
57. E.g., The Libel Act of 1792, 32 Geo. 3, c. 60 §1; see text accompanying notes 18–21 *supra*.
58. House of Commons Select Committee on Capital Punishment, *Report* viii–ix (1931); see L. Radzinowicz, *A History of English Criminal Law and Its Administration from 1750*, 1 (London, 1948): 4–5.
59. H. Kalven and H. Zeisel, *The American Jury* (Boston, 1966), p. 291.
60. *Id.* at 115.
61. *Id.* at 165.
62. *Id.* at 296.
63. See *id.* at 492–99.
64. Pound, *supra* note 54.
65. See note 34 *supra*.
66. See the opinion of Judge Leventhal in United States v. Dougherty, 473 F.2d 1113, 1130–37 (D.C. Cir. 1972), in which he deals with this issue from the perspective of the themes presented in this chapter in its earlier version (Kadish and Kadish, "On Justified Rule Departures by Officials," 59 *Calif. L. Rev.* 905 [1971]).
67. Kalven and Zeisel, *supra* note 59, at 498.
68. Williams v. Florida, 399 U.S. 78, 100 (1970).
69. See generally Cappelletti, "Judicial Review in Comparative Perspective," 58 *Calif. L. Rev.* 1017 (1970).
70. M. Mandelbaum, *History, Man and Reason: A Study in Nineteenth-Century Thought* (Baltimore, 1971), p. 134.
71. Gilmore, "The Age of Antiquarius: On Legal History in a Time of Troubles," 39 *U. Chi. L. Rev.* 475, 486–87 (1972).
72. See Dworkin, "Is Law a System of Rules?" *supra* note 11, at 38–39. Dworkin defines a principle as "a standard that is to be observed ... because it is a requirement of justice or fairness or some other dimension of morality"; he defines a policy as "that kind of standard that sets out a goal to be reached, generally an improvement in some economic, political, or social feature of the community" (pp. 34–35).
73. Goldstein, "Police Discretion Not to Invoke the Criminal Process," 69 *Yale L.J.* 543, 557 (1960). An exception is *N.M. Stat. Ann.* §39-1-1 (1954), making it the duty of peace officers to file complaints "if the circumstances are such as to indicate to a reasonably prudent person that such action should be taken."
74. See W. LaFave, *Arrest* (Boston, 1965), p. 76; Goldstein, *supra* note 73, at 557; Davis, *supra* note 7, at 84–88.
75. See Goldstein, *supra* note 73, at 547; cf., e.g., People v. Woodward, 220 Mich. 511, 515, 190 N.W. 721, 723 (1922).

76. The examples that follow are chosen from the data collected in LaFave, *supra* note 74, at 83–143.

77. Davis, *supra* note 7, at 84.

78. U.S. President's Comm'n on Law Enforcement and the Administration of Justice, *The Challenge of Crime in a Free Society* (Washington, D.C., 1967), p. 106.

79. Breitel, "Controls in Criminal Law Enforcement," 27 *U. Chi. L. Rev.* 427 (1960).

80. Davis, *supra* note 7, at 87.

81. Regina v. Commissioner of Police, [1968] 2 W.L.R. 893 (C.A.).

82. *Id.* at 902.

83. Davis, *supra* note 7, at 87.

84. Arnold, "Law Enforcement—An Attempt at Social Dissection," 42 *Yale L.J.* 1, 18 (1932). See also Snyder, "The District Attorney's Hardest Task," 30 *J. Crim. L.C. & P.S.* 167, 168 (1939).

85. State v. Winne, 12 N.J. 152, 96 A.2d 63 (1953).

86. Ferguson, "Formulation of Enforcement Policy: An Anatomy of the Prosecutor's Discretion Prior to Accusation," 1 *Rutgers L. Rev.* 507, 515 (1957).

87. Baker, "The Prosecutor—Initiation of Prosecution," 23 *J. Crim. L.C. & P.S.* 770 (1933). See also Baker and DeLong, "The Prosecuting Attorney—Powers and Duties in Criminal Prosecution," 24 *J. Crim. L.C. & P.S.* 1025, 1034, 1064 (1934).

88. City of Merced v. County of Merced, 240 Cal. App. 2d 763, 766, 50 Cal. Rptr. 287, 289 (5th Dist. 1966). See also *In re* Voss, 11 N.D. 540, 546, 90 N.W. 15, 18–19 (1902): "The duties of state's attorney are to be performed regardless of public sentiment, and he who administers that office in deference to sentiment opposed to the law is unfit to hold that office or to be an attorney at law."

89. See Baker and DeLong, *supra* note 87, at 1034–45; Note, "Prosecutor's Discretion," 103 *U. Pa. L. Rev.* 1057, 1058 (1955); e.g., *Cal. Penal Code* §335 (West 1971) ("Every District Attorney, Sheriff, Constable, or police officer must inform against and diligently prosecute persons whom they have reasonable cause to believe are offenders against the provisions of this Chapter [Gaming], and every such officer refusing so to do is guilty of a misdemeanor."); *Cal. Agric. Code* §8 (West 1971) ("The district attorney of any county in which a violation of any provision of this code [Agriculture] occurs shall, upon request of any enforcing officer or other interested person, prosecute such violation."); Board of Supervisors v. Simpson, 36 Cal. 2d 671, 227 P.2d 14 (1951) (duty to prosecute action to abate nuisance is mandatory).

90. Full-scale descriptions of the legal controls available may be found in F. Miller, *Prosecution: The Decision to Charge a Suspect with a Crime* (Boston, 1969), pp. 293–337; Note, *supra* note 89, at 1075–80.

91. See Remington and Rosenblum, "The Criminal Law and the

Legislative Process," 1960 *U. Ill. L.F.* 481, 498; Ferguson, *supra* note 86, at 523; Comment, "Private Prosecution: A Remedy for District Attorneys' Unwarranted Inaction," 65 *Yale L.J.* 209–15 (1955); Note, *supra* note 89, at 1076, 1079.

92. See note 90 *supra*.

93. See Comment, *supra* note 91, at 211–15.

94. Newman v. United States, 382 F.2d 479 (D.C. Cir. 1967); United States v. Brokaw, 60 F. Supp. 100 (S.D. Ill. 1945); 2 *Op. Att'y Gen.* 482, 486 (1831).

95. Confiscation Cases, 74 U.S. (7 Wall.) 454 (1868).

96. "It follows, as an incident of the constitutional separation of powers, that the courts are not to interfere with the free exercise of the discretionary power of the attorneys for the United States in their control over criminal prosecutions." United States v. Cox, 342 F.2d 167, 171 (5th Cir. 1965).

97. See Ferguson, *supra* note 86, at 510.

98. "Actually . . . the prosecutor is the 'father confessor' of the community, and whether or not a particular offender is prosecuted depends very largely upon the personal reactions (or judgment) of the prosecutor." Baker, *supra* note 87, at 770. "The prosecutor has more control over life, liberty and reputation than any other person in America. His discretion is tremendous." Jackson, "The Federal Prosecutor," 24 *J. Am. Jud. Soc'y* 18 (1940).

99. People v. Byrd, 12 Mich. App. 186, 197, 162 N.W. 2d 777, 782 (1968) (concurring opinion).

100. Newman v. United States, 382 F.2d 479, 481 (D.C. Cir. 1967).

101. United States v. Cox, 342 F.2d 167, 171 (5th Cir. 1965).

102. Howell v. Brown, 85 F. Supp. 537, 540 (D. Neb. 1949). See also Pugach v. Klein, 193 F. Supp. 630, 635 (S.D.N.Y. 1961); Kaplan, "The Prosecutorial Discretion," 60 *Nw. U.L. Rev.* 174 (1965); U.S. President's Comm'n on Law Enforcement and the Administration of Justice, *Task Force Report: The Courts* (Washington, D.C., 1967), p. 5.

103. See Davis, *supra* note 7, at 188–214; U.S. President's Comm'n on Law Enforcement and the Administration of Justice, *supra* note 102, at 5–9; Comment, "Discriminatory Law Enforcement and Equal Protection from the Law," 59 *Yale L.J.* 354 (1950); Note, "The Right to Nondiscriminatory Enforcement of State Penal Laws," 61 *Colum. L. Rev.* 1103 (1961).

104. See note 90 *supra*.

105. U.S. President's Comm'n on Law Enforcement and the Administration of Justice, *supra* note 102, at 16.

106. Tappan, "Habitual Offender Laws and Sentencing Practices in Relation to Organized Crime," in M. Ploscowe, ed., *Organized Crime and Law Enforcement* (New York, 1952), p. 123; Note, "Court Treatment of General Recidivist Statutes," 48 *Colum. L. Rev.* 238 (1948). See generally "Symposium on the Habitual Criminal," 13 *McGill L.J.* 533 (1967).

107. People v. West, 3 Cal. 3d 595, 608, 477 P.2d 409, 417, 91 Cal. Rptr. 385, 393 (1970).

108. Miller, "The Compromise of Criminal Cases," 1 *S. Cal. L. Rev.* 1, 27 (1927); McLaughlin, "Selected Excerpts from the 1968 Report of New York State Joint Legislative Committee on Crime, Its Causes, Control, and Effect on Society," 5 *Crim. L. Bull.* 255, 257 (1969).

109. Miller, *supra* note 108; Shelton v. United States, 242 F.2d 101, 113 (5th Cir. 1957) ("Justice and liberty are not the subject of bargaining and barter.").

110. People v. Byrd, 12 Mich. App. 186, 199, 162 N.W.2d 777, 783 (1968) (concurring opinion).

111. McLaughlin, *supra* note 108, at 268.

112. See Alschuler, "The Prosecutor's Role in Plea Bargaining," 36 *U. Chi. L. Rev.* 50, 51 (1968).

113. E.g., United States v. Williams, 407 F.2d 940, 947 n.11 (4th Cir. 1969); United States v. Jackson, 390 F.2d 130, 138 (7th Cir. 1968).

114. ABA Project on Minimum Standards for Criminal Justice, *Standards Relating to Pleas of Guilty* (New York, 1967), p. 45.

115. North Carolina v. Alford, 400 U.S. 25 (1971); Brady v. United States, 397 U.S. 742 (1970).

116. People v. West, 3 Cal. 3d 595, 604, 477 P.2d 409, 413, 91 Cal. Rptr. 385, 389 (1970), quoting Barber v. Gladden, 220 F. Supp. 308, 314 (D. Ore. 1963).

117. D. Newman, *Conviction: The Determination of Guilt or Innocence Without Trial* (Boston, 1966), p. 178.

118. Hart, *supra* note 1, at 138–44.

119. B. Cardozo, *The Nature of the Judicial Process* (New Haven, Conn., 1921), p. 129.

120. E.g., Hutcheson, "The Judgment Intuitive: The Function of the Hunch in Judicial Decision," 14 *Cornell L.Q.* 274 (1929).

121. Cardozo, *supra* note 119, at 136, 129.

122. J. Frank, *Law and the Modern Mind* (New York, 1930), p. 121.

123. "Generally a fiction is intended to escape the consequences of an existing, specific rule of law. Thus the fiction of 'inviting' in the 'attractive nuisance' cases is intended to escape the rule that there is no duty of care toward trespassers. But occasionally the matter is more obscure. In some cases a fiction seems to be intended to avoid the implications, not of any specific and recognized rule of law, but of some unexpressed and rather general and vague principle of jurisprudence or morals. Thus, the conclusive presumption that the donee of a gift accepts the gift, although it may have been delivered out of his presence and without his knowledge, assumes a general principle that title cannot pass to a man without his assent. The conclusive presumption that everyone knows the law is, apparently, intended to escape an assumed moral principle that it is unjust to visit the legal consequences of an act upon a person who does not know the law." L. Fuller, *Legal Fictions* (Stanford, Calif., 1967), p. 53.

124. *Id.* at 57, quoting *The Works of Jeremy Bentham*, ed. J. Bowring, 1 (1843): 243.

125. See Note, "Congress, the President, and the Power to Commit Forces to Combat," 81 *Harv. L. Rev.* 1771 (1968); Van Alstyne, "Congress, the President, and the Power to Declare War: A Requiem for Vietnam," 121 *U. Pa. L. Rev.* 1 (1972).

126. The tensions engendered by these overlapping grants of power have produced controversy in virtually every period of international crisis in American history. See Schlesinger, "Congress and the Making of American Foreign Policy," 51 *Foreign Affairs* 78 (1972).

127. See Herbers, "Nixon's Presidency: Crisis for Congress," *N.Y. Times,* March 5, 1973, p. 1, col. 1.

128. Both quotations are taken from Schlesinger, *supra* note 126, at 78, 113.

Chapter Three

1. E.g., De Boisblanc, "The Dilemma of the Disobedient: A Solution," 41 *Ind. L.J.* 521, 524 (1967). See H. L. A. Hart, *Punishment and Responsibility* (Oxford, Eng., 1962), pp. 6–7.

2. See J. Feinberg, *Doing and Deserving* (Princeton, N.J. 1970), p. 110; *Blackstone's Commentaries,* Jones ed., vol. 1 (San Francisco, 1915), Introduction, pp. 57–58.

3. Cf. Lerner, "Punishment as Justice and as Price," in S. Hook, ed., *Determinism and Freedom* (New York, 1958), p. 181; H. L. A. Hart, *The Concept of Law* (Oxford, Eng., 1961), p. 39; M. Howe, *Justice Holmes: The Proving Years* (Cambridge, Mass., 1963), pp. 74–80.

4. As was urged by Thomas Jefferson. See letter to Mrs. Adams, quoted in P. Freund et al., *Constitutional Law: Cases and Materials and Other Problems,* 3d ed., 1 (Boston, 1967): 18.

5. As seriously considered at the Constitutional Convention. See J. Butzner, ed., *Constitutional Chaff: Rejected Suggestions of the Constitutional Convention of 1787* (New York, 1941), pp. 54–57, 147–52; M. Farrand, ed., *The Records of the Federal Convention of 1787,* rev. ed., 2 (New Haven, Conn., 1937): 73 et seq.

6. Marbury v. Madison, 5 U.S. (1 Cranch) 137 (1803).

7. See discussion in United States v. Mitchell, 330 U.S. 75, 87–89 (1947).

8. Tileston v. Ullman, 318 U.S. 44 (1943).

9. Poe v. Ullman, 367 U.S. 497 (1961).

10. A comparable example is United Public Workers v. Mitchell, 330 U.S. 75 (1947), in which civil service employees discovered that their only means, in effect, of challenging the Hatch Act (imposing restraints on their political activities) was to violate it, suffer discharge, and sue for their jobs. Their federal declaratory judgment suit, based on their asserted desire to engage in partisan political activity in violation of the Hatch Act, was held to present a hypothetical for an advisory opinion rather than an actual case or controversy.

11. Griswold v. Connecticut, 381 U.S. 479 (1965).

12. See Note, "Declaratory Relief in the Criminal Law," 80 *Harv. L. Rev.* 1490 (1967); Annotation, "Validity, Construction and Application of Criminal Statutes or Ordinances as Proper Subject for Declaratory Judgment," 10 A.L.R.3d 727 (1966).

13. See, e.g., Dombrowski v. Pfister, 380 U.S. 479 (1965); Zeitlin v. Arnebergh, 59 Cal. 2d 901, 383 P.2d 152 (1963); Note, "The Chilling Effect in Constitutional Law," 69 *Colum. L. Rev.* 808 (1969).

14. See the birth control cases discussed *supra*. See also Younger v. Harris, 401 U.S. 37, 41–42 (1971); Boyle v. Landry, 401 U.S. 77 (1971).

15. See Zemel v. Rusk, 381 U.S. 1, 19 (1965).

16. See Watson v. Buck, 313 U.S. 387, 400 (1941); C. Wright, *Law of Federal Courts*, 2d ed. (St. Paul, Minn., 1970), pp. 196 et seq.

17. "It is a familiar rule that courts of equity do not ordinarily restrain criminal prosecutions. . . . [Their] imminence, even though alleged to be in violation of constitutional guarantees, is not a ground for equity relief since the lawfulness or constitutionality of the statute or ordinance on which the prosecution is based may be determined as readily in a criminal case as in a suit for injunction." Douglas v. Jeannette, 319 U.S. 157, 163 (1943).

18. "There are circumstances under which courts properly make exceptions to the general rule that equity will not interfere with the criminal processes, by entertaining actions for injunction or declaratory relief in advance of criminal prosecutions." Zemel v. Rusk, 381 U.S. 1, 19 (1965).

19. Justice Douglas dissenting in Poulos v. New Hampshire, 345 U.S. 395, 423 (1953). See also Wainwright v. New Orleans, 392 U.S. 593, 613 (1968): "The principle that a citizen can defy an unconstitutional act is deep in our system."

20. Walker v. City of Birmingham, 388 U.S. 307, 327 (1967) (dissenting opinion).

21. Quoted in Freund et al., *supra* note 4, at 20–21. Professor Dworkin has developed the implications of this argument in his "On Not Prosecuting Civil Disobedience," *New York Review of Books*, June 6, 1968, p. 14.

22. Constitution of the State of Hessen, German Federal Republic, Art. 147, in R. W. Füsslein, *Deutsche Verfassungen* (Berlin, 1951), p. 254.

23. See Dworkin, *supra* note 21, at 18.

24. The West German Supreme Court so held in a case discussed *infra*, pp. 155–56.

25. Wright v. Georgia, 373 U.S. 284 (1963).

26. *Id.* at 291–92.

27. See, e.g., United States v. Heliczer, 373 F.2d 241, 246, n. 3 (2d Cir. 1967); State v. Koonce, 80 N.J. Super. 160, 184, 214 A.2d 428, 436 (App. Div. 1965); Chevigny, "The Right to Resist an Unlawful Arrest," 78 *Yale L.J.* 1128, 1132, et seq. (1969); Note, "The Right to Re-

sist Unlawful Arrest: An Outdated Concept," 3 *Tulsa L.J.* 40 (1966).

28. ALI, Model Penal Code (Tent. Draft No. 8, 1958), Comments at 19.

29. John Bad Elk v. United States, 177 U.S. 529, 535 (1900); *Kenny's Outlines of Criminal Law*, ed. J. W. C. Turner (Cambridge, Eng., 1952), p. 114.

30. See notes 27 and 28 *supra*.

31. ALI *Proceedings* 254 (1958).

32. Chevigny, *supra* note 27, at 1137.

33. People v. Ah Teung, 92 Cal. 421, 28 Pac. 577 (1891).

34. *Id.* 92 Cal. at 425.

35. E.g., State v. Ferguson, 100 Ohio App. 191, 135 N.E.2d 884 (1955); State v. Adams, 143 W.Va. 325, 102 S.E.2d 145 (1958).

36. See the many cases reviewed in Annotation, "What Justifies Escape," 70 A.L.R.2d 1430 (1960). Apparently only one escape conviction has been upset on this ground since 1960. See A.L.R.2d, Later Case Services for vols. 67–72 at 482 (1967), and 1971 Supplement at 128.

37. People v. Hunt, 229 App. Div. 105, 242 N.Y.S. 105 (App. Div. 3d Dept. 1930).

38. *Id.* 242 N.Y.S. at 107. See also Beaulieu v. State, 211 A.2d 290, 293 (Me. 1965); People v. Hill, 17 Ill.2d 112, 160 N.E.2d 779, 781 (1959).

39. E.g., People v. Clark, 69 Cal. App. 520, 523, 231 Pac. 590 (1924); People v. Sherberg, 93 Cal. App. 2d 736, 743, 209 P.2d 796 (1949); People v. Hill, 17 Ill.2d 112, 160 N.E.2d 779, 781 (1959); Annotation, *supra* note 36, at 1433 n.b., 1437.

40. See cases discussed in Annotation, "Right to Punish for Contempt," 12 A.L.R.2d 1059 (1950).

41. See Z. Chafee, *Some Problems of Equity* (Ann Arbor, Mich., 1950), p. 296. E.g., Woodward v. The King, 2 Ch. Cas. 203 (1675).

42. See Cox, "The Void Order and the Duty to Obey," 16 *U. Chi. L. Rev.* 86 (1948); Moscowitz, "Contempt of Injunctions, Civil and Criminal," 43 *Colum. L. Rev.* 780 (1943).

43. Annotation, *supra* note 40, at 1079; Note, "Defiance of Unlawful Authority," 83 *Harv. L. Rev.* 626, 633 (1970). See United States v. United Mine Workers, 330 U.S. 258, 293 (1947).

44. Compare *In re* Sawyer, 124 U.S. 200 (1888); Howatt v. Kansas, 258 U.S. 181 (1922); *In re* Green, 369 U.S. 689 (1962); and Walker v. City of Birmingham, 388 U.S. 307 (1967).

45. For the case involving Lewis see United States v. United Mine Workers, 330 U.S. 258 (1947); for that involving King see Walker v. City of Birmingham, 388 U.S. 307 (1967).

46. United States v. United Mine Workers, 330 U.S. 258, 293 (1947).

47. *Id.* at 294. Cf. Professor Chafee's criticism of this qualification of the settled rule that orders beyond the jurisdiction of the court need

not be obeyed, as "unprecedented, vague and unnecessary." Chafee, *supra* note 41, at 376.

48. United States v. United Mine Workers, 330 U.S. at 311.

49. *Id.*

50. *Id.* at 308.

51. *Id.*

52. *Id.* at 312.

53. *Id.* at 309.

54. *Id.* at 311.

55. Indeed, the Alabama Supreme Court in a previous case quoted heavily from the Lewis decision in supporting the Alabama rule. Fields v. City of Fairfield, 273 Ala. 588, 143 So.2d 177, 180 (1962).

56. Walker v. City of Birmingham, 388 U.S. at 315.

57. *Id.* at 320–21. For a contrary view see *In re* Berry, 68 Cal.2d 137, 436 P.2d 273 (1968).

58. Poulos v. New Hampshire, 345 U.S. 395 (1953).

59. Yakus v. United States, 312 U.S. 414 (1944).

60. Falbo v. United States, 320 U.S. 549 (1944); McKart v. United States, 395 U.S. 185 (1969).

61. See Note, *supra* note 43, at 626, 630.

62. Yakus v. United States, 321 U.S. 414 (1944).

63. *Id.* at 468.

64. *Id.* at 446–47.

65. McKart v. United States, 395 U.S. 185 (1969).

66. Falbo v. United States, 320 U.S. 549 (1944).

67. McKart v. United States, 395 U.S. at 195.

68. *Id.* at 197.

69. Poulos v. New Hampshire, 345 U.S. 395 (1953).

70. *Id.* at 409.

71. Royall v. Virginia, 116 U.S. 572 (1886); Cantwell v. Connecticut, 310 U.S. 296 (1940); Thomas v. Collins, 323 U.S. 516 (1945).

72. Poulos v. New Hampshire, 345 U.S. at 414.

73. *Id.* at 423–24.

74. G. Williams, *Criminal Law: The General Part,* 2d ed. (London, 1961), p. 722.

75. *Id.* at 724; *Model Penal Code* (Tent. Draft No. 8, 1958), Comment at 6. See United States v. Holmes, 26 F. Cas. 360 (No. 15,383) (C.C. Pa. 1842); Hitchler, "Necessity as a Defense in Criminal Cases," 33 *Dick. L. Rev.* 138 (1929). Glazebrook agrees that the principle operates in the English common law, but prefers to regard it as a doctrine of statutory interpretation rather than as a discrete residual principle of general exculpation. "The Necessity Plea in English Criminal Law," 30 *Cambridge L. Rev.* 87 (1972).

76. Serjeant Pollard in Reniger v. Fogassa, 75 E. R. 29–30 (1550) quoted in Williams, *supra* note 74, at 725.

77. *Model Penal Code* (Tent. Draft No. 8, 1958), Comment at 8–9.

78. Art. 14 of the Criminal Code of the RSFSR, trans. in H. Berman, ed., *Soviet Criminal Law and Procedure* (Cambridge, Mass., 1966), p. 149. See also the Hungarian criminal code, in which a violation is considered defensible if it "caused no worse harm than the act it was intended to avert." *Criminal Code of the Hungarian People's Republic*, trans. L'Amberg (Budapest, 1962), § 26(2).

79. *German Draft Penal Code E 1962*, trans. N. Ross (American Series of Foreign Penal Codes No. 11), vol. 2 (South Hackensack, N.J., 1966), § 39, p. 36.

80. Art. 20. See Ass'n of German Democratic Lawyers, *Law and Legislation in the German Democratic Republic*, 2/68 (East Berlin, 1968), p. 29.

81. *Model Penal Code*, § 3.02 (Proposed Official Draft, 1962).

82. *N.Y. Penal Law*, § 35.05 (1967). See also *Ill. Rev. Stat.*, ch. 38, § 7.13 (1961).

83. St. Thomas Aquinas, *Summa Theologica*, Benziger Bros. ed., 1 (1947): 1022.

84. Cf. Williams, "The Defense of Necessity," [1953] *Current Legal Problems*, pp. 216, 224.

85. ALI, *Minutes of the Council* 209 (1958). The comment was made during a discussion of the proposed Model Penal Code defense of balance of evils. It is interesting to observe that the draftsman, Prof. Herbert Wechsler, promptly agreed (*id.*).

86. 18 *U.S.C.* § 242.

87. Screws v. United States, 325 U.S. 91 (1945).

88. *Id.* at 96.

89. C. K. Allen, *Law in the Making*, 7th ed. (Oxford, Eng., 1964), p. 479.

90. Baker, "Legislative Crimes," 23 *Minn. L. Rev.* 134 (1939); Bonfield, "The Abrogation of Penal Statutes by Non-enforcement," 49 *Iowa L. Rev.* 389 (1964).

91. See the arguments in Bonfield, *supra* note 90, at 409 et. seq.

92. Poe v. Ullman, 367 U.S. 497 (1961).

93. *Id.* at 502.

94. K. C. Davis, *Discretionary Justice* (Baton Rouge, La., 1969), p. 193.

95. W. LaFave, *Arrest* (Boston, 1965), pp. 131–32.

96. People v. Utica Daws Co., 225 N.Y.S.2d 128, 133 (4th Dept. 1962). See also People v. Harris, 182 Cal. App. 2d 837, 5 Cal. Rptr. 852 (App. Dept., Super. Ct. 160); Comment, "Discriminatory Law Enforcement and Equal Protection from the Law," 59 *Yale L.J.* 354 (1950); Note, "The Right to Nondiscriminatory Enforcement of State Penal Laws," 61 *Colum. L. Rev.* 1103 (1961).

97. NLRB v. Guy F. Atkinson, 195 F.2d 141 (9th Cir. 1952).

98. *Id.* at 143.

99. *Id.* at 149.

100. Davis, *supra* note 94, at 85.

101. *N.Y. Times,* Oct. 18, 1963, p. 17, col. 6.

102. United States v. Kartman, 417 F.2d 893 (9th Cir. 1969).

103. *Id.* at 896.

104. Redmund v. United States, 384 U.S. 264 (1966).

105. Memorandum for the United States, Richmund v. United States, No. 1056, Oct. Term 1965 (April 1966).

106. Jackson's letter is reproduced in H. Hart and A. Sachs, "The Legal Process," tent. mimeo. ed. (1959), pp. 1085–86. His argument also relied on prior practice. For a full documentation of the affair, see Hearings on the Nomination of Robert H. Jackson to be an Associate Justice of the Supreme Court, 77th Cong., 1st Sess., pp. 47–69 (1941).

107. Scott v. United States, 419 F.2d 264, 277 (D.C. Cir. 1969).

108. Abrams, "Internal Policy: Guiding the Exercise of Prosecutorial Discretion," 19 *U.C.L.A. L. Rev.* 1, 11 (1971).

109. Cf. the Israeli practice discussed in *id.* at 48; and the German practice discussed in Jescheck, "The Discretionary Powers of the Prosecuting Attorney in West Germany," 18 *Am. J. Comp. L.* 508, 512 (1970).

Chapter Four

1. H. L. A. Hart, *The Concept of Law* (Oxford, Eng., 1961), p. 91.

2. Hurst, "Problems of Legitimacy in the Contemporary Legal Order," 24 *Okla. L. Rev.* 224, 225 (1971).

3. See Touchy, "The New Legality," 53 *A.B.A.J.* 544 (1967).

4. See *Model Penal Code,* §3.02, Comment (Tent. Draft No. 8, 1958), p. 8.

5. *Id.* at 9.

6. See *Wis. Crim. Code* §939.47.

7. *Id.*

8. *N.Y. Penal Law* §35.05; for the quotation see Practice Commentary to *N.Y. Penal Law* §35.05, *McKinney's Consolidated Laws of N.Y.* (1967), Bk. 39, Penal Law 57. The mood of the statutory exclusion is clearer than its language. One would suppose that the essence of a lesser-evil defense is necessarily that as applied in the class of cases represented by the circumstances of the defendant's case the statute is "inadvisable." Interpreted literally, the statute appears to take back altogether what it purports to give.

9. Dworkin, "On Not Prosecuting Civil Disobedience," *New York Review of Books,* June 6, 1968, p. 14.

10. See page 65 *supra.*

11. See United States v. Dougherty, 473 F.2d 1113, 1134 (D.C. Cir. 1972).

12. Dennis v. United States, 384 U.S. 855 (1966).

13. *Id.* at 865.

14. See Annotation, "Reliance on Judicial Decision as Defense to Prosecution," 49 A.L.R. 1273 (1927).

15. James v. United States, 366 U.S. 213 (1961).

16. State v. O'Neil, 147 Iowa 513, 126 N.W. 454 (1910).

17. State v. Godwin, 123 N.C. 697, 31 S.E. 221 (1898). See also other cases discussed in Annotation, "Mistaken Belief as to the Constitutionality of Statute as Affecting Criminal Responsibility," 61 A.L.R. 1153 (1929).

18. United States v. Murdock, 290 U.S. 389 (1933).

19. United States v. Murdock, 284 U.S. 141 (1931). This decision was itself later overruled in Murphy v. Waterfront Commission, 378 U.S. 52 (1964).

20. Keegan v. United States, 325 U.S. 479 (1944).

21. *Id.* at 505. Cf. Warren v. United States, 177 F.2d 596, 600 (10th Cir. 1949): "One may not disobey a law even in the good-faith belief that it is unconstitutional and, on this ground, avoid the consequences of his act if the law is within the constitutional power of Congress."

22. United States v. Anthony, 24 F. Cas. 829 (No. 14,459) (C.C.N.D.-N.Y. 1873).

23. *Id.* at 831-32. For other holdings to the same effect see Hunter v. State, 158 Tenn. 63, 12 S.W.2d 361 (1929); Annotation, *supra* note 17.

24. Cf. *Model Penal Code*, §3.02, Comment (Tent. Draft No. 8, 1958), pp. 5–6: "The necessity must be avoidance of an evil greater than the evil sought to be avoided by the law defining the offense charged. The balancing of evils cannot, of course, be committed merely to the private judgment of the actor; it is an issue for determination in the trial. What is involved may be described as an interpretation of the law of the offense." See also LaFave and Scott, *Criminal Law* (St. Paul, Minn., 1972), p. 386.

25. 2 BGHSt. 194 (March 18, 1952). The decision is translated in G. Fletcher, "Comparative Criminal Theory," 2d ed. (mimeo., 1971), p. 72.

26. Fletcher, *supra* note 25, at 75. The holding is the basis for Section 17 of West Germany's new Penal Code, effective in 1973: "If in the course of the act the actor lacks the perception that he is acting wrongfully [*Unrecht*], he acts without culpability if he could not avoid making the mistake."

27. Fletcher, *supra* note 25, at 79. See also the court's decision in 4 BGHSt. 1 (1952) to the same effect. For a critique of this view, see K. Peters, "Überzeugunstäter und Gewissenstäter," in F. Geerds and W. Naucke, eds., *Beiträge zur gesamten Strafrechtswissenschaft: Festschrift für Helmuth Mayer* (Berlin, 1966), p. 257.

28. (1953) N.J.W. 513 (Nov. 28, 1952) (BGH); see Discussion in Ryu and Silving, "Euthanasia: A Study in Comparative Criminal Law," 103 *U. Pa. L. Rev.* 350, 358 (1954).

29. *Swiss Penal Code* §20, in S. Lowenstein, *Materials on Comparative Criminal Law as Based Upon the Penal Codes of Ethiopia and Switzerland* (New York, 1965), p. 406.

30. *Criminal Code of the Hungarian People's Republic*, trans. L'Amberg (Budapest, 1962), §24(2).

31. (1968) N.J.W. 212 (Oct. 10, 1967) (OLG Hamm).

32. See G. Radbruch, *Rechtsphilosophie*, 4th ed. (Stuttgart, 1950), p. 347; Hart, "Positivism and the Separation of Morals," 71 *Harv. L. Rev.* 593, 616–20 (1958); Fuller, "Positivism and Fidelity to Law—A Reply to Professor Hart," 71 *Harv. L. Rev.* 630, 648–57 (1958); Bodenheimer, "Significant Developments in German Legal Philosophy Since 1945," 3 *Am. J. Comp. L.* 379, 387–91 (1954).

33. Calif. Joint Legislative Comm. for Revision of the Penal Code, Tent. Draft No. 2 (1968), §500.

34. Wheeler, "The Law Above the Law," 1 *Center Magazine* 77, 80 (1968).

35. Wright, book review of Davis, *Discretionary Justice*, 81 *Yale L.J.* 575, 576 (1972).

36. K. C. Davis, *Discretionary Justice* (Baton Rouge, La., 1969), pp. 170–87.

37. *Id.* at chaps. 3, 4, 5.

38. Note Wright, *supra* note 35.

39. Davis, *supra* note 36; Kadish, "Legal Norm and Discretion in the Police and Sentencing Process," 75 *Harv. L. Rev.* 904 (1962).

40. United States v. United Mine Workers, 330 U.S. 258, 308–9, 312 (1947).

41. Shapiro, "The Impact of the Supreme Court," 23 *J. Legal Ed.* 77, 82–83 (1970).

42. Note 22 *supra*.

43. Griswold v. Connecticut, 381 U.S. 479 (1965).

44. Brown v. Board of Education, 347 U.S. 483 (1954).

45. West Virginia Board of Education v. Barnette, 319 U.S. 624 (1943), overruling Minersville School District v. Gobitis, 310 U.S. 586 (1940).

46. H. Laski, *The State in Theory and Practice* (New York, 1935), pp. 64–78.

47. Wigmore, "Program for the Trial of a Jury," 12 *J. Am. Jud. Soc'y* 166 (1929).

48. H. Kalven and H. Zeisel, *The American Jury* (Boston, 1966), p. 498.

49. J. Stephens, *A History of the Criminal Law of England,* 2 (1883): 110.

50. Wurzel, "Methods of Juridical Thinking," in *Science of Legal Method,* Modern Legal Philosophy Series, 9 (Boston, 1917): 286, 417.

51. See J. Frank, *Law and the Modern Mind* (New York, 1930), pp. 234–35.

52. Cf. Marshall, "The Protest Movement and the Law," 51 *Va. L. Rev.* 785, 795 (1965).

Chapter Five

1. H. L. A. Hart, *The Concept of Law* (Oxford, Eng., 1961), p. 92.

2. *Ibid.*, p. 132.

3. Max Weber, *The Theory of Social and Economic Organization*, trans. A. Henderson and T. Parsons (Glencoe, Ill., 1947). The quotations in the text appear at pp. 329–32.

4. "Pour qu'on ne puisse abuser du pouvoir, il faut que, par la disposition des choses, le pouvoir arrête le pouvoir." ("In order to avoid the abuse of power it is necessary, through the disposition of things, that power check power.") *De l'esprit des lois*, bk. 12, chap. 4, in *Oeuvres complètes de Montesquieu*, ed. André Masson (Paris, 1950–55), 1: 206. (Authors' translation.)

5. Montesquieu himself was apparently committed to what we have called "law and order" and "the rule of law": "La liberté est le droit de faire tout ce que les lois permettent; et si un citoyen pouvait faire ce qu'elles défendent, il n'aurait plus de liberté, parce que les autres auraient tout de même ce pouvoir." ("Liberty is the right to do all that the laws permit; and if a citizen could do what is prohibited, he would no longer have liberty, because others would have exactly the same power.") *Ibid.*, bk. 11, chap. 3, in *Oeuvres complètes de Montesquieu*, ed. André Masson (Paris, 1950–55), 1: 206. And later, he writes: "C'est le triomphe de la liberté, lorsque les lois criminelles tirent chaque peine de la nature particulière du crime. Tout l'arbitraire cesse; la peine ne descend point du caprice de législateur, mais de la nature de la chose; et ce n'est point l'homme qui fait violence à l'homme." ("Liberty triumphs when the criminal law derives each punishment from the particular nature of the crime. All arbitrariness ceases; punishment does not at all stem from the caprice of the legislator, but from the nature of the thing; and it is not at all man who is inflicting violence upon man.") *Ibid.*, bk. 12, chap. 4, p. 253. (Authors' translations.)

6. See *Corbin on Contracts*, vol. 6 (St. Paul, Minn., 1962), § 1322.

7. Poussard v. Spiers and Pond, 1 Q.B.D. 410 (1876).

8. Krell v. Henry, [1903] 2 K.B. 740.

9. Carroll v. Bowersock, 100 Kan. 270, 164 Pac. 143 (1917).

10. *Corbin on Contracts, supra* note 6, § 1331, pp. 356–57.

Index